HENRY A. WALLACE
AND AMERICAN
FOREIGN POLICY

Recent Titles in
Contributions in American History

Series Editor: Jon L. Wakelyn

J. Samuel Walker

HENRY A. WALLACE AND AMERICAN FOREIGN POLICY

CONTRIBUTIONS IN AMERICAN HISTORY,
NUMBER 50

GREENWOOD PRESS
WESTPORT, CONNECTICUT • LONDON, ENGLAND

Library of Congress Cataloging in Publication Data

Walker, J. Samuel.
  Henry A. Wallace and American foreign policy.

  (Contributions in American history ; no. 50)
  Bibliography: p.
  Includes index.
    1. Wallace, Henry Agard, 1888-1965. 2. United States—Foreign relations-
  1933-1945. 3. United States—Foreign relations—1945-1953. I. Title.
  E748.W23W28   973.917'092'4   75-44658
  ISBN 0-8371-8774-5

Library of Congress Catalog Card Number: 75-44658
ISBN: 0-8371-8774-5

First published in 1976

Greenwood Press, a division of Williamhouse-Regency Inc.
51 Riverside Avenue, Westport, Connecticut 06880

Printed in the United States of America

Acknowledgments

Excerpts from the book *The Price of Vision: The Diary of Henry A. Wallace, 1942-1946,* edited by John Morton Blum, copyright © 1973 by the Estate of Henry A. Wallace and John Morton Blum, reprinted by permission of Houghton Mifflin Company.

Excerpts from the J. P. Moffat Diary reprinted by permission of Harvard College Library.

FOR PAT

CONTENTS

PREFACE

This book is a study of Henry A. Wallace's views on foreign affairs throughout his entire career. Wallace's outspoken opposition to American foreign policy in the early cold war years and his presidential campaign of 1948 have attracted the attention of many scholars, and to a lesser extent, so have his ideas on international relations during World War II. However, his outlook on world affairs before 1941 has been virtually ignored. Wallace's foreign policy opinions during earlier periods are significant enough in themselves to merit careful review, but they also provide the basis for understanding his cold war critique. This study attempts to find the roots of Wallace's ideas on foreign affairs, search for continuity in his thinking, and suggest the reasons why he refused to join the cold war consensus that included a broadly based majority of Americans in the late 1940s. Finally, it seeks to explain why his attempt to challenge the assumptions underlying American diplomacy in the early cold war era proved so utterly futile.

I am indebted to the many people who kindly and generously assisted me in the preparation of this volume. Librarians and archivists in many repositories rendered invaluable services. I am particularly grateful to Earl Rogers and Robert McCown of Special Collections at the University of Iowa Library; Helen Ulibarri of National Archives; Alan Fusonie of the National Agricultural Library, Beltsville, Maryland; William J. Stewart, Raymond Teichman, and Donald Schewe of Franklin D. Roosevelt Library; Philip D. Lagerquist and Dennis Bilger of Harry S. Truman Library; and Louis M. Starr of the Columbia Oral History Collection.

I owe an especially deep personal and intellectual debt to Professor Wayne S. Cole of the University of Maryland. Professor Cole provided expert guidance in the writing of the original version of this manuscript as a doctoral dissertation, and has been a constant source of wisdom, encouragement, and contagious enthusiasm. Professor Keith Olson of the University of Maryland also patiently waded through the early drafts of this study, and I have greatly benefited from his friendly counsel and perceptive criticism. I have also profited from the comments of Richard M. Abrams, Charles J. Errico, Clifford B. Foust, John L. Gaddis, Irwin F. Gellman, Walter D. Jacobs, David R. Kepley, Horace Samuel Merrill, Lisle A. Rose, James H. Shideler, and E. B. Smith on various sections of the manuscript. Professor Walter Rundell, Jr., chairman of the History Department of the University of Maryland, furnished much appreciated funds for typing the original version of this volume. Mrs. Gladys Shimasaki typed my dissertation and subsequent drafts with remarkable skill and good humor.

My family has made this book possible in more ways than I can ever enumerate. My parents and my brothers Bob and Wally provided encouragement, moral support, and relief from the preoccupations of research and writing. My wife Pat has been a boundless source of inspiration and understanding. Her assistance as typist, proofreader, and critic of my prose and logic was exceeded only by the countless intangible ways in which she served as a collaborator in the preparation of this book.

J. Samuel Walker

HENRY A. WALLACE
AND AMERICAN
FOREIGN POLICY

1

The Third Henry Wallace

Henry Agard Wallace remains a controversial and enigmatic figure in the history of American foreign relations. Although he never held a position that dealt primarily with international affairs, he played an important role in foreign policy as Secretary of Agriculture and Vice President under Franklin D. Roosevelt and Secretary of Commerce under Harry S. Truman. After his dismissal from Truman's cabinet in September 1946, he emerged as the most prominent critic of America's "get-tough" posture toward the Soviet Union. His outspoken opposition to the cold war policies of the United States, culminating in his presidential candidacy on a third-party ticket in 1948, made him an isolated and widely vilified dissenter.

Wallace's views on foreign policy throughout his career defied easy generalizations and often seemed inconsistent and anachronistic. He was an unabashed idealist who spoke frequently and earnestly about achieving the millennium, but he was also practical enough that Roosevelt once called him "Old Man Common Sense." He shared a midwestern agrarian background with many noted isolationists, yet with the exception of an interlude during the 1920s, he was always a dedicated internationalist. Despite a conspicuous strain of Anglophobia, Wallace was an early advocate of aid for Great Britain's defense against Nazi Germany before Pearl Harbor. Although he vigorously protested Roosevelt's decision to extend diplomatic recognition to the Soviet Union in 1933, he sacrificed his public career and incurred a torrent of denunciation by urging a conciliatory stand toward the Soviets after World War II. Yet there were fundamental consistencies and strands of continuity that characterized Wallace's thinking on foreign affairs. The story of his political odyssey began with the man who influenced him most— his grandfather, the first Henry Wallace.

Born on a farm in Western Pennsylvania in 1836, the elder Henry Wallace was the offspring of Scots-Irish and staunchly Presbyterian parents. They decided that their son should enter the ministry, and as much from duty as devoutness, young Wallace went to seminary. Ordained in 1863, he and his bride settled in Iowa, and Wallace began his career as a preacher. It was not a happy experience. Bickering among the congregations he served, resistance to church reforms he advocated, a paltry salary, and family tragedy drained his strength and impaired his health. Finally, in 1877, he resigned the ministry, acquired land, and became a successful, prosperous farmer.[1]

Although Wallace quit the pulpit, he never gave up preaching. Soon after leaving the ministry, he began to write a column for the local newspaper espousing his views on agriculture, politics, religion, and other matters of interest to him. He became a popular and respected farm journalist, and eventually assumed the editorship of the prestigious *Iowa Homestead*. Under his leadership, the paper increased its circulation and influence, and he became widely and affectionately known as Uncle Henry Wallace. In 1895, however, his refusal to submit to demands of his publisher on editorial policy abruptly ended his association with the *Homestead*. Left without a vehicle to air his opinions and vent his energies, Wallace was despondent and restless. The problem was solved when his son, Henry Cantwell Wallace, at that time a professor at Iowa State College, persuaded the elder Wallace to serve as editor of a small farm journal that he and another professor owned jointly. The Wallace family bought full ownership of the paper, and under the slogan "Good Farming, Clear Thinking, Right Living" *Wallaces' Farmer* quickly emerged as one of the most influential and prosperous farm journals in the Midwest.[2]

Uncle Henry Wallace believed in God, democracy, and the land. "If I were to define the good man," he wrote in 1897, "I should say that he is the man who sincerely believes in a just, and therefore merciful, God, and who does his best every day of his life . . . to do

His will.'' He preached the virtues of Christian morality and Calvinist ethics, and insisted that the best guide to daily living was the Sermon on the Mount. Wallace was firmly convinced that the wellspring of the righteous life and America's democratic principles was agricultural civilization. Agrarian existence was the ''ideal human life,'' he believed, because it engendered courage, self-reliance, honesty, industriousness, and fear of the Lord. Uncle Henry had great faith in the inherent wisdom of the common people. ''They are the real source of what we call common sense, which, outside of Holy Writ, is the safest guide to all the affairs of life,'' he observed. ''They . . . stand for all that is best and purest in our civilization.'' Politically, Wallace described himself as an ''anti-monopoly Republican.'' He detested privilege and trusts, and was suspicious of cities and big business. But he also disliked the Populists, who were too loud and too shrill to suit his temperament. Although his instincts were progressive, they were never radical. The politician he most admired was his friend Theodore Roosevelt, whom he depicted in 1912 as ''altogether the biggest all-around man that walks in the United States today.''[3]

In foreign affairs, Uncle Henry inclined toward internationalism. He believed farmers could thrive under a system of either complete self-sufficiency or free trade, but he thought the latter would ultimately produce a more prosperous America. He supported high tariffs for infant industries, but feared that manufacturing interests manipulated tariff policies at the expense of farmers. Wallace protested a proposed reciprocal trade treaty with Canada in 1911 because it would have lowered tariffs on farm products entering the United States without making similar reductions on manufactured articles. Complaining that the agreement favored industry while hurting agriculture, he wrote: ''Whatever system of tariffs is adopted, it should be fair to both classes. . . . I am in favor of reciprocity, but not in favor of the present reciprocity law.'' Although not a doctrinaire pacifist, Uncle Henry despised war, and frequently attacked special interests that wanted to maintain a large army and navy. War preparations, he argued, benefited a few groups while the ''common people are saddled with taxes and higher living costs.'' He contended that ''a short and simple way'' to prevent war was to submit disputes between countries to international arbitration.[4]

Uncle Henry's ideas had a profound influence on his grandson. Born on a farm near Orient, Iowa, on October 7, 1888, the third Henry Wallace loved and respected his father, Henry Cantwell Wallace, but he idolized his grandfather. "Grandfather and I were very close, much closer than my father and I were," he later recalled. "You see, my father was only twenty-two when I was born. Naturally he had other things on his mind when I was young." As a boy, Henry A. Wallace displayed a keen, probing mind and a voracious curiosity. His primary interests were botany and genetics, and at a tender age, he was befriended and encouraged by the celebrated plant scientist George Washington Carver, who was at that time an obscure student at Iowa State College. Young Wallace attended the same institution a few years later, and received his degree in 1910. He was a serious, conscientious student who excelled in agriculture and genetics, but demonstrated interest in other areas as well. Shortly after graduation, he applied his scientific expertise by experimenting with various strains of corn and eventually producing the first hybrid corn for commercial use.[5]

Henry A. Wallace shared many of his grandfather's viewpoints. Although he began to question and ultimately rejected aspects of Calvinist dogma, he remained firmly and deeply committed to Christian ethics. Like Uncle Henry, he believed in the virtues and merits of agricultural life. "I want to see a strong rural civilization in the United States," he wrote in 1913, "because I think such a civilization is more competent to serve as a balance wheel for the nation than city civilization." He took an internationalist position on foreign policy issues. Wallace once recalled that the stories his grandparents told him of their visits to England and Ireland opened his eyes "to the vast world overseas." He echoed Uncle Henry's position on the tariff. Writing in *Wallaces' Farmer* in May 1913, he commended the free trade policies of Holland and expressed hope that the United States would follow a similar course. But he warned that tariffs should not be removed on agricultural products unless they were also removed on manufactured goods. The agrarian outlook, deep religious convictions, and internationalist orientation that Wallace inherited from his grandfather powerfully influenced his thinking about world affairs in future years.[6]

The outbreak of war in Europe in August 1914 shocked and dismayed Uncle Henry Wallace. "I am obsessed with the war in Europe; can't think of much else," he confided. He predicted that it would

be "the most terrible conflict the world has ever seen," but he hoped
it would result in "human liberty and a respect for human rights."
He believed that the war underscored the interdependence of the
countries of the world and pointed out that the United States could
not escape the effects of the conflict. But he vigorously supported
President Woodrow Wilson's call for strict neutrality, and urged
that the United States stay out of the war. Ultimately, Uncle Henry
believed, "we shall have to have an international court in which all
civilized nations are represented; and to enforce its decrees we must
have an international police on both land and sea, in which all civilized lands are represented." Greatly disturbed when a German sub-
marine sank the *Lusitania* in May 1915, Wallace resolved to discuss
his views with President Wilson. On a trip to Washington in October,
he secured an appointment with the President, who received him
"most cordially." He told Wilson that after the war, lasting peace
required "freedom of the seas and their policing by an international
fleet." The President, he said, "was the one man who could attract
the attention of all the world" and take steps to assure that no country
controlled the seas or impeded international trade. Wilson listened
"most attentively" and commented: "Of course you do not expect
me to give you a definite answer on this point." Uncle Henry replied
that he did not, but added that if his vision materialized, it would
"give us world peace for all time." Four months later, he died suddenly of a stroke. Henry Cantwell Wallace assumed editorship of
Wallaces' Farmer, while Henry Agard served as associate editor.[7]

The Wallaces supported American entry into World War I in
April 1917, maintaining that "this whole business is a struggle to
maintain the ideals upon which this great American republic was
founded, and for which, when the pinch comes, we are always ready
to fight." Henry C. Wallace aided the war effort in several civilian
capacities, and his son, despite a serious case of undulant fever, did
statistical work for the Food Administration and took on additional editorial duties because of his father's frequent absences.
He also read and admired Thorstein Veblen's wartime books, *Imperial Germany and the Industrial Revolution* and *The Nature of
Peace.* Veblen argued that although Germany had become a modern
industrial country, it had retained its archaic and autocratic political
institutions, which could be sustained only by constant preparation
for war. He suggested that German aggression and militarism would
be eliminated only if its "Dynastic State" were replaced by a more

democratic and inherently peaceful form of government. Veblen also attributed the roots of war to selfish interests who manipulated common people by appeals to patriotism and national honor in order to secure high tariffs and protect their overseas investments. He ridiculed nationalism, recommended the elimination of international trade barriers, and called for a "league of pacific nations" to guarantee peace. Perhaps because of Henry A. Wallace's regard for Veblen's analysis of Germany, *Wallaces' Farmer* rejected the idea of a negotiated agreement to end hostilities. It demanded Germany's unconditional surrender and a punitive peace settlement to eradicate Prussian militarism. "The good in Germany must . . . triumph over the bad, and those who have been guilty of this greatest crime in nineteen hundred years must be handed over to be judged at the bar of an outraged civilization."[8]

After the war ended, Henry A. Wallace served as president of the Iowa branch of the League of Nations Non-Partisan Association, while *Wallaces' Farmer* endorsed the Versailles Treaty and advocated American participation in the League. Although it admitted that the League covenant was imperfect, it argued that if the Senate failed to approve the Versailles Treaty, it would "dash to the ground the hopes of suffering humanity." When Senate passage of the treaty became increasingly problematical, *Wallaces' Farmer* condemned Wilson's obstinate refusal to accept reservations and the obstructionist tactics of legislators whose opposition to the President had "blinded them to their highest sense of duty to their country." It urged that everybody "come down from his high horse and be satisfied with the very best compromise possible." When the Senate defeated the treaty for the final time in March 1920, *Wallaces' Farmer* placed the primary blame on Wilson's stubborn unwillingness to consider reservations. A short time later, postwar adjustments caused a sudden collapse in farm prices, which had achieved unprecedented levels during the war. American agriculture fell into a serious depression, causing Henry A. Wallace to reassess his internationalist position.[9]

NOTES

1. Russell Lord, *The Wallaces of Iowa* (Boston: Houghton Mifflin Co., 1947), pp. 1-79; Edward L. and Frederick H. Schapsmeier, *Henry A. Wallace*

of Iowa: The Agrarian Years, 1910-1940 (Ames: Iowa State University Press: 1968), pp. 2-5.

2. Lord, *Wallaces of Iowa,* pp. 79-133; Schapsmeiers, *Agrarian Years,* pp. 6-10.

3. Henry Wallace, *Letters to the Farm Boy* (New York: Macmillan Co., 1900); Henry Wallace to Walter Hines Page, November 11, 1912, Henry Wallace [Uncle Henry] Papers, University of Iowa, Iowa City; Lord, *Wallaces of Iowa,* pp. 104, 112-13.

4. Wallace to Dan Wallace, February 25, 1911, Wallace to Walter Hines Page, March 13, 1913, Uncle Henry Papers; *Wallaces' Farmer,* April 28, 1899, p. 379, December 30, 1910, p. 1756, February 17, 1911, p. 271, May 19, 1911, p. 834, August 22, 1913, p. 1139, March 20, 1914, p. 501.

5. Schapsmeiers, *Agrarian Years,* pp. 16-27; Lord, *Wallaces of Iowa,* pp. 118-25, 140-59; "The Vice President," *Fortune,* 26 (November 1942): 144.

6. Henry A. Wallace, "Studying Agricultural Europe," *Wallaces' Farmer,* May 9, 1913, p. 797; Henry A. Wallace, *Statesmanship and Religion* (New York: Round Table Press, 1934), pp. 45-46; Henry A. Wallace, "Henry Wallace Tells of His Political Odyssey," *Life,* 40 (May 14, 1956): 174; Wallace interview, Columbia Oral History Collection, Columbia University, New York, pp. 106, 5177.

7. Henry Wallace to Dan Wallace, October 1, 1914, Uncle Henry Papers; Lord, *Wallaces of Iowa,* pp. 166-67; "The Vice President," p. 144; *Wallaces' Farmer,* August 7, 1914, p. 1086, August 28, 1914, p. 1165, September 11, 1914, p. 1221, October 9, 1914, p. 1349, January 1, 1915, p. 4.

8. Henry A. Wallace to W. D. Nettleton, July 7, 1931, Donald Murphy to Edward Schapsmeier, March 10, 1964, Henry A. Wallace Papers, University of Iowa; *Wallaces' Farmer,* April 13, 1917, p. 644, August 23, 1918, p. 1185, October 18, 1918, p. 1512; Henry A. Wallace, "Veblen's 'Imperial Germany and the Industrial Revolution,'" *Political Science Quarterly,* 55 (September 1940): 435-44; Thorstein Veblen, *Imperial Germany and the Industrial Revolution* (New York: Macmillan Co., 1915) and *The Nature of Peace* (New York: Macmillan Co., 1917).

9. *Wallaces' Farmer,* May 9, 1919, p. 1024, June 20, 1919, p. 1248, November 28, 1919, p. 2358, January 30, 1920, p. 339, March 26, 1920, p. 966; "Henry Wallace Tells of His Political Odyssey," p. 174.

2

The
Isolationist
Path

In a January 1919 article, Henry A. Wallace expressed concern that postwar adjustments would create difficulties for American farmers. He noted that the end of the Napoleonic wars had resulted in an agricultural depression in England because of the inevitable deflation of wartime prices. He warned readers that the recent conflict was likely to produce a similar effect, and cautioned them against assuming that high prices would continue indefinitely. In a book he wrote the same year, Wallace pointed out that U.S. export trade would probably decline in the postwar period because England and Germany were reluctant to buy high-priced American farm products. Even more importantly, the war had made the United States a creditor nation, which meant that it would have to import more than it exported so Europe could pay its debts. American farmers, he declared, would be required either to produce only to satisfy domestic needs, or to become so efficient that their goods could compete on the world market.[1]

For a short time, Wallace's fears appeared to be groundless. Agricultural prices remained high immediately after the war, causing farmers to believe their prosperity was going to be permanent. They continued producing to the hilt, and many increased their already considerable debts. The crash came in the summer of 1920. When the U.S. government terminated its foreign lending and European agriculture began to revive, the export market for American farm products declined drastically. Surpluses mounted and prices plummeted, plunging American agriculture into severe depression.[2]

The farm crisis marked the beginning of Henry A. Wallace's shift from internationalism. Assuming the editorship of *Wallaces' Farmer* in March 1921 when Henry C. Wallace became Warren G. Harding's Secretary of Agriculture, he called for an emergency tariff to provide assistance for beleaguered farmers. Wallace complained that foreign countries were dumping cheap farm products on an already glutted American market. He advocated a sliding scale tariff that would guarantee farmers cost of production for their goods but which would be removed when prices improved. Wallace also campaigned to persuade corn belt farmers to curb surpluses by cutting production. Under the slogan "Less Corn, More Clover, More Money," he wrote editorials and spoke before scores of meetings, urging farmers to reduce their acreage voluntarily. The effort proved futile. Farmers increased their corn acreage in 1921 and produced a bumper crop, thus further depressing a market already groaning under surpluses.[3]

Wallace's fruitless attempt to convince farmers to curtail production left him uncertain of the best way to combat the farm depression. "It would seem that the United States has before her two rather clear cut paths," he wrote his father in January 1922. "The one leads toward economic self-sufficiency with aloofness from Europe, and the other leads toward taking a very active interest in Europe, reorganizing Europe financially, investing liberally in European industries, and eventually taking a very vital interest in Europe's military and political affairs." Adopting the first path, Wallace contended, would involve placing prohibitive tariffs on both manufactured and farm products, adjusting agricultural production, and canceling European debts. The second alternative would require lowering tariffs on manufactured goods so that Europe could pay its debts and purchase American agricultural products by exporting industrial commodities to the United States. "The Republican party must either abandon the principle of a high tariff on manufactured goods, or it must take upon itself the responsibility of redirecting American agriculture so as to cut down the production of pork, corn, wheat and cotton," he asserted. Wallace did not indicate which alternative he preferred, but events soon pushed him down the isolationist path.[4]

Later in the same month, a National Agricultural Conference, called by Secretary Henry C. Wallace to discuss the farm crisis, convened in Washington. Henry A. Wallace wrote an address that was to be delivered to the meeting by A. Sykes, president of the Corn Belt Meat Producers' Association. The speech reiterated Wallace's conviction that high tariffs would impair Europe's ability to buy American exports, and that if the Republican administration insisted on a protectionist policy, it would have to assume responsibility for making necessary adjustments in agriculture. The proposed speech was moderate in tone and stated explicitly that it intended no criticism of the administration's tariff position. Nevertheless, it alarmed Henry C. Wallace, who had the address rewritten because he feared it would cause him political embarrassment. The secretary's action came too late to prevent the original version from appearing in *Wallaces' Farmer,* but the revised speech Sykes gave to the agricultural conference was completely innocuous.[5]

The incident made a profound impression on Henry A. Wallace. Since the Harding administration refused even to discuss tariff questions, he realized that there was no possibility that the United States would lower its trade barriers. The Republican protectionist stand effectively blocked the internationalist path he had outlined as a possible solution to the farm depression. The only alternative remaining was self-sufficiency and isolation. "It is time to stop thinking about the European market and begin to think about reducing our production to a home market basis," Wallace wrote on February 10, 1922.[6] He constantly reminded his readers that they could no longer sell profitably on a world market because of Europe's greatly decreased purchasing power. He pointed out that American farmers had sent record quantities of goods abroad in 1921, but the prices they had received were so low that it was imperative that they adjust their production to domestic requirements. In September 1922, when Congress passed the Fordney-McCumber bill, which set up the highest tariff schedule in American history, Wallace interpreted it as a step toward self-containment that would reduce the chances of the United States becoming involved in the affairs of Europe and Asia. He thought that the only way the United States could solve the farm depression was to adhere consistently to either a program of complete isolationism or a program of unqualified internationalism. Wallace argued that since the country had already moved in the direction of isolationism by raising tariff barriers, it should follow that path unambiguously by becoming self-sufficient. "When the people of the great middle west become fairly familiar with the point at issue," he stated, "we believe that they will be strong for the idea of a self-contained nation."[7]

Wallace's opinions about Europe reinforced his isolationism. European politics were a "quagmire of crookedness," he declared, characterized by a long tradition of "devious diplomacy and warfare." He saw little prospect of Europe changing its ways, and told his readers how fortunate they were to live in the United States, "the one really worth while nation of the world today." Like many Americans, Wallace felt disillusioned by the results of World War I, and concluded that Americans would be wise to stay out of European matters. One way to disengage from Europe, he believed, was to cancel the war debt. He feared American creditors would accept European property in payment of the debt, and the United States would become deeply involved in world affairs. "The more we see of European affairs," he observed, "the more we like the idea of being in a position to keep away from Europe as much as possible."[8]

Wallace was apprehensive that eastern manufacturers and financiers were taking the country in the opposite direction. Convinced that industrialists were counting heavily on overseas markets to increase sales, he warned that foreign trade would bring foreign entanglements because businessmen would insist that the government guarantee their markets. Even more alarming to Wallace was the steadily increasing volume of American foreign investment. It indicated to him that international bankers were following England's example and leading the country toward a financial empire. He predicted that economic expansion abroad would involve the United States in European diplomatic intrigue, cause unwarranted intervention in the internal affairs of other countries, and eventually foment a major war.[9]

Wallace continued to advocate a program of American self-containment through the end of 1923. His editorials repeatedly echoed the theme that American farmers must adjust production to domestic demand because the European market had disappeared as a satisfactory outlet for their surplus. He pointed out that Europe would not have sufficient buying power to purchase large quantities of American farm products for many years and that it was growing increasing quantities of its own food. Wallace suggested that the United States "treat Europe as tho she were located on another planet and readjust our agricultural and manufacturing situation accordingly." Such a scheme would not appeal to an "economic imperialist," Wallace wrote, "yet it has the merit of being a program that eliminates the necessity for huge armaments, that reduces the chances of war, and that makes a prosperous and stable existence possible for both the farmer and the industrial worker." His campaign for self-containment had little noticeable impact on farmers, however, who continued to produce surpluses.[10]

The prevailing sentiment in the Midwest regarding foreign affairs during the 1920s was isolationist. That isolationism was characterized by a profound disillusionment with American belligerency in World War I, opposition to political involvement with Europe, a deep-seated suspicion and antipathy for Wall Street and big business, a fear that the foreign activities and interests of eastern businessmen would lead to imperialism and war, intense nationalism, and Anglophobia. It did not mean that midwesterners were unconcerned about foreign affairs or that they contemplated a cessation of trade with Europe. Wallace's views reflected the predominant mood of the 1920s, but his call for self-sufficiency entailed a more complete isolationism than most Americans were willing to accept. He later admitted that farmers regarded a plan that required them to stop producing for export as "visionary and impractical."[11]

In December 1923, Wallace abandoned his campaign for self-containment and began to promote an export plan advanced by two midwestern businessmen, George N. Peek and General Hugh S. Johnson. The Peek-Johnson plan sought to ensure "equality for agriculture" by erecting a two-price system for agricultural products. Peek and Johnson recognized that tariff protection was useless for agricultural goods produced in surplus and that American farmers had to sell their commodities at world prices while buying manufactured goods at protected prices. They proposed to make the tariff effective for agriculture by setting up a government corporation that would buy surplus products and sell them abroad at the world price. Farmers would be assessed an "equalization fee" to pay the losses incurred by the corporation. But by dumping the price-depressing surplus abroad, American farmers would receive a better return for their products at home. For several years, the Peek-Johnson plan, introduced in Congress as the McNary-Haugen bill in January 1924, provided the basis for a widespread movement to end the agricultural depression.[12]

The economic nationalism embodied in the McNary-Haugen bill appealed to Henry A. Wallace. In December 1923, he criticized a proposal of former Secretary of Agriculture E. T. Meredith because it did not contain any provision "for dumping the surplus of wheat and hog products on the European market at a lower price than the same product is sold on the American market." In the same month, Wallace later recalled, his diligent efforts at the Iowa Farm Bureau convention helped persuade it to become the first organization to approve a resolution supporting the McNary-Haugen plan. *Wallaces' Farmer* became one of the few farm papers to champion the bill in 1924, exhorting its readers to write their respective members of Congress and build a "prairie fire of farm enthusiasm" for the export plan.[13]

Farmers deserved the protection that the McNary-Haugen bill would provide, Wallace reasoned, because the government was largely responsible for their miseries. During the war, it had encouraged farmers to increase their productivity, and patriotically, they had done so. After the war, however, the reversal of credit balances had drastically reduced Europe's purchasing power, causing a sharp decline in farm prices. American agriculture needed a system to assure it of a fair price for its products on the domestic market. Business and industry prospered because they had adequate tariff protection and dumped their surplus abroad; labor prospered because of government legislation. Therefore, farmers were justified in demanding the export plan because it would make the tariff effective for agriculture. Europe would not retaliate against the dumping of agricultural surpluses because it would be happy to receive cheap food from the United States. Furthermore, the McNary-Haugen plan, since it dealt with a temporary emergency growing out of the war, would not continue indefinitely.[14]

Wallace emerged as a major figure in the battle for the McNary-Haugen bill and campaigned vigorously for its enactment. With characteristic zeal, he wrote dozens of editorials, spoke before farmers' meetings, attended conferences, and journeyed to Washington on several occasions to promote the export plan. The arguments he presented in favor of the proposal in early 1924 remained basically unchanged during the five years he fought for McNary-Haugenism. Wallace recognized that the export plan was imperfect and never regarded its principles as inviolable. But in light of other possible solutions, he contended that the McNary-Haugen plan represented the best available and most politically feasible method to combat the farm problem.[15]

One conceivable alternative to the export plan was reducing tariffs on both agricultural and manufactured products, but Wallace realized that lowering trade barriers was a political improbability. Moreover, he argued that farmers had "no particular grudge against the protective system." He believed that they would eventually benefit from it because the American population would expand enough to use all that U.S. farmers produced. While admitting that he had "no very definite convictions on either free trade or protection," Wallace demanded that farmers be given justice under one system or the other. The McNary-Haugen bill would ensure fair treatment for farmers by making the tariff work for them. But defeat of the export plan, Wallace warned, would force farmers to exercise their only remaining option of working to eliminate trade barriers. He threatened that "if the conservatives of the east insist that natural forces take care of the farming situation and defeat the McNary-Haugen bill, the farmer must also insist that natural forces take care of American industry and work for free trade in manufactured products."[16]

President Calvin Coolidge offered another alternative to the McNary-Haugen plan. He suggested that farmers produce only for domestic needs and profitable foreign markets. Wallace had advocated a similar position, but farmers had not responded favorably. He continued to urge his readers to reduce their acreage, because he recognized that controlled production would be necessary even if the export plan became law.[17] But he also expressed grave reservations about drastically curtailing agricultural output, and pointed out that a series of crop failures would create food shortages in the United States. Cutting production to domestic levels would also be a "brutal thing" because it would cause millions of Europeans to starve. Furthermore, Wallace argued that the ideal of a self-sufficient country must apply to industry and finance as well as agriculture. He suspected manufacturers of encouraging a reduction in agricultural output to avoid sharing the profits of foreign trade with farmers and to clear the way for importing increasing quantities of cheap food from Argentina and Australia. If those eastern interests were really serious about promoting self-sufficiency, Wallace asserted, they should invest their money to increase consumer prosperity and demand at home rather than sending millions of dollars abroad.[18]

The steady expansion of American economic activity abroad continued to trouble Henry Wallace, who had become firmly convinced that foreign trade and investment led to imperialism and war. He declared that the United States "should not follow in the footsteps of England and meddle in affairs all over the world." European commercial rivalries had helped precipitate war in 1914, he believed, and the peace that had followed had done little to remove the causes of war. The only way to abolish war, Wallace insisted, was by refusing to guarantee the foreign investments of "economic adventurers."[19] But it appeared to him that the United States had begun to pursue a policy of economic imperialism that imitated the patterns of European diplomacy. The presence of American gunboats in China and marines in Central America, the American refusal to free the Philippines, and the dramatic increase of foreign loans deeply disturbed Wallace. He feared that in order to protect the profits of a few individuals, the United States would engage in foreign intervention and war that would be costly in money and lives and inimical to American ideals. Noting the rising nationalistic feelings in China, India, and the Philippines, he commented: "Young nations like young people want to be allowed the privilege of making their own mistakes." While the people of those countries did not fear political domination by the United States, they were "very suspicious of our efforts at financial and trade control."[20]

Wallace repeatedly reminded his readers that only a few investors benefited from economic expansion overseas, but that the entire country, including farmers, paid the costs. "No farmer has investments in Nicaragua, Mexico or China," he pointed out, "but the farmer is helping to pay for the armed forces that go to protect American investments in those countries, and he will continue to pay heavily both in taxes and in blood, if those imperialistic adventures abroad lead to a major war." Wallace favored a military force strong enough to ensure the national security of the United States, but opposed a large navy "needed only to back up the sort of foreign trade that is interested in collecting exorbitant interest rates and in exchanging manufactured goods for twice their value in raw material.'' Farmers wanted the most defense for the lowest possible price, he asserted, and had no inclination to pay the costs of collecting bad debts for foreign investors. An ardent advocate of disarmament, Wallace denounced rising military expenditures in England, France, and the United States. ''It seems that the Allied powers crushed German militarism only to take some of its characteristics for their own,'' he complained.[21]

Wallace assailed the huge volume of American lending to Europe. Although loans might temporarily enable Europeans to purchase American farm products, ultimately the only way that Europe could pay its debts and restore effective purchasing power was by exporting its manufactured articles. But American tariff policy prevented Europe from selling its goods to the United States. As Europe became saddled with increasing interest payments on American loans, Wallace believed, its ability to buy American farm exports would be further impaired. Moreover, the loans to Europe gave financial interests in the United States an enormous amount of influence in European affairs. The world power of American investors exceeded that of English financiers before the war, Wallace stated, and would inevitably lead the United States to imperialism and war.[22] He suggested that instead of sending money abroad in exchange for paper promises, American investors use their surplus capital to develop natural resources at home and to increase the purchasing power of farmers. Those investments would not be so lucrative as foreign lending, Wallace admitted, but they would be much safer and more beneficial to the country as a whole. He also thought that one way, though ''not a very important way,'' for the U.S. government to improve farm buying power was to cancel the European war debt.[23]

The policies of the Coolidge administration enraged Wallace, because the ''eastern administration'' refused to assist farmers in any meaningful way. It was primarily concerned, he insisted, with providing cheap food for the East and ensuring prosperity for industry and labor. After three unsuccessful attempts, the persistent efforts of farm leaders finally pushed the McNary-Haugen bill through Congress in February 1927. Coolidge promptly replied with a scathing veto message that Wallace thought was marked by ''intemperance of language'' and ''ignorance of the situation of agriculture and of the provisions of the bill.'' Proponents of the export plan again persuaded Congress to pass the McNary-Haugen bill in May 1928, and again Coolidge responded with a veto message that Wallace described as a "storm of abuse" that was "a slap in the face for agriculture." He was incensed that Coolidge approved a ship subsidy to aid the merchant marine at the same time he rejected the export plan for farmers.[24]

Thoroughly disgusted with the Republican administration and suspicious of the Democrats, Wallace proposed the formation of a new political party to serve western and southern interests. The idea aroused little enthusiasm, however, and in the presidential campaign of 1928, Wallace supported Democrat Al Smith because of his endorsement of McNary-Haugenism.[25] Wallace continued to advocate the McNary-Haugen plan as the best available solution to the farm problem until after Herbert Hoover's overwhelming victory in the election of 1928. Congress was unlikely to reconsider the export plan seriously, he pointed out, when sixty percent of western farmers had voted for a man who adamantly opposed McNary-Haugenism. For all practical purposes, the McNary-Haugen bill was dead. In December 1928, Wallace began to express reservations about the principle of dumping either industrial or agricultural surpluses abroad. But he believed that the battle for McNary-Haugenism, despite its ultimate futility, had educated thousands of farmers to understand the tariff better. "With the situation as it is now developing I would expect the majority of the thoughtful McNary-Haugenites to become free-traders sooner or later," he declared.[26]

Although he did not immediately abandon his isolationism, the demise of McNary-Haugenism started Wallace back on the road to internationalism. He had often stated that if the export plan were defeated, farmers would respond by attacking the protectionist system. Nevertheless, he watched with foreboding as Congress convened in April 1929 and took up tariff revision. Wallace predicted that Congress would raise tariffs on agricultural products that farmers produced in surplus—an action that would be of no value to them. But farmers would be expected to support increased rates on manufactured products that they consumed, so the end result of tariff revision would be detrimental to them. Farmers would receive "the superficial appearance of protection while the substance of protection is being given to manufacturers." Wallace concluded that the best course of action was to oppose any change in the tariff schedule, because farmers were unlikely "to beat the industries at the log-rolling game." Eventually, after farmers had learned more about the tariff, he believed they would strive to reduce duties on manufactured goods. Wallace did not condemn high tariffs on principle, but on the practical ground that they would only benefit farmers if some means were devised to make protection work for agriculture. But any such scheme appeared to be a political impossibility.[27]

The Smoot-Hawley tariff bill that passed the House of Representatives in June 1929 confirmed Wallace's worst fears. He declared that it would "do the farmers of the United States tens of millions of dollars of damage every year." Denouncing the proposed tariff as "iniquitous," he pointed out that it raised rates on corn, hogs, eggs, and beef, which did nothing to help farmers. But it also increased rates on a wide variety of industrial commodities, which hurt farmers because they would pay higher prices for those products. Convinced that the Smoot-Hawley bill was a "strictly selfish log-rolling proposition," Wallace told his readers to insist that the Fordney-McCumber tariff continue unchanged, and urged them to consider seriously the merits of "wholesale reduction" of tariff rates. Congress adjourned in November 1929 without passing the new tariff, but Wallace remained apprehensive about the future.[28]

To combat the agricultural depression Herbert Hoover set up a Farm Board and asked farmers to cut production voluntarily. Wallace attacked that program as inadequate and inherently defective. He argued that a scheme to make the tariff effective for agriculture would work better than Hoover's plan, but that the best solution would be "the continual, gradual reduction of the tariff on manufactured products."[29] The prospects for decreased tariff rates on industrial goods looked bleak, however. Wallace renewed his assault on the Smoot-Hawley bill as Congress reconsidered the measure in the spring of 1930. The tariff, he maintained, was "nothing but selfish grabbing" that would injure farmers because they were not skilled at "outgrabbing the other fellow." The assertion that Smoot-Hawley would assist farmers, Wallace exclaimed, was "pure bunk." When Congress passed the tariff bill, he urged Hoover to veto the "new monstrosity," but the President signed it in June 1930. Wallace was dismayed, and expressed the hope that there would not be another general revision because changes in the tariff schedule worked to the advantage of special interests. "Very probably we wouldn't feel so indignant about it if the farmer were ever one of those favored groups," Wallace commented. "He never is tho [*sic*]. We believe he never will be."[30]

The Smoot-Hawley Tariff Act signaled the end of Henry Wallace's isolationism. For ten years he had sought a solution to the farm depression by pursuing the isolationist path, but he had found it to be a blind alley. His campaign for American self-containment had been rejected by farmers as impractical, and expanding foreign investment had made it untenable. From 1924 through 1928 he had fought for the dumping scheme embodied in the McNary-Haugen bill, only to be frustrated by Coolidge's vetoes and Hoover's election. Wallace had voiced no particular opposition to high tariffs in principle, but the passage of Smoot-Hawley had persuaded him that farmers would never receive just and equitable treatment under the protectionist system. Convinced that the United States would never adopt a viable isolationist program, Wallace turned to the internationalist path as the only remaining alternative.

NOTES

1. Henry A. Wallace, *Agricultural Prices* (Des Moines: Wallace Publishing Co., 1920), pp. 68-69, 71; "Farming Depression in England Following the Napoleonic War," *Wallaces' Farmer,* January 31, 1919, pp. 247, 250.

2. James H. Shideler, *Farm Crisis, 1919-1923* (Berkeley: University of California Press, 1957), Chap. 2; Wayne D. Rasmussen, ed., *Readings in the History of American Agriculture* (Urbana: University of Illinois Press, 1960), p. 227; Donald L. Winters, *Henry C. Wallace as Secretary of Agriculture, 1921-1924* (Urbana: University of Illinois Press, 1970), pp. 64-65.

3. Shideler, *Farm Crisis,* pp. 86-87; Jack Alexander, "Henry A. Wallace: Cornfield Prophet," *Life,* 9 (September 2, 1940): 85; *Wallaces' Farmer,* March 18, 1921, pp. 504-505, April 1, 1921, p. 576, April 8, 1921, p. 608. Wallace's editorials in *Wallaces' Farmer* will be cited by the appropriate issue of the paper. His signed articles in *Wallaces' Farmer* will be cited by the title of the article and the appropriate issue.

4. Henry A. Wallace to Henry C. Wallace, January 3, 1922, Henry C. Taylor Papers, Wisconsin State Historical Society Archives, Madison.

5. Henry A. Wallace speech, "Relation of the Tariff to Farm Relief in the United States," September 6, 1929, Henry A. Wallace Papers, University

of Iowa; "High Tariff and Foreign Trade," *Wallaces' Farmer,* February 3, 1922, p. 135; Henry A. Wallace, Review of Shideler, *Farm Crisis* in *American Historical Review,* 63 (April, 1958): 707; Winters, *Henry C. Wallace,* p. 150.

6. Wallace, "Relation of the Tariff to Farm Relief," Wallace Papers; *Wallaces' Farmer,* February 10, 1922, p. 173; Russell Lord, *The Wallaces of Iowa* (Boston: Houghton Mifflin Co., 1947), p. 238.

7. *Wallaces' Farmer,* February 17, 1922, pp. 212-13, April 28, 1922, p. 550, September 29, 1922, p. 1132, November 3, 1922, p. 1292, November 24, 1922, p. 1390; Henry A. Wallace, "Controlling Agricultural Output," *Journal of Farm Economics,* 5 (January 1923): 16-25.

8. *Wallaces' Farmer,* May 19, 1922, p. 639, September 22, 1922, p. 1104, October 13, 1922, p. 1188, October 20, 1922, p. 1229, November 10, 1922, p. 1324.

9. Ibid., September 15, 1922, p. 1073, October 6, 1922, p. 1157, October 13, 1922, p. 1188, January 19, 1923, p. 76, August 3, 1923, p. 1054.

10. Ibid., February 16, 1923, p. 251, March 2, 1923, p. 338, July 27, 1923, p. 1031, September 7, 1923, pp. 1174-75, September 14, 1923, p. 1215.

11. "The South and the Export Plan," ibid., January 15, 1926, p. 67; Wayne S. Cole, *Senator Gerald P. Nye and American Foreign Relations* (Minneapolis: University of Minnesota Press, 1962).

12. Gilbert C. Fite, *George N. Peek and the Fight for Farm Parity* (Norman: University of Oklahoma Press, 1954), pp. 38-40.

13. Ibid., p. 66; *Wallaces' Farmer,* January 25, 1924, p. 128, February 29, 1924, p. 336; Wallace to E. T. Meredith, December 26, 1923, Wallace Papers; Wallace draft of letter to Hugh S. Johnson, March 14, 1940, Secretary's Office—Letters Sent, Record Group 16 (Records of the Office of the Secretary of Agriculture), National Archives, Washington, D.C. (hereafter Record Group and National Archives will be abbreviated as RG and NA).

14. *Wallaces' Farmer,* December 28, 1923, p. 1754, January 4, 1924, p. 6, February 15, 1924, p. 253, April 18, 1924, pp. 620-21.

15. Ibid., April 18, 1924, p. 620, November 12, 1926, p. 1473; Wallace draft of letter to Hugh S. Johnson, March 14, 1940, Secretary's Office-Letters Sent, RG 16, NA; Lord, *Wallaces of Iowa,* pp. 267-68.

16. *Wallaces' Farmer,* May 16, 1924, p. 760, April 24, 1925, p. 606, May 15, 1925, p. 698, June 26, 1925, p. 872, September 25, 1925, p. 1230, June 4, 1926, p. 818, July 23, 1926, p. 987, "The South and the Export Plan," p. 67.

17. Ibid., February 13, 1925, p. 208, January 15, 1926, p. 69; Fite, *Peek and Farm Parity,* pp. 111-12.

18. *Wallaces' Farmer,* March 7, 1924, p. 376, April 18, 1924, p. 620, June 5, 1925, p. 782, December 23, 1927, p. 1670.

19. Ibid., February 22, 1924, p. 293, November 7, 1924, p. 1440, January 23, 1925, p. 105, January 29, 1926, p. 142.

20. Ibid., July 17, 1925, p. 942, August 14, 1925, p. 1035, November 27, 1925, p. 1552, February 19, 1926, p. 268.

21. Ibid., November 7, 1924, p. 1440, March 27, 1925, p. 456, September 18, 1925, p. 1199, October 30, 1925, p. 1420, September 9, 1927, p. 1146, December 30, 1927, p. 1697, March 30, 1928, p. 514.

22. Ibid., August 28, 1925, p. 1091, July 30, 1926, p. 1006, November 5, 1926, p. 1441, March 25, 1927, p. 468.

23. Ibid., August 21, 1925, p. 1059, May 21, 1926, p. 755, December 21, 1926, p. 1712, August 5, 1927, p. 1020, October 7, 1927, p. 1281, September 28, 1928, p. 1308.

24. Ibid., June 25, 1926, p. 893, March 4, 1927, p. 344, June 1, 1928, p. 844, June 8, 1928, p. 869; *Des Moines Register,* May 24, 1928.

25. Wallace speech, "Party Changes Needed," Chester Davis Papers, Western Historical Manuscripts Collection, University of Missouri, Columbia; Lord, *Wallaces of Iowa,* pp. 275-76; Edward L. and Frederick H. Schapsmeier, *Henry A. Wallace of Iowa: The Agrarian Years, 1910-1940* (Ames: Iowa State University Press, 1968), pp. 110-12.

26. Henry A. Wallace, "Stabilization of Farm Prices and the McNary-Haugen Bill," *Annals of the American Academy of Political and Social Science,* 142 (March 1929): 402-405; *Wallaces' Farmer,* December 14, 1928, p. 1724.

27. Wallace, "Relation of the Tariff to Farm Relief," Wallace to Ralph Snyder, April 29, 1929, Wallace to William Hirth, April 17, 1929, Wallace Papers; *Wallaces' Farmer,* February 1, 1929, p. 152, February 22, 1929, p. 276, May 10, 1929, p. 724, May 17, 1929, pp. 756-57, May 24, 1929, p. 791.

28. Wallace, "Relation of the Tariff to Farm Relief," Wallace Papers; *Wallaces' Farmer,* May 17, 1929, p. 756, July 5, 1929, p. 971, September 20, 1929, p. 1270, "The New Tariff and Agriculture," June 14, 1929, pp. 873, 878, 891.

29. *Wallaces' Farmer,* September 6, 1929, p. 1190; *Wallaces' Farmer and Iowa Homestead,* February 15, 1930, p. 298, August 2, 1930, p. 1295, August 9, 1930, p. 1318. In 1929, *Wallaces' Farmer* merged with *Iowa Homestead,* and beginning October 25, both names appeared in the paper's title.

30. Ibid., February 1, 1930, p. 182, March 29, 1930, p. 639, May 17, 1930, p. 959, May 31, 1930, p. 1032, July 19, 1930, p. 1246; Wallace to Charles Brand, July 7, 1930, Wallace Papers.

3

The International Path

Henry Wallace's disenchantment with isolationism would have guided him toward internationalism under any circumstances, but his recognition that the depression was no longer peculiar to American agriculture further impelled him in that direction. As economic catastrophe spread throughout Europe in 1930, he expanded his vision and broadened the scope of his thinking. The deepening world crisis confirmed and intensified the isolationism of many Americans, but it stirred Wallace to speak out forcefully for international solutions to end the depression. On October 11, 1930, he published an analysis of the depression that reflected a distinctly internationalist point of view. The United States, he wrote, had contributed significantly to the onset of world depression. Although it had not been "deliberately selfish," its policies had demonstrated "selfish ignorance" that had led to "international misunderstanding and widespread depression." Its tariff program was particularly reprehensible because it provoked retaliation from other countries and produced a general increase in trade barriers. It was a "terrible thing," Wallace argued, that countries should erect tariff walls just when developments in transportation, communication, and scientific knowledge made possible unprecedented world prosperity through "free exchange of goods." Convinced that "the whole world has become one world for the first time in history," he admonished farmers to recognize that foreign affairs directly affected them. As the most powerful country in the world, he declared, it was time that the United States assume the world responsibilities it had abnegated since 1918.[1]

Wallace discerned three primary causes of the world depression—changes in international economic relationships, monetary deflation, and technological progress. As he had done so often during the 1920s, he pointed out that World War I had fundamentally transformed America's world economic position. America had ceased to be a debtor nation and had emerged from the war as Europe's creditor. Unfortunately, the United States had refused to act as a mature and responsible creditor state. Instead of lowering tariffs to enable Europe to repay its war debts and purchase American products, the United States aggressively sought to increase its exports while raising tariffs to unprecedented levels and insisting on repayment of the war debts. "Not even God himself" could make such a policy work over a long period of time. During the 1920s, America had succeeded in expanding exports and underwriting Europe's buying power only by loaning vast sums of money abroad. But the curtailment of those loans and Europe's reluctance to keep borrowing when it had no way to discharge its debts had caused the whole system to collapse.[2]

Wallace's recommendations for counteracting the damage caused by the country's failure to act properly as a creditor state underscored the internationalist orientation in his thinking that emerged in the latter part of 1930. Although he had advocated self-containment for a time during the 1920s, he now criticized the "narrow minded insularity of the American people" and ridiculed isolationists as people who had "decided that the world is too boisterous a place for them." Nobody had worked harder than Wallace for enactment of the McNary-Haugen bill, but now he warned that such a plan would arouse the animosity of other countries and lead to "worldwide overproduction." He had attacked the Smoot-Hawley tariff because it would harm the interests of farmers, but now he emphasized that it had provoked retaliation abroad and drastically reduced the total volume of world trade. During the 1920s, Wallace advocated cancellation of the war debt first as a means to disengage from Europe, and later as a rather unimportant way to enhance the purchasing power of farmers. In 1930, however, he strongly urged cancellation of the debt and lowering of tariffs as methods of "oil-ing the international economic machine'' and promoting international good will.[3]

Wallace believed that canceling the intergovernmental war debts would help foster world trade by increasing Europe's purchasing power, but also stressed the salutary psychological effect of voiding Europe's obligations. It would be a "great gesture of good will," he wrote, that would "create world-wide confidence" and dispel "international suspicion and hatred." Wallace argued somewhat paradoxically that the country should also use the debts "as a club" to accomplish worthy ends. He suggested that the United States insist that if it invalidated the debts, Britain and France must nullify an equal amount of the German reparations. Wallace also thought that America could link debt cancellation with disarmament by demanding that Europe employ the voided debts for economic, social, and cultural improvement rather than for military expenditures. He believed that European countries would eventually default on their payments, so the United States should extract some benefit from the debts while it could. Denying that cancellation would raise taxes for farmers, Wallace asserted that the advantages of restored world confidence and increased world trade would outweigh the monetary loss incurred by invalidating the debts. He acclaimed President Hoover's decision to declare a one-year moratorium on war debts in June 1931, and contended that a "wave of world confidence" had resulted from Hoover's action.[4]

Wallace repeatedly urged a gradual reduction of tariff barriers by the United States. "Probably no nation in time of peace has ever aroused more world-wide resentment than did the United States . . . by means of the Hawley-Smoot tariff," he wrote. It had triggered reprisals from foreign countries, sharply curbed American exports, and "brought the world to a state of strong commercial conflict." America's tariff policies, Wallace believed, not only obstructed international trade, but also created discord between countries and increased the chances of war. He suggested that the United States negotiate trade treaties with Europe whereby America would agree to accept manufactured goods from Europe if it would remove tariffs on American farm products. Wallace constantly asserted that the United States could help combat the world depression by acting like a mature creditor state. Its policies on war debts and tariffs during the 1920s had caused "an explosion." "We will have more explosions of this sort if we continue to follow the same policy that we have followed since the Great War," he declared.[5]

A second major cause of the worldwide depression that Wallace identified was monetary deflation. He pointed out that insufficient quantities of gold and the contraction of credit throughout the world had caused a general price decline, with disastrous consequences for both individuals and countries in debt. He favored inflationary policies at home and abroad and urged international cooperation to achieve permanent monetary stability so that both extreme inflation and deflation could be averted. Wallace described the gold standard as "a relic of barbarism," but considered it "still necessary as a symbol of world monetary unity." Since the United States and France controlled most of the world's gold supply, he thought they should provide leadership in restoring world confidence and insuring a better distribution of gold to facilitate international trade. Wallace also supported remonetization of silver, as long as it was done sensibly to raise world price levels and not simply to accommodate silver interests. He thought it imperative to convene an international conference to work out a system of expanding credit, raising prices, assuring monetary stability, and remonetizing silver. "The world is now one world in an economic sense," he declared. If the United States refused to cooperate with other countries on vital economic questions, it would "suffer most deeply" for its "smart-alek aloofness."[6]

The third fundamental cause of the depression, Wallace believed, was technological progress. Modern inventions expanded production and improved efficiency, but they also created unemployment. The problem was serious in industry, but it was even more acute in agriculture. Tractors, trucks, combines, and other machinery enabled farmers to increase their output greatly, but left them with price-depressing surpluses. In order to enjoy the benefits of modern technology, Wallace contended, it was necessary to develop social machinery to ensure a fair distribution of abundance. In that way, living standards would be raised everywhere in the world and "the millennium would surely be with us."[7]

The "fundamental cure" for world depression, Wallace wrote, entailed "changing the human heart." The economic system was based "on short-sighted human selfishness" and was ill-equipped to promote cooperation and provide equitable distribution of wealth.

"What we need is effective social machinery to distribute the produce of our mechanical machinery more fairly among the different
nations, the different classes and different individuals of the world,"
Wallace argued. If people demonstrated a burning desire for social
justice and renounced greed, hatred, and fear, the "promised land"
could be attained. He cautioned farmers against blaming the depression on scapegoats and urged them "to fight the ignorance and
prejudice which divides nation from nation and class from class."
He declared that if the United States acted responsibly and unselfishly
on war debts, tariffs, and monetary policy, it could lead the world
toward unprecedented prosperity. "The United States is now in a
position to take action to enable the nations of the world to enter a
veritable millennium," he proclaimed.[8]

While Wallace hoped for the millennium, he also feared that if
the United States and European countries failed to end the depression and provide economic justice, they would succumb to the
blandishments of Bolshevism. During the 1920s, he had demonstrated an ambivalent attitude toward the Soviet Union. Shortly
after the October Revolution of 1917, he had described the Bolsheviks as "anarchists" who were a cross between American Wobblies
and "the more lawless of the working people in the cities." In 1921,
he chastized Soviet leaders for their insensitivity toward peasants
and declared that under communism, "Russia has gone to pot."
Throughout the decade, Wallace warned that when agricultural
production increased in Russia and it began to export wheat in large
quantities, American farmers would have to adjust their crops
accordingly.[9] But he gradually perceived some virtues in the Soviet
system. He thought it a good idea to honor "economic heroes"
who contributed to Russia's welfare, and rebuked the United States
for over-glorifying sports heroes. Wallace was interested in Russia's
agricultural techniques, and noted it was making great strides through
cooperative farming. He applauded Soviet leaders for attempting
to increase the purchasing power of farmers, and for developing an
equitable system of land taxation. "With all their mistakes, the
people of Soviet Russia may yet stumble onto ideals which may be
worth a lot to us here," Wallace suggested.[10]

As depression became worldwide in 1930, however, Wallace became increasingly alarmed that the Soviets would attempt to undermine stability and disrupt capitalism. He noted the Soviet govern-

ment's monumental effort to increase its exports, even though it subjected the Russian people to enormous sacrifice and strain. He thought the Soviets purposely "played havoc" with farm prices in order to "create discontent in the United States." "It is sort of funny that the Russians should try to cause hard times in the United States by sending us goods," Wallace mused. "Goods are wealth and ought to make us happy." He contended that the Soviets were also anxious to sell abroad in order to buy U.S. machinery. Within ten or fifteen years, they would utilize that machinery to increase production greatly and wield awesome economic power.[11] The best way to combat the "Russian menace," Wallace argued, was to make certain that the United States provided a better life for its people than the Soviets did for theirs. It was imperative to establish world confidence, stabilize prices, and end the depression, "or the whole world may sooner or later fall under the spell of Soviet Russia."[12]

In December 1931, Wallace outlined two paths to end the depression. Echoing the arguments he had presented to his father ten years earlier, he wrote that America could either adopt a program of self-containment, or it could develop "world consciousness." The isolationist path entailed raising prohibitive tariff barriers, abstention from exporting goods or capital abroad, and careful planning to effect necessary readjustments in the domestic economy. Since farmers sent large quantities of their products overseas, agricultural output would have to be sharply curtailed, and about one-fourth of the rural population would have to emigrate into the cities to find work. The international path, on the other hand, meant that the United States would have to lower its tariff gradually, accept goods from abroad, cancel intergovernmental war debts, intelligently lend money to foreign countries, and play an active role in world affairs. Both alternatives presented grave dangers and great difficulties, but Wallace insisted that it was essential that Americans choose and adhere to one path or the other. He contended that America's most grievous mistake since 1918 had been attempting to follow both paths at once by expanding exports while refusing imports.[13]

Wallace stated unequivocally that he preferred the path of internationalism, which, he believed, would generate greater prosperity in the long run. Moreover, he maintained, "those who take the message of Christianity seriously must incline to the idea of world cooperation." Wallace feared that isolationism would require a

massive bureaucracy and probably lead to "state socialism." Ultimately, it could introduce "a dictatorship either of the proletariat
or of a Mussolini." He realized that the American people leaned
toward isolation, but worried that they failed to understand how
rigorous such a program would have to be to provide prosperity.
Wallace urged a nonpartisan effort to educate the public about the
advantages and disadvantages of the two paths. He suggested that a
prominent isolationist, Senator William E. Borah, and an outstanding internationalist, perhaps Nicholas Murray Butler or former
Illinois governor Frank O. Lowden, travel throughout the country
debating the merits of their positions in the same way that Abraham
Lincoln and Stephen Douglas had done before the Civil War. Wallace
believed deeply in the inherent wisdom of the American people, and
was confident that once they fully understood the situation, they
would discard their "ancient prejudices" and adopt an internationalist program. He suggested that the United States could take a
modest step toward promoting world cooperation and good will by
joining the World Court.[14]

Wallace realized that even if the United States adopted internationalist policies, it would take several years to combat the depression effectively. While the country gradually lowered tariffs, negotiated trade agreements, and made credit arrangements with foreign
countries, farm prices would remain disastrously low. If agricultural
surpluses continued to accumulate, and the distress of farmers were
not alleviated, Wallace feared that revolution would engulf the
countryside. Therefore, immediate action to shrink the surplus and
raise farm prices was essential. Although it was inconsistent with
his internationalist position, Wallace supported as a temporary
emergency measure a proposal known as the voluntary domestic
allotment plan.[15]

The allotment plan envisioned cutting agricultural output by sub-
sidizing the portion of production that was consumed at home.
After domestic demand for farm goods was determined, farmers
could voluntarily enter agreements to reduce their acreage by a percentage that would correspond with internal requirements. For that
part of their crop, they would receive benefit payments financed by
a tax levied on processors of agricultural commodities. The allotment plan aimed at making the tariff effective for agriculture by
guaranteeing farmers a return equal to the current world price plus

the tariff for the portion of their production that was used domestically. Although Wallace described the scheme as "rather crude," he thought it was the best available proposal for restricting acreage and could be made practical if the United States decided to follow "the route of state socialism." However, he still hoped that the country would select the path of world cooperation. The allotment plan would be useful in raising farm prices while an internationalist program was gradually being implemented. In the long run, however, he urged the United States to act "from an international point of view instead of from a narrow national standpoint."[16]

What the United States needed to fight the depression, Wallace wrote in 1930, was a "thoughtful, unified effort behind resolute leadership. The leadership, unfortunately, has been slow to manifest itself." He had little confidence in Herbert Hoover, and hoped that the Democrats could provide more effective leadership. As early as June 1931, Wallace expressed certainty that Franklin D. Roosevelt would be the Democratic presidential nominee in 1932, but he was less certain that Roosevelt could "make the Democrats behave themselves in a position of responsibility." Wallace first met Roosevelt in August 1932, shortly after the Democratic convention selected the New York governor as its presidential candidate. He was greatly impressed with Roosevelt's charm, vigor, open mind, and sympathy for agricultural problems. Wallace campaigned vigorously for the Democratic nominee, telling his readers: "With Roosevelt, the farmers have a chance—with Hoover, none." He was delighted that Roosevelt endorsed the domestic allotment plan and pleased with his tariff position. Wallace hailed Roosevelt's election victory and voiced optimism that the incoming president could overcome the "reactionary element" in the Democratic party and build a "genuine progressive party."[17]

During the interregnum, Wallace continued to advocate a policy of internationalism. But he noted the ever-growing trend of economic nationalism in Europe, and realized that it pushed an effective international program even further into the future. Therefore, it was of paramount importance to "provide an orderly retreat for American agriculture" through the domestic allotment plan. Wallace advised Roosevelt to appoint George N. Peek as Secretary of Agriculture. Protesting against suggestions that he deserved that position, Wallace wrote: "I sincerely trust that fate will not carry me

into that hell down in Washington." But when Roosevelt offered
him the post in February 1933, he quickly accepted. In his final editorial, he told his readers: "I will try to do my part in Washington.
No doubt I shall make mistakes, but I hope it can always be said
that I have done the best I knew."[18]

After Wallace departed Iowa for Washington, he never returned
to live in his native state. But his attitudes and viewpoints always
reflected his agrarian background and his observations and experiences during the 1920s and early 1930s. He had tried and rejected
isolationism, and become firmly convinced that, in the long run,
the only way to combat the world economic crisis effectively was to
foster international cooperation, both economically and spiritually.
Wallace's outlook on world affairs and foreign policy issues also
stemmed from his antipathy for Wall Street, big business, and special
interests. He continued to oppose commercial imperialism and interference in the internal affairs of other countries, and demonstrated a strain of Anglophobia and distrust of European diplomacy
in general. He sympathized with colonial peoples, in part because it
often seemed that the Midwest had been relegated to a colonial
status by the industrial Northeast. Wallace remained a "small 'd'
democrat" who deeply believed in the inherent wisdom and common sense of ordinary people. Although not a doctrinaire pacifist,
he was a staunch advocate of reducing armaments. Those characteristics frequently reappeared during his long and tempestuous
public career.

NOTES

1. *Wallaces' Farmer and Iowa Homestead,* October 11, 1930, p. 1628.
2. Henry A. Wallace pamphlet, "Causes of the World Wide Depression
of 1930," Winter, 1930-1931, Henry A. Wallace Papers, University of
Iowa; *Wallaces' Farmer and Iowa Homestead,* June 13, 1931, p. 746.
3. Wallace, "Causes of the Depression," Wallace Papers.
4. Wallace to Frank D. Ruppert, October 23, 1930, Wallace to A. M.
Simmons, June 23, 1931, Wallace Papers; *Wallaces' Farmer and Iowa
Homestead,* November 8, 1930, p. 1766, December 27, 1930, p. 1977, January
24, 1931, p. 102, July 25, 1931, p. 867.
5. Wallace, "Causes of the Depression," Wallace to Alexander Legge,
November 18, 1930, Wallace to E. G. Brockway, May 9, 1931, Wallace to
Lloyd Thurston, January 11, 1932, Wallace Papers; *Wallaces' Farmer and*

Iowa Homestead, January 31, 1931, p. 130, May 9, 1931, p. 632, July 4, 1931, p. 807, October 31, 1931, p. 1153.

6. Wallace, "Causes of the Depression," Wallace to R. D. Kellogg, October 8, 1931, Wallace to Burton K. Wheeler, February 15, 1932, Wallace Papers; Wallace to William Hirth, August 20, 1932, William Hirth Papers, Western Historical Manuscripts Collection, University of Missouri; *Wallaces' Farmer and Iowa Homestead,* April 18, 1931, p. 540, August 15, 1931, p. 927, October 3, 1931, p. 1085, "Restoring the 1926 Price Level," October 31, 1931, pp. 1151, 1169-70.

7. Wallace, "Causes of the Depression," Wallace Papers.

8. Ibid., Wallace to Mark Hyde, December 10, 1930, Wallace to Lee H. Yager, February 1, 1932, Wallace to W. H. Wilfong, February 23, 1932, Wallace Papers; *Wallaces' Farmer and Iowa Homestead,* September 12, 1931, p. 1010, June 25, 1932, p. 353, "Dragons That Devour Prosperity," May 14, 1932, p. 271.

9. *Wallaces' Farmer,* January 11, 1918, p. 37, April 1, 1921, p. 577, June 24, 1921, p. 905, November 18, 1921, p. 1397, June 9, 1922, p. 713, May 4, 1923, p. 691; *Wallaces' Farmer and Iowa Homestead,* May 10, 1930, p. 916.

10. *Wallaces' Farmer,* November 24, 1922, p. 1390, October 3, 1924, p. 1288, November 14, 1924, p. 1472, November 12, 1926, p. 1473; *Wallaces' Farmer and Iowa Homestead,* February 1, 1930, p. 183, April 19, 1930, p. 788.

11. Wallace to Mark Hyde, July 31, December 10, 1930, Wallace Papers; *Wallaces' Farmer and Iowa Homestead,* June 21, 1930, p. 1135, September 6, 1930, p. 1419, September 27, 1930, p. 1551, October 4, 1930, p. 1582, March 7, 1931, p. 317, October 31, 1931, p. 1152.

12. *Wallaces' Farmer and Iowa Homestead,* April 11, 1931, p. 509, April 25, 1931, p. 572, May 30, 1931, p. 701, June 6, 1931, p. 721.

13. Wallace to Thomas T. Kerl, December 4, 1931, Wallace to Paul deKruif, December 30, 1931, Wallace speech, "Agriculture and National Planning," March 22, 1932, Wallace Papers.

14. Wallace to Thomas T. Kerl, December 4, 1931, Wallace to Charles A. Beard, April 7, 1932, Wallace to Franklin D. Roosevelt, April 11, 1932, Wallace to George F. Chipman, April 16, 1932, Wallace to Clark M. Eichelberger, April 21, 1932, Wallace to H. E. Morrow, May 4, 1932, Wallace to Nicholas Murray Butler, July 9, 1932, Wallace to Frank O. Lowden, July 13, 1932, Wallace to Smith W. Brookhart, November 5, 1930, February 23, 1932, Wallace Papers.

15. Wallace to William E. Borah, May 20, 1932, Wallace to Grover Arbeiter, September 23, 1932, Wallace Papers; Wallace to M. L. Wilson, April 20, 1932, M. L. Wilson Papers, Montana State University Archives, Bozeman.

16. Van L. Perkins, *Crisis in Agriculture: The Agricultural Adjustment Administration and the New Deal, 1933* (Berkeley: University of California Press, 1969), pp. 27-28; Wallace to Franklin D. Roosevelt, April 11, 1932, Wallace to Grover Arbeiter, September 23, 1932, Wallace to Walter Parker, October 13, 1932, Wallace Papers; Wallace to M. L. Wilson, April 20, 1932, Wilson Papers; "Voluntary Domestic Allotment Plan," *Wallaces' Farmer and Iowa Homestead,* December 24, 1932, p. 678.

17. Wallace to W. H. Brock, June 24, 1931, Wallace to Henry J. Morgenthau, Jr., August 19, 1932, Wallace Papers; *Wallaces' Farmer and Iowa Homestead,* June 27, 1931, p. 787, October 1, 1932, p. 512, October 29, 1932, p. 565, November 26, 1932, p. 617; Russell Lord, *The Wallaces of Iowa* (Boston: Houghton Mifflin Co., 1947). pp. 320-22.

18. Wallace to R. E. Mallory, November 11, 1932, Wallace to Franklin D. Roosevelt, November 17, 1932, February, 1933, Roosevelt to Wallace, February 3, 1933, Wallace Papers; *Wallaces' Farmer and Iowa Homestead,* February 18, 1933, p. 73, March 4, 1933, p. 97; *New York Times,* January 22, 1933.

4

The
Planned Middle
Course

Forty-four years old when he became Secretary of Agriculture in March 1933, Henry Wallace was something of an anomaly in Washington. Careless of appearance and rumpled in dress, he walked over two miles to work every day in all kinds of weather, played awkward but determined tennis on public courts, and occasionally Indian wrestled in his office with aide James LeCron. He did not smoke, drink, curse, or enjoy off-color stories.[1] Never a glad-hander or back-slapper, he was basically a shy person who felt uncomfortable with strangers and often appeared detached and aloof. One close associate, M. L. Wilson, later commented: "There wasn't anybody that I know of who could say he knew Henry Wallace intimately." Although Wallace had many friends and a group of capable advisors in the Department of Agriculture, he was essentially a loner who arrived at positions more on the basis of his own independent thinking than on the advice or suasion of others. He detested politicos, favor seekers, and pleaders for special interests. After refusing the request of one lobbyist for special consideration, the Agriculture Secretary told him solemnly: "Unless we learn to treat each other fairly, this country is going to smash."[2]

Although Wallace was not humorless, he was serious minded, earnest, and intense. "He gave the impression of laboring under immense strain," J. Pierrepont Moffat wrote in his diary after meeting the Agriculture Secretary for the first time. Wallace possessed a brilliant, probing, wide-ranging mind. His insatiable curiosity spurred him to delve into genetics, statistics, economics, politics, history and religion. His many books, articles, and editorials on subjects ranging from breeding corn to building the millennium reflected the breadth of his interests. Wallace's writings were clearly presented and cogently argued, but his private conversations were less lucid. "His power of expression fell short of the power of his ideas," commented Moffat. Though not an accomplished public speaker, Wallace's fervor and earnestness compensated partly for his lack of polish.[3]

In his first few weeks as Secretary of Agriculture, Wallace concentrated on drafting and securing congressional approval of legislation to aid farmers. On May 12, 1933, Congress passed an omnibus farm bill that granted broad powers to the Secretary of Agriculture and largely left to his discretion the decision of how best to deal with the emergency. Wallace preferred acreage reduction through the domestic allotment plan. But George N. Peek, the newly appointed director of the Agricultural Adjustment Administration (AAA), remained an unreconstructed McNary-Haugenite who was committed to the principle of dumping exports abroad. Since the farm act bestowed considerable power to the AAA executive, Peek's appointment presented a problem to Wallace. Although wary of Peek because he was "full of the old McNary-Haugen ideas," Wallace thought he could "learn how to handle" his administrator.[4] He told Peek that there were "extraordinary difficulties" in trying to increase foreign trade, and expressed opposition to subsidized farm exports because they would lead to "international jams of one kind or another." The best course of action, Wallace contended, was "to act for the moment as if we were a self-contained agricultural economy."[5]

Wallace had not retreated to isolationism. He thought it essential that the United States assume its responsibilities as a creditor state and work to regain its foreign markets, but he saw no immediate prospect for restoring an effective demand abroad for American farm products. He objected to increasing exports by extending credit to China so it could buy American wheat and cotton. Reminding President Roosevelt of America's disastrous lending policies in the 1920s, Wallace argued that the loan was unsound unless Americans were willing to import large quantities of Chinese goods.[6]

He maintained that "everything possible" should be done to reduce world trade barriers, but asserted that tariffs and other international issues were "so controversial . . . that they had best be left for later consideration."[7]

Meanwhile, Wallace centered his attention on controlling domestic production by taking remedial action to curtail cotton and hog output. Enactment of the farm bill in May had come too late to discourage cotton farmers from increasing their acreage during spring planting, although prices were already distressingly low. A similar situation existed in corn-hog country, where farmers faced another grievous winter because of an already glutted market. Reluctantly, Wallace and his advisors decided that the situation compelled extreme measures to prevent new surpluses from further depressing prices. In the late summer of 1933, farmers destroyed ten million acres of cotton and slaughtered six million pigs, and received millions of dollars from the AAA for their cooperation. Wallace later commented that "to have to destroy a growing crop is a shocking commentary on our civilization," but it had been "made necessary by the almost insane lack of world statesmanship during the period from 1920 to 1932."[8]

Only unfavorable weather during 1933 had averted the need to plow up wheat. Wallace believed that cooperation among the world's leading wheat exporters could help alleviate difficulties caused by the wheat surplus in future years. As a result of maladjustments stemming from World War I, the world wheat supply had exceeded demand for several years. As surpluses had accumulated, prices had fallen. A bushel of wheat that had sold for $3.10 in 1920 brought 42¢ in November 1932.[9] At the suggestion of Pietro Stoppani of the League of Nations, the four major wheat exporting countries—the United States, Canada, Australia, and Argentina—agreed to discuss the world wheat situation. Wallace initially showed little enthusiasm for the wheat conference, preferring to mark time until Congress enacted farm legislation. But once Congress passed the Agricultural Adjustment Act, he became committed to achieving an international agreement on wheat.[10]

The wheat conference took place in London during the summer of 1933. The four countries appeared willing to combat the world wheat surplus by reducing their wheat acreage by 12 1/2 to 15 percent. The American negotiator in London, Henry J. Morgenthau,

Sr., informed Wallace, who directed the U.S. delegation, that he hoped a tentative agreement would quickly be consummated. But complications developed because Australia depended heavily on wheat exports and hesitated to curb production. Wallace responded to the Australian recalcitrance by threatening to use his power under the AAA to dump American exports abroad. If the wheat conference failed, he told Morgenthau, "we have the legal authority and economic resources to engage in competitive export dumping which would drive world market prices of wheat in Australia and Argentina down to zero." Wallace admitted that such action would be "deplorable," but maintained it would be necessary unless the other exporters agreed to crop control.[11]

Morgenthau relayed Wallace's warning, and the Australian delegate changed tactics. His government would not join an accord, he declared, unless European countries also cooperated. Morgenthau protested, and Wallace again blustered about dumping, but he wanted an agreement. He consented to include the nations of Europe in the wheat conference. After lengthy negotiations, the importing countries of Europe agreed to attempt to restrict their production of wheat to current levels, to encourage increased consumption of wheat, and to reduce trade barriers, while the Danubian wheat growing countries accepted a combined export quota. The four major exporting countries quickly reached settlement, agreeing to reduce production by 15 percent or otherwise remove surplus wheat from world markets, and to restrict the total volume of exports during 1934 and 1935. They allocated a percentage of the total exports to each country, giving the United States about 8 1/2 percent of the projected world market for 1934 and up to 20 percent for 1935. Wallace secured Roosevelt's approval of the final accord, and on August 25, 1933, the United States and twenty other countries signed the international wheat agreement.[12]

Wallace was satisfied with the agreement, and declared that it was a "momentous step," which would be "a landmark in international efforts to solve the economic depression." While the World Economic Conference had floundered in London during the summer of 1933, wheat growing countries had agreed to combat price-depressing surpluses. The United States had retained a share of the world market without resorting to export dumping. The wheat agreement soon faltered and eventually failed, largely because of unexpectedly abundant crops in Argentina. But for the time being Wallace was euphoric about its prospects for success and hopeful of continued progress on the international front.[13]

Although the Soviet Union participated in the conference, it was the only important wheat growing country that refused to reduce acreage or specify the degree to which it would withhold wheat exports. Wallace feared that the Soviets might sabotage world recovery and stability, and he expressed grave reservations about proposals to extend credit to Russia. He again reminded Roosevelt of the "fatal mistakes" of the Republicans in loaning money abroad without providing means for repayment. In the case of the Russians, however, Wallace was less concerned about their ability to requite loans than their intention to disrupt world capitalism and undermine religion. He feared that under the guise of repaying loans, the "centralized government of iron men" would dump goods on the world market in a manner calculated to "cause discontent among the proletariat" by creating "price chaos among the capitalistic nations." "The Russian leadership is so utterly without religion," he wrote Secretary of State Cordell Hull, "and so bitter regarding certain things which we hold dear, that I don't like to place ourselves in their hands by giving them the opportunity to disorganize our markets when the time for repayment comes."[14]

When President Roosevelt announced on October 20, 1933 that he had initiated steps to normalize diplomatic relations with the Soviet Union, Wallace suggested that recognizing Russia would lead to difficulties in foreign trade that would be deleterious to American interests. The following day, he confided that he was "scared to death about this Russian thing" because it would "eventually lead us to disaster." It appeared to Wallace that the United States was in danger of doing "the Hoover thing over again" by lending money to increase exports. After examining data on trade between the United States and the Soviet Union, he concluded that Russian offers to buy American farm products were only part of their "come-on game." Wallace believed the administration should resist the pressure of special interests who favored diplomatic recognition of the Soviet Union in hopes of gaining new markets subsidized by an American loan. He also privately voiced his concern to Roosevelt about the impact of recognition on religion in the United States. Wallace's fears of the harmful effects of recognizing Russia proved to be greatly exaggerated, and he soon grew increasingly more alarmed by the rising tide of world fascism than by the threat of a revolution exported from Moscow.[15]

During Wallace's first hectic months as Secretary of Agriculture, he continued to ponder the two paths—isolationism or international cooperation—that the United States could follow to overcome the depression. He had tried and ultimately rejected the isolationist path during the 1920s and although he preferred internationalism, he realized that it presented a maze of difficulties. He remained convinced that the United States must commit itself to one of the alternatives, or perhaps, some combination of the two. "So far we have made no clear cut decision," Wallace wrote, "and I think it is extremely important that these issues be defined in a striking, clear cut way so that all of our people may see." Wallace endeavored to inform the American public of its alternatives in speeches, press conferences, and reports. But the most articulate statement of his position came in February 1934, when he published a pamphlet appropriately titled *America Must Choose.*[16]

Wallace began his analysis by pointing out that any path the United States decided to follow involved "enormously difficult adjustments." The days of unfettered individualism had ended, and Americans must realize that new programs of controlled production were permanent, "much as we all dislike them." Each alternative—isolationism, internationalism, or a middle course—required careful planning. It was imperative that the issues be openly and intelligently debated before Americans determined in which direction to go. The decision must not be made "behind closed doors, either in Washington or on Wall Street." Only after the American people had chosen a path could they begin to combat the depression effectively.[17]

One possible approach to ending the economic morass was isolationism. The New Deal already had taken steps in that direction by reducing acreage because "our millions of surplus acres breed nothing but confusion, poverty and waste." Production control was not necessarily incompatible with world cooperation, Wallace observed, but the United States could not seek world agreements until it was ready to act as a creditor nation. Although the administration had no intention of withdrawing from world markets, it recognized that a large volume of foreign trade could not be restored precipitately.

The actions taken had been temporary measures to meet the emergency. "We are sparring with the situation until the American people are ready to face facts," Wallace wrote.[18]

If the United States opted for a course of absolute isolationism, Wallace argued, planning would be much more stringent than the few tentative steps already taken. The burden of the isolationist path would fall on farmers, who would have to retire as many as one hundred million acres of land from production. Moreover, isolationism would require "a completely army-like nationalist discipline in peace time," and "regimentation of agriculture and industry far beyond that which anyone has yet suggested." Isolationism presented a viable solution to the crisis, but Wallace found "the spiritual price too high."[19]

Although Wallace spurned the isolationist path, he realized that the international path was also fraught with difficulty. Other countries were demonstrating a marked propensity for nationalism, and it was questionable whether the United States could embark on a course of internationalism against the tide of world events. Furthermore, the path of world cooperation demanded a drastic decrease in tariff rates, which would require the United States to import nearly a billion dollars more foreign products than it had in 1929. Such importation would severely injure some American industries and a few agricultural interests. Nevertheless, Wallace contended that Americans could never tolerate "the pain of a pinched-in national economy" and ought to consider seriously the merits of world trade. He maintained that a system of international trade would not only expand American exports, but would be less likely to lead to commercial imperialism and war than would a continuation of one-way trading patterns and economic nationalism. If the United States failed to give other nations the means to pay for goods it sent abroad, Wallace argued, the result would be to increase pressures to exact payment by force. He suggested that the United States lead the way "toward larger, more rational and more decent trade designs" which would promote prosperity and lessen the chances for war.[20]

Having outlined the two extremes, Wallace admitted that those ideals were seldom approached, and that actual conditions would force the United States to middle ground. But he did not want the country to arrive at a position by haphazard compromise and indecision. He proposed a "planned middle course" that stood exactly halfway between the two extremes. Since isolationism hurt agriculture more than industry, while internationalism was more harmful to manufacturing, Wallace advised permanent retirement of 25 million acres of good farm land, and tariff reductions that would increase imports of manufactured articles by a half billion dollars annually. That way, he believed, the United States could increase its foreign trade and avoid the mistakes of the "Old Deal," which had attempted to sell goods abroad without accepting foreign products in return. By means of programs such as the AAA, the planned middle course would also help rectify maldistribution of income at home, and increased domestic purchasing power would partially supplant the constant need for new foreign customers. "There is no more effective way to melt surpluses in any country than to put buying power in the hands of the people there," Wallace declared. Having presented his ideas, he urged the American people to consider the whole question thoughtfully, objectively, and unselfishly. The Agriculture Secretary held the firm but unrealistic conviction that the public would arrive at a clear-cut decision after carefully weighing the merits of each position according to what was best for the general welfare rather than what best served their parochial interests.[21]

America Must Choose received wide distribution and a generally favorable response. By May 1934, 65,000 copies had been sold, and it had been reprinted in newspapers with a combined circulation of over ten million. *Commonweal* praised the pamphlet and noted that it had "attracted extraordinary and deserved attention." The *New Republic* described it as "an extraordinarily able presentation, broad-minded and fair in spirit." President Roosevelt commended *America Must Choose* for "its clarity of statement" and told Wallace it was "the kind of thing that makes the people of this country think."[22]

One critic of Wallace's pamphlet was the distinguished historian Charles A. Beard. In his book, *The Open Door at Home,* Beard advocated an essentially isolationist position for America and recommended that the country become as self-sufficient as possible while closely regulating whatever foreign trade was necessary. Beard chastized Wallace as a pleader for agricultural interests, because, as Beard saw it, the Secretary favored making tariff adjustments that would hurt industry in order to keep millions of acres of farm land in production. Wallace denied that assertion, pointing out that his middle course divided the burdens of building a planned economy between agriculture and industry. He also expressed doubts about the soundness of Beard's proposals, which he thought outlined admirable objectives but reflected better historical than economic thinking. Wallace believed that Beard's plan would take ten years to implement, and although it might "be permissible for a historian to neglect the time factor," policy makers could not. He also rebuked Beard for ignoring the severe dislocations that his program would inflict on farmers and agricultural industries, and for failing to recognize that the open door at home required strict regimentation that would arouse the opposition of the American people. Wallace hoped that Beard's ideas would be studied and debated, but he still preferred the planned middle course.[23]

The success of the middle path depended on reduction of world trade barriers, and Wallace vigorously supported Cordell Hull's reciprocal trade program because it represented the greatest hope for expanding foreign markets. Many American farm products—particularly wheat, cotton, hogs, and tobacco—relied heavily on overseas markets, and Wallace maintained that mutual agreements between countries to remove trade restrictions would greatly benefit farmers. If the United States refused to lower tariffs and permit more imports, it would force a "drastic transformation" in the domestic economy. On the other hand, Wallace told the House Ways and Means Committee in March 1934, passage of the pending reciprocal trade agreements bill would ease the "exceedingly difficult job of eliminating surplus acres" by lessening the amount of land retired from production. He admitted that lowering tariffs would result in dislocations and unemployment in some "inefficient" industries, but he contended that high tariffs created similar hardships in efficient industries that produced for export. Wallace wanted gradual and carefully planned tariff reductions to minimize the distress of people working in enterprises dependent on protection, but he insisted that the advantages of reciprocity outweighed the drawbacks. Congress eventually concurred, and the Reciprocal Trade Agreements Act, passed in June 1934, gave the President authority to adjust tariff rates by as much as fifty percent.[24]

Roosevelt's attitude toward American foreign trade policies remained a matter of conjecture, however, and throughout 1934, a battle raged within the administration between Secretary Hull and George Peek over the best method to increase exports. Peek's tenure as head of the AAA had been brief and stormy, ending in December 1933, after Wallace complained that Peek was overstepping his authority. Roosevelt then horrified Hull by appointing Peek special advisor to the President on foreign trade. Peek's idea that trade should be expanded through dumping, export subsidies, and barter agreements contrasted sharply with Hull's multilateral approach, and a controversy soon developed around the reciprocal trade agreements. Hull urged extending unconditional most-favored-nation status to countries with whom the United States concluded agreements, meaning that a reduction in duties on a commodity granted to one country would also apply to all countries that gave the United States the same most-favored-nation treatment. Peek espoused the conditional most-favored-nation policy, which involved negotiating pacts on a bilateral basis and lowering tariffs on a commodity for other countries only if they made equal concessions to the United States. Hull intended to torpedo American tariff barriers and promote freer trade on a world basis, while Peek aimed to safeguard the American protective system.[25]

Wallace stood squarely behind Hull. The Agriculture Secretary observed that most foreign trade was not conducted on a bilateral basis, but usually involved more complex arrangements among three of four countries. He feared that bilateral agreements would interfere with existing trade patterns, diminish the volume of world trade, and "further accentuate the marked trends in the direction of intense economic nationalism." Wallace reiterated his views in a letter to Roosevelt, arguing that bilateral trade was "highly prejudicial" to the welfare of American farmers. He pointed out that in past years, for example, the United States had shipped agricultural goods to European nations, which had sent industrial commodities to South American countries, which in turn had traded tropical products to the United States. But the devices of economic nationalism had disrupted that kind of circular trade. Wallace asserted that Peek wanted to "play the same game" of nationalism, striving "to get as large a share of the winnings as possible," while Hull was attempting "to change the rules of the game" by stimulating a greater volume of world commerce. The proponents of multilateralism eventually prevailed, and in late 1935, Peek left the administration.[26]

Although Wallace endorsed Hull's position on reciprocity, he watched carefully to make certain that the State Department's agreements promoted the interests of American farmers. Disturbed by the course of negotiations with Cuba, Wallace protested to Hull that since the United States had substantially reduced sugar tariffs, Cuba should assent to significantly lower duties on American lard and pork products. Cuba provided a major outlet for pork products, so a satisfactory accord would mitigate the problem of controlling corn and hog production and help win the support of farmers for reciprocity. Otherwise, Wallace warned: "I feel certain that both your Department and my Department will be severely and perhaps fairly criticized by our farmers." Ultimately, Cuba granted additional concessions, American agricultural exports increased, and Undersecretary of State Sumner Welles thanked Wallace for his "tremendously effective assistance."[27]

The Cuban negotiations gratified Wallace, but he was primarily concerned with increasing exports to the European industrial countries that had always provided the most important markets for American farm products. "The success of the reciprocal trade agreements program, so far as agriculture is concerned, will be determined largely by the extent to which this end is achieved," he wrote. An accord signed with Belgium in February 1935, annoyed Wallace because the Belgians made "no significant concessions" on agricultural products, and because he suspected the State Department of circumventing the Department of Agriculture while conducting negotiations on the agreement. He complained to Assistant Secretary of State Francis B. Sayre that the United States was making no progress in working out trade agreements with Great Britain and Germany, which would greatly benefit farmers, while discussing pacts with countries that would require concessions from American agriculture. Although Wallace believed that many agricultural duties were too high and deserved to be lowered, he contended that the "major emphasis" of the reciprocal trade program should focus on reducing tariffs on industrial products.[28]

Despite his reservations, Wallace remained committed to the principle of reciprocal trade. An agreement signed with Canada in November 1935 rankled cattle, potato, lumber, and dairy interests because of decreased tariffs on those products, but Wallace publicly defended the pact and asserted it would benefit both countries. He pointed out that Canada had lowered duties on over a hundred American farm products, while the United States had agreed to permit only limited quantities of certain Canadian goods to enter the country under reduced tariffs. Upbraiding its opponents as "implacable enemies of agriculture," Wallace argued that the agreement would help "undo the terrific damage" caused by the Smoot-Hawley tariff.[29]

Both during and after his tenure as Secretary of Agriculture, Wallace advocated the planned middle course. He was firmly committed to expanding American exports and achieving world cooperation on economic matters, but he did not regard foreign trade as a cure-all for America's economic ills. Under his leadership, the Department of Agriculture undertook a number of programs designed to increase domestic buying power and diminish the need for foreign markets, including acreage reduction, soil conservation, and food stamp distribution. Wallace also advanced a plan for a crop storage system that he called the "ever-normal granary." It was intended to prevent food shortages in times of adverse weather and to stabilize farm prices by stockpiling agricultural surpluses in government-operated warehouses. Wallace argued that the ever-normal granary would benefit both farmers and consumers. By extending government loans to growers, it would ensure them a fair return for their goods when surpluses existed, and by releasing reserves when shortages occurred, it would keep consumer prices from rising too high. It would avoid the mistakes of Herbert Hoover's Farm Board by combining crop storage with acreage reduction. Congress approved the ever-normal granary plan in 1938.[30]

While he strived to implement new domestic programs, Wallace persistently promoted economic internationalism. During the early New Deal period, he worked for the cause of world cooperation both as a publicist and as a policy maker who played direct roles in the International Wheat Agreement of 1933 and in the formulation of the reciprocal trade agreements. During the latter part of the 1930s, he continued to defend the principle of reciprocity as a means to fight the depression and foster world peace. "The most significant fact" about the reciprocal trade program, Wallace declared in 1937, was that it led "in the direction of peace instead of in the direction of hard feelings" between nations. He also urged international commodity agreements among producers of wheat and cotton to combat world surpluses, and proposed the idea of an international ever-normal granary to stabilize world grain supplies and prices. Wallace deplored the growing trend toward economic nationalism in the world, and warned that such programs would lead to "paralysis for all" and the "flaming cataclysm of international war." He continued to oppose commercial imperialism, but modified his position of the 1920s by arguing that economic nationalism was much more likely to lead to foreign intervention and war than was the planned middle course.[31]

NOTES

1. *New York Herald Tribune,* March 6, 1934; *Washington Times-Herald,* April 16, 1938; Russell Lord, *The Wallaces of Iowa* (Boston: Houghton Mifflin Co., 1947), pp. 336, 446; Frank Kingdon, *An Uncommon Man: Henry Wallace and Sixty Million Jobs* (New York: Readers Press, 1945), Chap. 1.

2. James LeCron, Mordecai Ezekiel, Louis Bean, M. L. Wilson, John B. Hutson, interviews, Columbia Oral History Collection; Lord, *Wallaces of Iowa,* pp. 338, 451; Interview with Louis Bean, September 4, 1974.

3. J. P. Moffat Diary, October 10, 1933, Houghton Library, Harvard University, Cambridge, Massachusetts; LeCron, Ezekiel interviews, Columbia Oral History Collection; Lord, *Wallaces of Iowa,* p. 363.

4. Wallace to Donald Murphy, April 20, 1933, Wallace to Dante Pierce, April, 1933, Henry A. Wallace Papers, University of Iowa; Arthur M. Schlesinger, Jr., *The Coming of the New Deal* (Boston: Houghton Mifflin Co., 1958), pp. 46-48.

5. Wallace to George N. Peek, April 29, 1933, Foreign Trade File, RG 16, NA; Wallace to Peek, May 12, 1933, George N. Peek Papers, Western Historical Manuscripts Collection, University of Missouri.

6. Henry A. Wallace, *Democracy Reborn,* Russell Lord, ed., (New York: Reynal and Hitchcock, 1944), p. 42; Wallace to Franklin D. Roosevelt, May 27, 1933, Official File 150-A, Franklin D. Roosevelt Papers, Franklin D. Roosevelt Library, Hyde Park, New York.

7. Wallace to Edmund Platt, March 22, 1933, Wallace to F. T. Robson, March 27, 1933, Wallace to D. L. Thompson, May 29, 1933, Secretary's Office—Letters Sent, RG 16, NA.

8. Schlesinger, *Coming of the New Deal,* pp. 59-63; Henry A. Wallace, *New Frontiers* (New York: Reynal and Hitchcock, 1934), pp. 167-81, 200.

9. Wallace, *New Frontiers,* p. 171; *New York Times,* May 21, September 3, 1933.

10. P. Stoppani to Norman Davis, February 24, 1933, 561.311 F1/1, Wallace to Cordell Hull, March 27, 1933, 561.311 F1/3, RG 59 (Records of the State Department), NA.

11. *Foreign Relations of the United States: 1933,* Vol. I, pp. 797, 799-800; *New York Times,* June 8, 22, 1933.

12. *Foreign Relations: 1933,* Vol. I, pp. 801-802, 809, 811-12, 815-21, 823-24; Wallace to Hull, November 10, 1933, Department of Agriculture Press Release, August 15, 1933, Radio Speech by Francis Deak, November 16, 1933, International Wheat Conference File, RG 16, NA.

13. *Foreign Relations: 1933,* Vol. I, p. 825; *Report of the Secretary of Agriculture: 1933* (Washington: Government Printing Office, 1933) pp. 36-37.

14. Wallace to Roosevelt, September 29, 1933, Wallace to Hull, September 29, 1933, Wallace Papers.

15. Wallace to Dante Pierce, October 21, 1933, Wallace to Frank C. Walker, October 28, 1933, Wallace Papers; Henry Morgenthau, Jr., Farm Credit Diary, October 25, 1933, Morgenthau Diaries, Roosevelt Library; Nils A. Olsen to Wallace, October 21, 1933, Foreign Trade File, RG 16, NA; Harold L. Ickes, *The Secret Diary of Harold L. Ickes: The First Thousand Days, 1933-1936* (New York: Simon and Schuster, 1953), Vol. I, p. 111.

16. Wallace to Dan Wallace, October 21, 1933, Secretary's Office—Letters Sent, RG 16, NA; *Report of the Secretary of Agriculture: 1933*, pp. 6-7; *New York Times,* November 15, 24, 1933.

17. Henry A. Wallace, *America Must Choose* (New York and Boston: Foreign Policy Association and World Peace Foundation, 1934), pp. 1-3.

18. Ibid., pp. 4-7.

19. Ibid., pp. 8-11, 14-17.

20. Ibid., pp. 12, 18-25.

21. Ibid., pp. 26-33.

22. "Secretary Wallace Urges Spiritual Cooperation," *Literary Digest,* 117 (May 26, 1934): 29; "The Campaign of Reason," *Commonweal,* 19 (March 9, 1934): 505; "Shall We Trade Abroad?" *New Republic,* 78 (March 7, 1934): 87; Roosevelt to Wallace, March 5, 1934, President's Personal File 41, Roosevelt Papers.

23. Charles A. Beard, *The Open Door at Home: A Trial Philosophy of National Interest* (New York: Macmillan Co., 1934); Henry A. Wallace, "Beard: The Planner," *New Republic,* 81 (January 2, 1935): 225-27.

24. Wallace to Oscar Ronken, December 21, 1933, Foreign Trade File, Wallace to W. H. Thompson, October 25, 1933, Wallace to Perley Morse, March 10, 1934, Secretary's Office—Letters Sent, RG 16, NA; U.S. Congress, House, Committee on Ways and Means, *Hearings on Reciprocal Trade Agreements,* 73rd Cong., 2nd Sess., 1934, pp. 45-61.

25. Gilbert C. Fite, *George N. Peek and the Fight for Farm Parity* (Norman: University of Oklahoma Press, 1954), pp. 265-71; Cordell Hull, *The Memoirs of Cordell Hull* (New York: Macmillan Co., 1948), Vol. I, pp. 360-62, 370-74.

26. Wallace to Daniel Roper, February 15, 1934, Secretary's Office—Letters Sent, Wallace to Roosevelt, November 27, 1934, Foreign Trade File, RG 16, NA; Fite, *Peek and Farm Parity*, pp. 281-85.

27. Wallace to Hull, August 17, 1934, Sumner Welles to Wallace, October 4, 1934, Foreign Trade File, RG 16, NA; *Report of the Secretary of Agriculture: 1934* (Washington: Government Printing Office, 1934), pp. 14-15.

28. Wallace to Clifford Gregory, November 14, 1934, Wallace to Francis B. Sayre, February 8, July 11, 1935, Foreign Trade File, RG 16, NA; Arthur W. Schatz, "The Reciprocal Trade Agreements Program and the 'Farm Vote,' 1934-1940," *Agricultural History,* 46 (October 1972) : 501.

29. Wallace speeches, "How the Canadian Trade Agreement Will Affect Farmers," November 21, 1935, "Farmers and the Export Market," December 10, 1935, Wallace Papers; *New York Times,* November 21, December 11, 1935; Schatz, "Reciprocal Trade Agreements," pp. 502-503.

30. Wallace, *New Frontiers,* pp. 225-38; Wallace, *Democracy Reborn,* pp. 87-88, 95, 117-18; Wallace speech, "The Joseph Plan in Modern America," May 16, 1935, Wallace Papers; Murray R. Benedict, *Farm Policies of the United States, 1790-1950* (New York: Twentieth Century Fund, 1953), pp. 375-86.

31. U.S. Congress, Senate, Committee on Finance, *Hearings on Extending Reciprocal Trade Agreement Act,* 75th Cong., 1st Sess., 1937, pp. 159-81; Wallace to A. G. Black, July 12, 1938, 561.311 F1 Advisory Committee/693, RG 59, NA; Henry A. Wallace, *Whose Constitution: An Inquiry into the General Welfare* (New York: Reynal and Hitchcock, 1936), p. 139; Wallace draft of article, "The Farmer Looks for Customers," April 2, 1939, Wallace Papers.

5

God, Man, and the Guru

Since the early 1920s, Henry Wallace's thoughts on foreign affairs had been shaped by his attempts to find solutions for economic depression. In groping for ways to combat the farm depression and then the world depression, he had taken a number of different positions before settling on the planned middle course. But Wallace did not believe that the answer to the depression lay only in economic planning. Although he once spent hours trying to persuade a friend that "economics precedes everything," he also maintained that "back of the economic endeavors stand the religious longings." He was convinced that the great depression was a religious as well as an economic crisis. Wallace found solace in his belief that the bewildering world conditions provided fertile ground for "spiritual growth" and that a "new order" might "arise in some measure out of the chaos." His religious philosophy displayed a prominent strain of mystical idealism that played a critical role in molding his outlook on world affairs.[1]

Wallace was an intensely religious man whose quest for eternal truths led him far beyond the bounds of conventional organized religion. Raised as a Presbyterian, he had begun to question the tenets of Calvinism as a young man, and for a time his scientific training had made him doubt the existence of God. His skepticism proved transitory, and when he again felt a need to believe in God, he found spiritual satisfaction in the Roman Catholic mass. But as

Wallace began to examine the intellectual foundations of Catholicism, he found that his studies destroyed "the spiritual beauty of the mass." During the 1920s he drifted into the Liberal Catholic Church, a small sect that combined the liturgy of high Anglicanism with an extremely flexible doctrine. It provided a common ritual for its members without requiring adherence to a specific dogma, while affirming the reality of revealed truth through mystical experiences.[2]

Wallace's views on religion displayed characteristics of mysticism. His perceptions of Divinity were more spiritual than intellectual, and although he was wary of people who feigned mysticism, he professed: "I have had enough experience with this kind of thing myself to believe there is something to it." It was a mistake, he observed, "for scientific and common sense people to shut the door to some of these things which they cannot understand." He confided to one correspondent that he was "fundamentally . . . a searcher for methods of bringing the 'Inner light' to outward manifestation." Wallace believed in a transcendent and immanent God, but he disdained "the lukewarmness, the wishy-washy goody-goodiness and the infantile irrelevancy" of Christian orthodoxy. He defined religion in a broad sense as "the force which governs the attitude of men in their inmost hearts toward God and toward their fellowmen." After becoming Secretary of Agriculture, he used his office to preach the urgent need for Americans to readjust their attitudes toward their countrymen and the world at large.[3]

Throughout their history, Wallace stated, Americans had demonstrated a spirit of bold, rugged, free-wheeling individualism. Those qualities had served the pioneers well when they battled adversity and deprivation to conquer the wilderness. But those men, "grabbers and exploiters that they were," had never learned to live with one another or with other countries. America had inherited from its frontier experience a philosophy of fierce competitiveness, laissez-faire economics, and unbridled materialism that was inapplicable in the twentieth century. The old frontier had ended, Wallace pointed out, and science and technology had produced an era of plentitude that replaced the scarcity economics of pioneer days. Americans must discard the obsolete aspects of their frontier legacy, he insisted, and develop new social machinery to meet the demands of an age of material abundance. Vast new frontiers challenged the country, but those frontiers did not appear on any map. They entailed a quest for spiritual growth that would create "a new state of heart and mind" and check "unrestrained selfishness" that was "ruinous to everyone."[4]

"The keynote of the new frontier is cooperation," Wallace declared, "just as that of the old frontier was individualistic competition." Americans must learn to subordinate their immediate, self-serving goals to the broader vision of working for the general welfare. Such an ideal was attainable, Wallace believed, even though it required a spiritual reformation even greater than that of the sixteenth century. If the American people would cleanse their hearts of "bitterness, prejudice, hatred, greed and fear," the potential for economic, cultural, and spiritual fulfillment was limitless. Modern technology had solved the problem of material scarcity, and only man's spiritual paucity prevented him from enjoying the fruits of abundance. "If the tiny spark of divine spirit found in each individual could be fanned into an all-consuming flame," the message of the Sermon on the Mount could be implemented and a veritable heaven on earth could be achieved.[5]

The New Deal, Wallace asserted, was taking strides to construct the social machinery necessary to effect the cooperative ideal. While affirming the sacredness of individual rights and retaining democratic institutions, it attempted to restrict special privilege for the few and provide economic justice for the many. He felt certain that the New Deal was progressing toward his goal of "economic democracy," and emphasized that it placed "human rights above property rights." Wallace assailed those who wanted to perpetuate "the law of the jungle" by seeking special favors to enhance short-term profits, particularly pressure groups, segments of the press, some farm and labor organizations, and many businessmen. He derided the supposedly realistic people whose pursuit of narrow, selfish interests would eventually prove to be "thoroughly impractical." If their philosophy continued to predominate, and if men became more myopic in their social vision, then a disaster even worse than that of 1932 was likely to occur. Wallace argued that "from the hardheaded material point of view, the Sermon on the Mount is practical."[6]

The American people not only should adhere to the "higher law of cooperation" at home, Wallace maintained, but should recognize that they lived in a spiritually unified world. Affirming his belief in the universal fatherhood of God and brotherhood of man, he lamented that national boundaries had obscured the common bonds shared by all religions. He cited the need for a genuinely catholic faith that would embrace Buddhists, Mohammedans, Jews, and Christians. Wallace urged Americans to reject "pagan nationalism," acknowledge the brotherhood of man, and realize that the world was one. "The aim of a truly religious people," he wrote, "should be to appeal to those things that bind humanity together and bind humanity to God." The spirit of nationalism that raised barriers between countries was "a negation of true religion." The world needed a "New Deal among nations" that would promote the co-operative ideal on an international basis.[7]

The countries of the world could take a dramatic step toward achieving spiritual maturity and ushering in a "Golden Age," Wallace believed, by adopting a treaty to protect cultural and artistic treasures, especially in time of war. For several years, a White Russian artist named Nicholas Roerich had unsuccessfully promoted an international agreement to preserve cultural monuments. Wallace, who deeply admired Roerich, actively campaigned for the pact after becoming Secretary of Agriculture. His relationship with Roerich resulted in the most extraordinary episode of his career, but it also underscored the connection between his religious convictions and his views on international relations.[8]

Nicholas Roerich was a Russian-born painter, poet, archeologist, philosopher, and mystic. Short, soft-spoken, and completely bald, he wore a flowing, double-pointed beard, and gazed from penetrating, deep-set eyes. Driven from his homeland after the Bolshevik Revolution, he traveled widely in Asia during the 1920s, painting and doing archeological work. His expeditions created enough turmoil for the British Foreign Office to label him as an "unbalanced" person. But his paintings attracted world-wide acclaim, and in 1929, a group of admirers erected the 29-story Roerich Museum in New York City to exhibit his work.[9]

Roerich had proposed a treaty to protect artistic treasures as early as 1904, and in 1914 had suggested it to Czar Nicholas II. It was not until 1929, however, that Roerich and his associates formally drafted a treaty according to international law. They adopted the "Banner of Peace," a red circle surrounding three spheres on a field of white, as the symbol to identify the monuments to be safeguarded by the Roerich Pact. The artist requested the support of President Hoover and asked the State Department to initiate international action on the proposed agreement. The State Department showed little enthusiasm for the treaty, however, arguing that the Hague Convention of 1907 and the Kellogg-Briand Pact made the Roerich Pact superfluous, and expressing doubt that "futile, weak, and unenforcible" accords accomplished anything.[10]

Henry Wallace had become interested in the Banner of Peace as early as 1929, and he admired Roerich's paintings, which, he said, "gave him a smooth feeling inside." He esteemed Roerich's philosophy, which had much in common with his own. Both affirmed a belief in the fundamental unity of all religions, the brotherhood of man, and the need for a transformation of the human heart to achieve cooperation. Roerich's mystical insights also attracted Wallace because they seemed to offer illumination in his enduring search for eternal truth.[11]

Although Wallace met Roerich only once, he was in frequent contact with officials of the Roerich Museum.[12] In a remarkable series of letters he wrote in 1933 and 1934 to Frances R. Grant, vice-president of the museum, he described his spiritual yearnings and commented on contemporary events and personalities. Some of those communications were later published by Wallace's political opponents and dubbed the "Guru letters" because of his occasional references to Nicholas Roerich as the "Guru." Wallace told Miss Grant that her "quiet confidence" reassured him when his faith in "the ultimate" was shaken "by the shoving of a busy world and petty cross currents." He reported seeing visions of Roerich in his morning meditations and that those meditations gave him renewed strength. He complained of the constant tension under which he labored, but expressed confidence that it marked "the first crude beginnings of a new age."[13]

The "Guru letters" contained many coded references and some disparaging remarks about Wallace's associates. He labeled Cordell Hull as the "Sour One" and called the State Department the "Old House." Wallace characterized Roosevelt either as the "Flaming One" or the "Wavering One," depending on whether or not he approved of the President's actions. Roosevelt was "undoubtedly an agent through which great forces are working," the Agriculture Secretary told Miss Grant, "but he is as provoking to me in the density of his perceptions at times as I doubtless am to you."[14]

Wallace related the progress of negotiations that led to the diplomatic recognition of the Soviet Union, which he called the "Tigers." He worried that Roosevelt was too tractable in his attitude toward the Russians, and confided that he had sent "an effective tiger letter" to Roosevelt and Hull. Nicholas Roerich had no love for the Soviet regime, and although he and his admirers may have reinforced Wallace's opposition to recognizing Russia, they did not induce him to take that position.[15]

The "Guru letters" also featured allegorical allusions that were meaningful to those steeped in Roerich's philosophical musings. Wallace referred to the "Dark Ones," "Steadfast Ones," and "dugpas," and often beseeched the blessings of the "Great Ones."[16] The letters were decidedly unconventional and possibly bizarre, but they accurately reflected Wallace's admiration for Nicholas Roerich, his personal quest for spiritual satisfaction, and his adherence to the principles represented by Roerich's Banner of Peace.

Wallace lobbied aggressively in the summer and fall of 1933 to secure the endorsement of the Roosevelt administration for the Banner of Peace. He assured Roerich of his full support for the "endeavor to furnish a symbol for the thought that beauty and knowledge should tie all of the nations together in appreciation of a common human purpose."[17] The artist, as usual, was out of the country, but Wallace arranged for Roerich Museum officials to see President Roosevelt and other government authorities.[18] He also wrote long letters to Roosevelt and Secretary Hull, reviewing the history and outlining the objectives of the Roerich Pact. Wallace suggested to the President that despite the world trend toward nationalism, the Banner of Peace presented an opportunity to enhance the spiritual and cultural unity of mankind, and to forge "a 'New Deal' in international relationships."[19]

State Department officers remained unimpressed by the merits of the Roerich Pact. They reminded Wallace of the department's previous objections to the Banner of Peace, pointing out that the Hague Convention of 1907 had provided guarantees against wanton destruction of cultural, artistic, and scientific treasures in wartime, and adding that modern weapons made such agreements obsolete. An international conference to discuss the Roerich Pact was to be held in Washington, D.C., in November 1933, and Wallace urged Secretary Hull to attend or designate an official representative of the American government to do so. Hull demurred, conveying his personal sympathy for the pact, but declaring that the United States should not become involved with the movement. Wallace persevered, however, arguing that the United States should advance beyond the attitude taken by the Hoover administration on the Banner of Peace and "begin to make some real progress toward doing our part in holding up international ideals." He again asked Hull to appoint a delegate to the upcoming convention, and requested the Secretary of State to send it a message of greeting.[20]

Irritated by Wallace's persistence, Hull solicited Roosevelt's advice. The President was more receptive to the idea of the Roerich Pact than was Hull, and asked the Secretary of State to discuss it with him. Shortly thereafter, Hull softened his position. He drafted a message of welcome to the Banner of Peace Convention and named Wallace to serve as its American delegate.[21]

The Third International Roerich Peace Banner Convention met at the Mayflower Hotel in Washington, D.C., on November 17 and 18, 1933. Although the most vociferous, Wallace was not the only American dignitary to support the Roerich Pact. Senator Robert F. Wagner of New York acted as Honorary Chairman of the conference, and fourteen U.S. senators, two congressmen, sixteen governors, the superintendent of the U.S. Military Academy, and several college presidents served as honorary members. In his address to the meeting, Wallace compared the Banner of Peace to the Red Cross, and deplored the nationalistic "hatreds and prejudices of these terrible times." He realized the Roerich Pact was no substitute for the need to deal with "hard economic facts," but he hoped it would draw the world closer together and smooth the way for successful economic and disarmament agreements. Representatives from thirty-five countries culminated the conference by unanimously adopting a resolution to recommend the Banner of Peace to the governments of every nation in the world.[22]

Less than a month after the Washington meeting, a Pan-American conference in Montevideo, Uruguay, recommended that all governments in the Western Hemisphere sign the Roerich Pact. But the State Department continued to drag its feet. One official, J. Pierrepont Moffat, noted that most countries had sent minor functionaries to the Banner of Peace Convention and regarded the Roerich Pact as "a good joke." Undersecretary of State William Phillips advised

Wallace that the State Department would view the pact more favorably if the countries of Western Europe displayed greater interest in it. He also suggested that the treaty, if finalized, should not include Roerich's name.[23] Irked by Phillips' opinions, Wallace replied that it seemed "entirely natural" that the pact should bear the name of its originator, and argued that Roerich's name would "enhance the value of the measure." Moreover, he asserted, the Pan-American conference demonstrated the wide support among Latin American countries for the Banner of Peace. The Agriculture Secretary denied that the Hague Convention of 1907 adequately protected cultural treasures and requested that the United States sign the Roerich Pact to show that it stood "for a new humanity among the nations of the earth . . . based on united vigilance for the things of the spirit."[24]

Wallace's efforts eventually succeeded. In July 1934, Roosevelt directed Hull to follow the procedures necessary to subscribe to the Roerich Pact and designated Wallace as U.S. plenipotentiary.[25] On April 15, 1935, Wallace and twenty Latin American representatives signed the pact at the White House. Roosevelt broadcast a statement acclaiming the Banner of Peace, and Wallace described the occasion as a step toward a "spiritual New Deal which places that which is fine in humanity above that which is low and sordid and mean and hateful and grabbing." The following day, the Agriculture Secretary sent a series of letters proposing that Nicholas Roerich be considered for the Nobel Peace Prize.[26]

Roerich did not witness the fruition of his life-long project. In March 1934, Wallace had appointed him to lead an expedition to the hinterlands of Mongolia to search for specimens and information on the drought-resistant grasses of Asia. Sponsored by the Department of Agriculture's Bureau of Plant Industry, the project also included Roerich's son, George, and two of the bureau's expert botanists, Howard MacMillan and James Stephens. The State Department expressed concern about the venture because the Roerichs were White Russians and not American citizens, and because the explorers would travel in Manchuria and North China, a hotbed of international tension and intrigue in the early 1930s. Wallace dismissed those doubts and assured the State Department that the mission would create no political difficulties.[27] The Agriculture Secretary was also unmoved by reservations voiced by Knowles Ryerson, chief of the Bureau of Plant Industry. Ryerson worried that the important objectives of the mission would be aborted by Roerich's lack of scientific expertise, and also feared for the safety of his two men. Wallace reported Ryerson's apprehensions to George Roerich, and said that he "placed responsibility for the lives of these two men on the Guru." He requested the younger Roerich to "ask the Guru to use his powers to give them confidence and joy" so that they would return from the expedition "singing your praises."[28]

The expedition got underway in May 1934, and quickly ran into problems. MacMillan and Stephens had planned to meet the Roerichs in Tokyo, but the artist and his son left Japan before the botanists arrived. The Roerichs journeyed to Mukden, where Japanese officials detained them. Their suspicions were aroused by the Roerichs' vagueness about the purposes of their trip and their lack of proper diplomatic credentials. The only official identification the Roerichs carried was a handwritten letter from Wallace on plain stationery with no letterhead. The American consulate eventually resolved that imbroglio, and the Roerichs continued on to Manchuria. There they met the emperor of the Japanese puppet state of Manchukuo and presented him with an insignia of the Roerich Museum. That action enraged the State Department because Roerich led an expedition sponsored by the American government, and it refused to recognize the existence of Manchukuo.[29]

Meanwhile, MacMillan and Stephens, despite Japanese obstructions and inclement weather, tried to catch up with the elusive Roerichs. The botanists finally overtook them in Harbin, Manchuria, but the Roerichs still avoided seeing them. MacMillan vented his grievances in long, bitter letters to Knowles Ryerson. He complained of the Roerichs' evasiveness, and accused them of political agitation among White Russian elements in Harbin that aroused the suspicions of the Japanese. He also asserted that the Roerichs displayed little interest in gathering drought-resistant grass seeds. George Roerich, on the other hand, told Wallace that the botanists were delaying the expedition and refusing to obey instructions, and added that Frances Grant would pass on further information about the situation.[30] A short time after Miss Grant visited Wallace in Washington, he recalled MacMillan and Stephens for "serious insubordination." When Ryerson protested and attempted to explain the reasons for the botanists' disaffection, the Agriculture Secretary retorted that the "rumors" about the Roerichs were "ridiculous" and "extremely malicious." He relieved Ryerson as chief of the Bureau of Plant Industry and transferred him to the Division of Subtropical Horticulture. The expedition's first season ended after gathering a great deal of bitterness but few drought-resistant seeds.[31]

In late 1934, the Roerichs decided to move their operations from Manchuria to Mongolia. They asked Wallace to secure authorization from the War Department to obtain arms and ammunition from the American military detachment in Tientsin, China. Wallace complied, telling the War Department that the Roerichs needed the weapons for their personal protection because of "unsettled conditions" in the Gobi area. The Roerichs, who had already alarmed the Japanese by their activities among the 70,000 White Russians in Harbin, received ten firearms in Tientsin, recruited a small band of White Russian Cossack soldiers, and proceeded to Mongolia. In June 1935, the *Chicago Tribune* reported that the Roerichs and their entourage, flaunting their American diplomatic protection, were arousing "considerable suspicion" among Mongolian authorities. Disturbed by accounts of Roerich's political activities, Wallace wrote to Louis Horch, president of the Roerich Museum, stating that he was "exceedingly anxious" to ascertain that the artist was confining himself to a search for seeds. He believed that the newspaper stories were unfounded, but he asked Roerich to move the expedition to a less sensitive region.[32]

Roerich vehemently denied that he was dabbling in Asian politics, and denounced the reports in the *Tribune* and other newspapers as "gross insinuations." Shortly thereafter, however, Wallace received information that the American military attaché in Moscow had learned that the Soviet Union was troubled by the expedition, and feared that the Roerichs' "armed party" intended "to rally former White elements and discontented Mongols." Convinced by that report that Roerich was doing more than looking for drought-resistant grasses, Wallace quickly resolved to terminate the mission. He curtly informed the artist of his decision on September 16, 1935.[33]

The expedition was not a total loss, and the Roerichs sent a relatively large number of seed specimens to the Department of Agriculture. But that did not assuage Wallace's utter disillusionment with Nicholas Roerich. Believing that the artist had betrayed his trust, Wallace came to revile Roerich as keenly as he once had admired him. He embarked on a concerted effort to exorcise Roerich from his life. The Agriculture Secretary sent letters of apology to Knowles Ryerson, James Stephens, and Howard MacMillan. He wrote Roerich's wife to inform her that he wanted no contacts of any kind with the Roerich family.[34]

Wallace informed the U.S. ambassadors from every country in the world that although he had played an active role in promoting the Banner of Peace, he had lost faith in Nicholas Roerich and those "who continue fanatically in their policy of aggrandizing a name rather than an ideal." To underscore his point, he asked the State Department to refrain from using Roerich's name in connection with the treaty to protect cultural treasures, and to take no further steps to secure plates or prints of the Banner of Peace. He told Joseph Grew, U.S. ambassador to Japan, of his complete disenchantment with Roerich because of the artist's political activities in Asia. In a letter to Governor Herbert Lehman of New York, Wallace condemned the American admirers of Roerich who regarded him "as a superman and were determined to stop at nothing in helping him to work out some extraordinary phantasy of Asiatic power."[35]

After his bitter experience with Roerich, Wallace's interest in mystical pursuits waned.[36] But his belief in the fundamental unity of mankind, the need to achieve a new spirit of cooperation at home and abroad, and the practicality of the Sermon on the Mount remained unshaken.

NOTES

1. Paul deKruif to Henry A. Wallace, August 25, 1934, Secretary's Personal File, RG 16, NA; Wallace to J. F. Corbett, October 14, 1931, Wallace to Charles Roos, December 31, 1931, Henry A. Wallace Papers, University of Iowa.

2. Henry A. Wallace, *Statesmanship and Religion* (New York: Round Table Press, 1934), pp. 44-47; Paul Appleby interview, Columbia Oral History Collection; Charles S. Braden, *They Also Believe: A Study of Modern American Cults and Minority Religious Movements* (New York: Macmillan Co., 1949), Chap. 8.

3. Wallace to Mark Hyde, July 14, 1930, Wallace to L. E. Johndro, October 24, 1931, Wallace Papers; Louis Bean interview, Columbia Oral History Collection; Wallace, *Statesmanship and Religion,* pp. 46, 88, 116.

4. Henry A. Wallace, *New Frontiers* (New York: Reynal and Hitchcock, 1934), pp. 3-13, 269-87; Wallace, *Statesmanship and Religion,* pp. 5-10, 115-

39; Wallace, *Democracy Reborn,* Russell Lord, ed., (New York: Reynal and Hitchcock, 1944), pp. 57-64.

5. Wallace, *New Frontiers,* pp. 263-87; Wallace, *Statesmanship and Religion,* pp. 115-139; Wallace speech, "Machinery, Economics, and Religion," August 18, 1933, Wallace Papers.

6. Wallace, *New Frontiers,* pp. 11, 37-67, 251-53, 282-87; Wallace, *Statesmanship and Religion,* pp. 92-96, 115.

7. Wallace, *Statesmanship and Religion,* pp. 79-81, 100-106, 130-33; Wallace to S. J. Truscott, February 25, 1936, Criticisms File, RG 16, NA.

8. Wallace radio speech given immediately before the Roerich Peace Pact Conference, November 17, 1933, Wallace Papers; *The Roerich Pact and the Banner of Peace* (New York: Roerich Pact and Banner of Peace Committee, 1947), pp. 5-8.

9. "The Silver Valley," *Time,* 50 (December 29, 1947): 21; "The 'Guru Letters,'" *Newsweek,* 31 (March 22, 1948): 27; F. A. Sterling to Secretary of State, September 29, 1925, 031.11 R62, RG 59, NA; Norman D. Markowitz, *The Rise and Fall of the People's Century: Henry A. Wallace and American Liberalism, 1941-1948* (New York: Free Press, 1973), p. 336.

10. Nicholas Roerich to Herbert Hoover, February 26, 1930, 504.418 B1/2, J. P. Cotton to Roerich, April 29, 1930, 504.418 B1/20, Treaty Division Policy Memorandum, n.d., 504.418 B1/17, RG 59, NA; *The Roerich Pact,* pp. 6-7.

11. Wallace to Cordell Hull, August 31, 1933, 504.418 B1/42, RG 59, NA; Bean interview, Columbia Oral History Collection; Nicholas Roerich, *Fiery Stronghold* (Boston: Stratford Co., 1933).

12. Wallace to Carl Gewitz, April 5, 1960, Wallace Papers; Mrs. Louis L. Horch to the author, July 27, 1973.

13. Wallace to Miss Grant, June 18, 1933, Wallace to F.R.G., ca. September 1933, Wallace to F., ca. November 1933, Wallace to Miss Grant, date undetermined, Samuel Rosenman Papers, Roosevelt Library. Wallace often signed the letters with a crossed W. The "Guru letters" must be used with extreme caution because they may include forgeries perpetrated by Wallace's political opponents. The Republican National Committee obtained copies of the letters and considered publishing them to embarrass Wallace when he ran as Roosevelt's vice-presidential candidate in 1940, but ultimately decided against it. In 1948, when Wallace ran for president on a third-party ticket, Westbrook Pegler printed some of the letters in his syndicated newspaper column. A portion of the correspondence is written in Wallace's scrawl, while part of it is typewritten. Although some of the letters may be fabrications, many of them can be authenticated from their context. I have used only those letters that I am convinced are genuine. There is no evidence to support William O. Douglas' contention that Wallace attended seances and spoke to spirits through a medium. See William O. Douglas, *Go East, Young Man* (New York: Random House, 1974), pp. 338-39.

14. Wallace to F.R.G., July 17, 1933, Wallace to M., December 12, 1933, Wallace to unspecified recipient, ca. October 1933, Rosenman Papers.

15. Wallace to F., ca. November 1933, Wallace to unspecified recipient, ca. October 1933, Wallace to unspecified recipient, late September 1933 (the "tiger letters" were sent September 29), Rosenman Papers; Roerich, *Fiery Stronghold,* p. 158.

16. Wallace to F.R.G., ca. September 1933, Wallace to Miss Grant, date undetermined, Wallace to unspecified recipient, ca. October 1933, Rosenman Papers.

17. Wallace to Nicholas Roerich, June 17, 1933, Rosenman Papers. This was an official letter written on Department of Agriculture stationery.

18. Wallace to Jesse Jones, August 25, 1933, Wallace Papers; Wallace to Marvin McIntyre, November 10, 1933, Official File 723, Franklin D. Roosevelt Papers, Roosevelt Library; Hull to Wallace, September 29, 1933, 504.418 B1/66, RG 59, NA.

19. Wallace to Hull, August 31, 1933, 504.418 B1/42, RG 59, NA; Wallace to Roosevelt, September 18, 1933, Official File 723, Roosevelt Papers.

20. Unsigned draft of State Department memorandum sent to Wallace, September 2, 1933, 504.418 B1/43, Hull to Wallace, September 29, 1933, 504.418 B1/66, Wallace to Hull, October 2, 11, 1933, 504.418 B1/83, 90, RG 59, NA.

21. Hull to Roosevelt, October 11, 1933, with attached message from Roosevelt to Hull, Official File 723, Roosevelt Papers; Wallace to F.R.G., ca. September 1933, Rosenman Papers; Hull to Wallace, October 18, 1933, 504.418 B1/84, RG 59, NA.

22. *The Roerich Pact,* pp. 8, 44-47; Louis L. Horch to James C. Dunn, October 31, 1933, 504.418 B1/99, RG 59, NA; Wallace speech, "The Red Cross and the Banner of Peace," November 17, 1933, Cordell Hull Papers, Library of Congress, Washington, D.C.

23. *The Roerich Pact,* p. 8; J. P. Moffat Diary, December 4, 1933, Houghton Library, Harvard University; James C. Dunn to Richard Southgate, February 27, 1934, 504.418 B1/107, William Phillips to Wallace, January 11, 1934, 504.418 B1/110, RG 59, NA.

24. Wallace to Phillips, January 18, April 8, 1934, 504.418 B1/111, 112, RG 59, NA.

25. Charles M. Barnes to Sidney Y. Smith, August 1, 1934, 504.418 B1/119, Hull to Roosevelt, August 10, 1934, 504.418 B1/122, RG 59, NA. Roosevelt's reasons for supporting the Banner of Peace are obscure. Wallace later recounted that Roosevelt had met Roerich through his mother, Sara Roosevelt, and that the President spoke kindly of the artist. Wallace interview, Columbia Oral History Collection, pp. 5102-5104. For a time in late 1934, Roosevelt received and apparently replied to allegorical letters from Roerich's wife, Helena. See Official File 723, Roosevelt Papers.

26. Wallace speech, "Signing of the Roerich Pact Symbolizes International Cultural Unity," April 15, 1935, Wallace to Dr. Fredrik Stang, April 16, 1935, Wallace Papers; *Washington Post,* April 16, 1935. The Senate approved the Roerich Pact on July 10, 1935.

27. Knowles Ryerson to Wallace, February 5, 1934, Roerich Expedition Records, RG 54 (Records of the Bureau of Plant Industry, Soils and Agricultural Engineering), "Conversation between Secretary of Agriculture, Mr. Ryerson, Mr. Hornbeck, and Mr. Jacobs," April 5, 1934, 102.7302 MacMillan, Howard G. and Stephens, James L./3/10, RG 59, NA; Wallace to Roerich, March 16, 1934, Wallace Papers.

28. Interview with Knowles A. Ryerson, April 24, 1975; Wallace to George [Roerich], Spring 1934, Rosenman Papers.

29. George Roerich to Howard MacMillan, May 23, 1934, MacMillan to Ryerson, June 9, 1934, Roerich Expedition, RG 54, Memorandum to the Secretary, July 5, 1934, 102.7302 MacMillan, Howard G. and Stephens, James L./25, RG 59, NA; Interview with Ryerson.

30. MacMillan to Arthur Garrels, July 20, 1934, MacMillan to Ryerson, July 20, 22, 25, 31, August 17, 1934, George Roerich to Wallace, July 20, 1934, Roerich Expedition, RG 54, NA.

31. Wallace to George C. Hanson, September 27, 1934, Wallace to Nicholas Roerich, September 27, 1934, Wallace to Cabot Coville, October 17, 1934, Wallace to E. N. Bressman, October 22, 1934, Roerich Expedition, RG 54, NA; Ryerson to MacMillan, August 11, 1934, Wallace to Ryerson, October 20, 1934, Wallace Papers; Interview with Ryerson.

32. George Roerich to Wallace, November 30, 1934, Wallace to the Secretary of War, December 1, 1934, Wallace to Louis L. Horch, July 3, 1935, Roerich Expedition, RG 54, NA; *Chicago Tribune,* June 24, 1935.

33. Nicholas Roerich to Wallace, July 27, 1935, R. Walton Moore to Wallace, August 24, 1935, Wallace to F. D. Richey, August 30, 1935, Wallace to Nicholas Roerich, September 16, 1935, Roerich Expedition, RG 54, NA.

34. Wallace to Stephens, November 6, 1935, Wallace to MacMillan, November 6, 1935, Roerich Expedition, RG 54, NA; Wallace to Ryerson, October 11, 1935, Wallace to Mrs. Nicholas Roerich, September 24, 1935, Wallace Papers; *New York Times,* September 7, 1935.

35. Wallace to Oswald Aranha, October 23, 1935, Wallace to Joseph Grew, October 24, 1935, Wallace to Herbert Lehman, January 18, 1936, Wallace Papers; Wilber J. Carr to C. Wynne, January 2, 1936, 504.418 B1/230, RG 59, NA.

36. Wallace to Raymond Suppes, September 9, 1936, Secretary's Personal File, RG 16, NA; James LeCron interview, Columbia Oral History Collection.

6

The Specter of War

The deepening crises in Europe and Asia in the late 1930s and the increasing possibility of another great war sorely troubled Henry Wallace. Like the overwhelming majority of his countrymen, he loathed the thought of American involvement in a foreign conflict. He hoped that Europe would not again plunge into war, but he informed his uncle that he had little confidence in Europe's ability to "behave itself." Wallace believed that the American people had learned from World War I "that war is a bad business, a murderous business, and that all you can collect from it afterward is increasing grief." He feared that a European war would jeopardize the farm program, disrupt New Deal reform, and create major maladjustments in the American economy. In 1936, he suggested that in the event of a foreign conflict, the United States would be wise to adopt a policy of complete commercial and financial isolation rather than risk belligerency by continuing to trade with Europe. He admitted that such a program would pose enormous difficulties, but maintained that it would be preferable to participation in war.[1]

At the same time that he abhorred the thought of war, Wallace despised the theory and practice of fascism. Like many Americans, he was torn between his hope for peace and his desire to stop fascist aggression. He favored collaboration with other countries to curb the activities of the dictators. Wallace applauded President Roosevelt's "quarantine speech" of October 5, 1937, in which the President condemned the actions of the dictators in general terms and forwarded a vague proposal for international cooperation to "quarantine" aggressors. Adolph Hitler's maneuvers in early 1938 further persuaded the Agriculture Secretary that America should not stand aloof from the world crisis. Shortly after Nazi troops rolled into Austria, he urged Roosevelt to combat the recession the country was then suffering by cooperating with business and striving to win its support. Wallace argued that the United States must attain prosperity and domestic harmony to present a united front in world affairs and help discourage "the depredations of Germany, Italy, and Japan." "If you can furnish strong leadership via the Americas and other democracies, including Russia," he wrote the President, "you will have rendered a profound service to this generation and the generations to come."[2]

The Agriculture Secretary's thinking reflected a modified attitude toward the Soviet Union and an intensified interest in Latin America. In late 1936, a friend had written to Wallace expressing concern that the failure to solve the depression in Europe, combined with the success of the Soviet experiment, laid the groundwork for "a 'revolt of the Masses' such has never been seen before." Those fears were similar to ones Wallace had expressed in 1933 when he opposed the recognition of the Soviet Union. But he had altered his views considerably in three years and replied to his correspondent: "It seems to me at the present time there is far greater danger from fascism than from communism." A few months later, an official of the Department of Agriculture who had traveled widely in the Soviet Union reported that he sensed an air of intrigue and suspicion of foreigners that was greatly reinforced by the purge trials then being conducted. Wallace was not surprised by the information, and he suggested that there might be "more justification for the situation . . . than appears on the surface" because of European tensions.[3]

The crisis in Europe heightened Wallace's awareness of the urgent need for closer ties with Latin America. Soon after becoming Agriculture Secretary, Wallace developed a keen interest in Latin America and regularly attended a weekly luncheon club that featured tamales and frijoles, an informal atmosphere, and conversation strictly in Spanish. But it was not until tensions mounted in Europe that Wallace began to press for improved relations with Latin America. In an address to the American Farm Bureau Federation on December 9, 1936, he stated that the risk of the United States getting into war stemmed from its export trade with Europe. That danger could be averted by desisting as much as possible from trade with Europe and Asia, and by building closer economic bonds with Latin America. Asserting that farmers disliked Europe and the League of Nations because both symbolized war, Wallace declared: "Both our hearts and our heads lead us increasingly to Pan-America." But he pointed out that bettering hemispheric relations would require U.S. farmers to import more Latin American agricultural goods.[4]

The problem of expanding imports from Latin America, Wallace admitted, was "a somewhat difficult one." Realizing that American growers would object to any large increase in competitive farm imports, he recommended that the United States embark on a program to encourage its southern neighbors to produce more noncompetitive tropical products which could be sold in the United States without hurting American farmers. The resulting growth of trade would help cement hemispheric ties.[5] Otherwise, Wallace feared, dictators "intent on destroying democracy" might make economic and political inroads among the people of Latin America.[6]

Wallace concluded that Nazi Germany presented a threat to the Western Hemisphere long before most Americans did. Hitler's demands at Munich in September 1938 convinced him that the dictator planned "to take one bite at a time." He told General Hugh Johnson that the Germans intended to apply internal and external pressures on both North and South America and that the United States "must begin to plan for contingencies at once if we are to avoid eventual war." Wallace also detested Naziism because it violated his religious and economic credos. He denounced the rigidly nationalistic economic policies followed by the fascist dictatorships that explained "at least a part of present-day war-mongering." He was repelled by Hitler's glorification of a master race that denied his belief in the universal brotherhood of man. As an expert geneticist, Wallace spoke with authority when he assailed Germany's "mumbo-jumbo of dangerous nonsense" that provided "pseudo-scientific support for the exaltation of one race and one nation as conquerors."[7]

In April 1939, shortly after Hitler occupied all of Czechoslovakia and Benito Mussolini seized Albania, President Roosevelt proposed to send a personal message to the two strongmen, asking for pledges that they refrain from further aggression. Wallace advised Roosevelt against making the appeal, declaring that "the two madmen respect force and force alone." The gesture, he said, would be like "delivering a sermon to a mad dog." The Agriculture Secretary's judgment was sound. When Roosevelt issued his plea, Hitler and Mussolini responded with sardonic insults and undisguised contempt. Wallace confided to a friend that he anticipated a war in Europe within a year or two because Hitler would not be "diverted by anything but a full appreciation of force." His hatred of Germany had not increased his admiration for Britain. "England in my opinion is continuing to retreat from Hitler with secret promises which can be fulfilled only at other people's expense," he wrote. "I would not be at all surprised if she would suggest at the appropriate moment giving Germany a foothold in such a spot as to most embarrass us."[8]

On September 1, 1939, Hitler invaded Poland and Europe plunged into war. Wallace announced that the primary effort of the Department of Agriculture would be to keep the United States out of war and shield American farmers and consumers from the harmful effects of the conflict. Apprehensive that farmers would abandon crop control in hopes that the war would create a vast demand abroad for American products, he urged them to avoid "the same old trap with the inevitable repercussions coming afterward." While conceding that prices had risen during World War I, he reminded farmers that prices had been lower the year after the war than they had been in 1914. Any temporary gains farmers might achieve as a result of hostilities would be "paid for twice over" by the depression that followed. Far from presenting a solution to the farm problem, Wallace argued, the war made agricultural adjustment more necessary and difficult than ever.[9]

The "only bright thing" about the war, Wallace remarked, "is the splendid way in which it is bringing this hemisphere together." Shortly before the European conflict began, he had called for improved cultural and economic ties in the New World. He regretted that North and South America knew so little about each other, and suggested that the time had come to build a "genuinely inter-American" culture. Wallace advocated cultural exchanges, increased study of Latin American history and language, an inter-American

University, and a Pan-American highway as methods to promote hemispheric understanding. But cultural links needed to be buttressed by "a firm basis of economic reciprocity." Noting that eighty percent of Latin America's exports were agricultural, Wallace again recommended that the United States assist the Latin American countries in producing more goods that complemented its economy so that two-way trade could be established. The United States would readily accept more tropical products from Latin America, particularly rubber, quinine, hemp and other commodities that Asian countries normally supplied. Wallace regarded his plan as a practical way to cultivate better relations among the Americas and believed that the outbreak of war in Europe made his vision of Pan-Americanism a necessity.[10]

In October 1939, in an address to the Commonwealth Club in San Francisco, Wallace reiterated his plea for closer inter-American bonds and demonstrated his disgust and dismay with Europe. He denounced the economic nationalism of Europe that had undercut the "courageous and persistent" efforts of the United States to restore "peace and sanity and normal trade" to the world. He condemned the diplomatic intrigue, climaxed by the Nazi-Soviet Pact, that proved "that almost any type of realignment is possible in the Old World." Wallace lambasted Europe for its economic imperialism and squabbling over colonies. But above all, he decried the dictatorships that represented "everything that is abhorrent to Americans." The Agriculture Secretary expressed gratification that the New World lived by different principles than the Old and was committed to "equality among nations" and "respect for their rights and territories." He acknowledged that the United States had been guilty of transgressions in its past, but argued that there still existed a "wide gulf" between the ways of the Old World and the New World. Persuaded that the United States should turn away from Europe, Wallace asserted that the country should concentrate on conserving the fertility of its soil and building cultural and economic ties with Latin America. It should also erect a strong hemispheric defense, "so that regardless of which ideology comes out on top in the Old World, we can guard our New World civilization."[11]

Wallace's fulminations against Europe were consistent with the views of American isolationists and recalled his sentiments during the 1920s. His inclinations were distinctly noninterventionist regarding the war in Europe, but he had not abandoned his internationalism. Although the United States should place its strongest emphasis on Pan-Americanism, he declared, it should not "entirely forget" the people of Europe. Even though they were "caught in systems of iniquity," they were "part of the universal brother-hood of man." As long as it did not involve the risk of war, the United States should "furnish leadership looking toward international peace and international trade among the people of the Old World." Ultimately, the American people should work for the fulfillment of Woodrow Wilson's vision of a League of Nations to preserve lasting peace.[12]

Wallace's address reflected a new intensity in his long-standing repugnance for European politics and his faith in the superior virtue of the United States. Yet his devotion to the ideal of internationalism remained intact, as did his commitment to the planned middle course. Wallace had once suggested that if war broke out in Europe, the United States could avoid involvement only by complete economic isolation. But he did not adhere to that proposal after the outbreak of hostilities. Four days after the war began, he told an International Cotton Conference that "international cooperation on an equitable and sensible basis is the only practical way to solve world problems." Wallace did not advocate terminating trade with warring countries, and was disturbed that trade routes for agricultural exports to Britain and France might be disrupted. He approved the 1939 Neutrality Act, which repealed the arms embargo but reenacted the stipulation that belligerents must pay for American exports in cash and transport them in their own vessels. The Agriculture Secretary believed that the cash-and-carry provision would allow foreign shippers to haul American exports to belligerent areas while freeing U.S. ships to trade with Latin America.[13]

Early in 1940, Wallace appeared before congressional committees to testify in favor of extending the Reciprocal Trade Agreements Act. As always, he argued that the trade agreements eased but did not replace the need for crop control, and that they had benefited American farmers. But the war, he believed, gave added significance to the reciprocal trade program because it, along with international commodity agreements, could "be an extremely important factor in the economic reconstruction of the post-war world." If the United States had adopted a policy of reciprocal trade after the first World

War, Wallace asserted, it would have prevented the "ultimately terrible disaster." During the 1920s America had expanded its exports by loaning vast sums of money abroad while refusing to accept imports or cancel war debts. The cessation of loans had placed Germany in "a totally impossible situation" because it had no way to pay its debts. The ensuing financial crisis and depression had "created the rise of Hitler beyond a question." Wallace urged Congress to continue the reciprocal trade program in order to avoid a repetition of such tragic consequences. If the United States extended credit to reconstruct Europe after the war, Wallace insisted, it must be prepared to accept goods from the countries to which it floated loans.[14]

Although Henry Wallace did not regard Britain and France with the same malevolence he held for the fascist dictatorships, he had blurred the distinction in his generalized denunciations of Europe after the war began. He became more discriminating after March 1940. In that month, Wallace reread Thorstein Veblen's books, *Imperial Germany and the Industrial Revolution* and *The Nature of Peace,* and, once again, was influenced by Veblen's analysis. According to Wallace, Veblen recognized that Germans were not genetically superior, but had benefited by borrowing advanced technology from Britain and France. Germany had advanced rapidly from "living in the spirit of the Middle Ages" to becoming a modern industrial state. But it had not developed the political institutions that accompanied modernization in other Western European countries; it retained its archaic "Dynastic State." Veblen believed that modern technology would inevitably erode the foundations of dynastic autocracy, but that process could be impeded by war. Therefore, the German government engaged in constant preparation for war in order to sustain itself.[15]

Hitler, Wallace contended, was a modern manifestation of the "Prussian imperial spirit." The Nazis had inherited the militaristic and imperialistic legacy of the Prussian state, and censorship, education, economic concentration, and historical tradition combined to make the Germans "psychologically very strong." Severe difficulties would arise if Germany, contrary to Veblen's expectations, should demonstrate the ability to maintain its economic efficiency and militarism over a long period of time. Under those circumstances, the whole world, including the Western Hemisphere, "would be confronted with a situation fraught with difficulty, danger, and the possibility of ultimate tragedy."[16]

Impressed by Veblen's insight, Wallace suggested to Roosevelt that he read sections of *The Nature of Peace.* He told Roosevelt that Veblen had foreseen the events that occurred between 1915 and 1940, and had explained "the bandit character" of both Germany and Japan. Simply eliminating Hitler would not solve the current crisis, Wallace stated, because he only personified the deeply ingrained militaristic spirit of Germany. It was impossible to read Veblen "without being gravely concerned with what will happen if England and France make a premature peace with Germany," as Wallace thought they had done after World War I. In order to assure a lasting peace, Germany had to be thoroughly defeated and cleansed of its Prussian imperial spirit.[17]

Veblen's influence, combined with Hitler's stunning blitzkrieg in Western Europe in the spring of 1940, prompted Wallace to reconsider his position regarding the war in Europe. He became much more outspoken in calling for vigorous action to ensure defeat of the Axis powers. Although he still hoped the United States could avoid belligerency, he doubted whether it was "possible to handle the great evils in the world . . . by the pacific spirit." Wallace urged military, economic, and spiritual preparedness and supported aid to the Allies as the best means to thwart the Nazis while maintaining peace in the Western Hemisphere. He thought the United States should arm itself quickly and efficiently in order to "command the fear and respect on the part of every aggressor."[18]

The Agriculture Secretary pressed for economic preparedness to meet the Nazi threat. He wanted to protect the American economy from the disruptions and distortions caused by the war in Europe. In an effort to maintain pre-war export levels, he urged the President to purchase large quantities of gold from Britain and France and suggested a complex scheme to extend short-term credit to them so they could buy American products. Otherwise, he feared, severe dislocations would occur in the American economy, the Allies would be unable to obtain needed provisions, and they would lose the war.[19]

If Hitler conquered Britain and France, Wallace believed, the Western Hemisphere would be his next objective. Therefore, he advocated military and economic cooperation between the United States and Latin America. The New World "must hang together," he declared, "or surely we shall hang separately." Wallace feared that if Germany gained control of Europe, it could extend its influence in the Western Hemisphere by exploiting the fact that many Latin American countries had surpluses of the same goods that the United States overproduced. Shortly after the fall of France in June 1940, he joined with the Secretaries of State, Treasury, and Commerce in urging Roosevelt to establish an Inter-American Trading Corporation that would present a united front to Germany. Wallace envisioned the cartel corporation as a "clearing house for all export and import transactions between the New World and the Old" if the Nazis subjugated all of Europe. It would deal with hemispheric surpluses by regulating the sale of exports, setting up an ever-normal granary, and distributing remaining overstocks to the needy of both North and South America.[20]

Wallace maintained that Americans must be spiritually as well as militarily and economically prepared to repel the Nazi menace. The Prussian militarist spirit, he wrote, was a "veritable anti-Christ" that threatened the foundations of American democracy. The people of the United States must "summon every possible source of spiritual strength" to meet the German challenge to the sacredness of the individual, freedom of religion, and freedom of expression.[21]

Wallace expressed frustration at the reluctance of Americans to respond to the need for preparedness. But although he thought "the ways of democracy are often hard in times of an emergency," he avowed that "the wise thing to do is to take the public into our confidence." He did not want the country to abandon democratic procedures at home in its effort to defeat the enemies of democracy abroad. Wallace was convinced that the people of the United States would realize that the only way to ensure peace throughout the Western Hemisphere was by maximum preparedness on all fronts. He assured friends that the administration had no intention of entering the war, but he favored sending airplanes and munitions to aid the Allies in their desperate struggle against Hitler. Declaring that the President had done "a masterful job in the field of defense and diplomacy," he voiced his confidence that the American people would support Roosevelt in the upcoming presidential election.[22]

Wallace believed that the world crisis made Roosevelt's leadership indispensable. In October 1939, he had publicly called for a third term for Roosevelt, asserting that "the war situation obviously makes it clear that the President's talent and training are necessary to steer the country . . . to safe harbor." Wallace spoke out during a debate over revision of the Neutrality Act, despite Roosevelt's plea for a moratorium on partisan politics on war-related issues. Obviously embarrassed, the White House rebuked Wallace by saying: "It would have been kind and polite of the speaker to have consulted the victim before he spoke."In the spring of 1940, as German armies overran most of Europe, Wallace became more certain that the American people should grant Roosevelt a third term. "Recent world events," Wallace wrote, "have made it all the clearer that we need in the next Administration the leadership of President Roosevelt."[23]

The Democratic party nominated Roosevelt as its standard-bearer in July 1940, and at the President's insistence, selected Wallace as his running mate. The Agriculture Secretary was not Roosevelt's first choice for the vice-presidential nomination, but after Cordell Hull shunned his overtures, the President turned to Wallace. Wallace had a number of attributes that appealed to Roosevelt. He was a fervent New Dealer and a dedicated internationalist who, if the need arose, could be counted on to carry out Roosevelt's policies on both domestic and foreign issues. He would give the Democratic ticket geographical balance, and hopefully, his prestige in the Middle West would help compensate for the unpopularity of Roosevelt's foreign policies in isolationist agricultural regions. Roosevelt worried about Democratic strength in the Midwest, especially since the Republican vice-presidential candidate, Charles McNary, was popular among farmers. Finally, although Wallace was not an intimate confidant, Roosevelt respected his judgment and ability. Many Democrats did not share the President's regard for Wallace, however, and the convention selected him only after an acrimonious floor battle and Roosevelt's threat to decline the presidential nomination if the party rejected his choice for running mate. Roosevelt's dictatorial demand aroused so much indignation among party regulars that Wallace thought it prudent to postpone his acceptance speech.[24]

Wallace officially accepted his nomination for vice-president in Des Moines, Iowa, on August 29, 1940, in an address that indicated the strategy and set the tone for the Democratic campaign. He lauded Roosevelt's program for peace and preparedness, and his commitment to democratic ideals. The President had tried to promote international understanding and warn the American people of the menace that the "satanic doctrine" of Naziism posed to the Western Hemisphere. But his efforts had been constantly obstructed by Hitler abroad, and by "continuous and bitter partisan opposition at home." Wallace went on to identify domestic opponents of Roosevelt as accomplices of Hitler. Attacks on the President "played into the hands of Hitler," Wallace asserted, because the dictator would like nothing more than "to get rid of the unyielding Roosevelt." While he admitted that Republican leaders did not "willfully or consciously" abet Naziism, Wallace declared that the "replacement of Roosevelt, even if it were by the most patriotic leadership that could be found, would cause Hitler to rejoice." The Republicans were the "party of appeasement," because influential business elements in the GOP would follow the path to enslavement by trading with a German-dominated Europe. "For the sake of profit in 1941, they would sell out their own future and their children's freedom."[25]

President Roosevelt hailed Wallace's address as "a grand speech and splendidly given before an appreciative nation." Other observers, both of isolationist and internationalist persuasion, were less enthusiastic. The *New York Times* attacked the speech as an "irresponsible . . . attempt to arrogate patriotism for the Democratic Party." The Indianola, Iowa *Record* remarked sadly that Wallace seemed "to have degenerated from an economist into a demagogue," and jibed: "By gosh, it took guts to stand up in public . . . and denounce Hitler right there in Des Moines where everybody loves him so much." Oswald Garrison Villard called the address "a new low for American politics" and expressed astonishment "that as fine a man as Henry Wallace has been would lend himself to anything of that kind."[26]

Undaunted by the criticism, Wallace continued his assault. "Some people don't like what I said in my acceptance speech," he observed. "They said I was running Roosevelt against Hitler. That's exactly what I was doing." Wallace admitted that the Republican nominee, Wendell L. Willkie, was also "running against Hitler," but added: "I'm sure we all want the man who can run the fastest." When Roosevelt announced that he had sent fifty outdated destroyers to Britain in return for American bases on British holdings in the Western Hemisphere, Wallace acclaimed the action. He denounced Republican opponents of the destroyer deal for obstructing the

President's efforts for peace and suggested there might be something "sinister" in their motives. Although he did concede that neither Willkie nor most Republicans advocated a policy of appeasement, he stated: "But you can be sure that every Nazi, every Hitlerite and every appeaser is a Republican." The friends of the dictators, Wallace asserted, hoped to take advantage of the "ignorance and lack of leadership" of the Republican nominee, whose inexperience prevented him from understanding "Nazi plots."[27]

Wallace was worried that a Republican victory might result in economic appeasement of Hitler. If Germany defeated Britain and consolidated its control of Europe, he believed, big businessmen and Wall Street interests that dominated the Republican party would insist on maintaining trade with the "totalitarian tyrant states." That policy would play into Hitler's hands, because he would use his enormous economic power to achieve political conquest without war. Once powerful businesses became dependent on trade with a German Europe, Hitler's American agents could easily manipulate them to serve Nazi ends. Declaring that "he that sups with the devil needs a long spoon," Wallace suggested that instead of falling to Hitler's inveiglements, the United States should concentrate on preserving and reclaiming its natural resources and promoting improved relations with Latin America. Only after the Western Hemisphere demonstrated economic and military strength along with a spirit of unity would it be safe to trade with a Nazi Europe. Meanwhile, Wallace continued to berate the "economic appeasers" who thought they could do business with the "fanatic mad dog" Hitler.[28]

The vice-presidential nominee continued to attack Republicans as the party of appeasement throughout the campaign. Some commentators thought his speeches were merely election year oratory, but in fact, Wallace's rhetoric reflected his deep-seated and genuine fear that a Republican triumph would imperil U.S. security. "We are involved in economic warfare with the totalitarian states," he wrote even before the campaign started, "and the wrong kind of appeasement in the economic field might cost us our liberty." When relations with Japan deteriorated during the fall of 1940, Wallace predicted that the Republicans would charge that Roosevelt was leading the United States toward war in the Pacific. "The methods they will use will be close to treason in my opinion," he confided to the President. Even in the final stages of the campaign, when the Democrats decided to shift strategy and tone down their innuendos, Wallace did not change his style. Just before election day, he condemned Willkie for "trying to catch votes" by saying that he would keep the country out of war, and again asserted that a Republican victory would permit Germany to make inroads in the United States. The American people went to the polls on November 5, returning Roosevelt to the White House, and for the first and only time, placing Henry Wallace in an elective office.[29]

The Vice-President-elect had little time to relax after the arduous campaign. Shortly after the election, Wallace represented the United States at the inauguration of Manuel Avila Camacho, who had been chosen President of Mexico the previous summer. Avila Camacho, who was more pro-American and anti-Nazi than his opponent, had won an overwhelming victory, but election procedures had been blatantly fraudulent. Supporters of the defeated candidate protested angrily, occasional violence broke out, and ominous rumors persisted that Avila Camacho's enemies planned an uprising to prevent him from assuming office. The appointment of Wallace to attend the inauguration represented the first official acknowledgement of Camacho's claim to office by the United States, and removed any doubts about its position on the election.[30]

Wallace and his entourage left Texas by automobile on November 26, 1940, and began a triumphant procession down the Mexican peninsula. In Monterrey, between fifty and a hundred thousand people cheered the Vice-President-elect, throwing flowers, singing, and according to observers, generating unprecedented enthusiasm for the American visitor. That pattern continued until Wallace reached Mexico City. There he was met by partisans of Avila Camacho's opponents, who pelted the Americans with rocks, shouted obscenities, and started a riot. The next day, however, when Wallace appeared for Avila Camacho's inauguration, the Mexican Chamber of Deputies accorded him a moving welcome, spontaneously rising and bursting into prolonged applause "with a cordiality that has seldom been shown to representatives of a foreign nation." Two days later, Wallace addressed the Mexican legislative body, declaring in Spanish that Pan-Americanism was "the most practical idea for the people of this hemisphere."[31]

After the ceremonial events ended, Wallace and Mexican officials held a series of high-level talks about Mexican-American differences. The discussions proved to be inconclusive, and Wallace returned home. But the trip was not futile. He promoted the Good Neighbor policy, won the affection of the Mexican people by his use of their native language and by his sincere concern for their problems, and established a close personal relationship with Avila Camacho. President Roosevelt thought that the mission had produced "exceedingly useful results."[32]

After his inauguration as vice-president in January 1941, Wallace continued to exhort the American people about the menace of Hitler's Germany. He asserted that despite the dangers of Naziism, the United States appeared overconfident and complacent in its attitude toward the world crisis. He urged the country to redouble its effort to crush the Prussian imperial spirit and vanquish the "forces of evil." A German victory in Europe, the Vice-President maintained, would threaten America's democratic institutions and its national well-being. "Those who believe the United States can live peacefully and well in a world of triumphant nazi-ism simply do not know what they are talking about," he stated. Contending that democracy and religion were basically the same because the "central core" of both affirmed the dignity of the individual, Wallace argued that "the world crisis is fundamentally religious in character." Naziism represented the antithesis of democracy because in its fanatical devotion to the state, it rejected the sanctity of individual rights, the brotherhood of man, and the fatherhood of God. Therefore, the United States must combat the German threat through hemispheric preparedness and aid to Great Britain. The country should extend aid to the beleaguered British, Wallace believed, not primarily to save Britain, but to promote the security and increase the chances of peace in the Western Hemisphere. "In helping Britain, we are driven by the most selfish of motives—self preservation," he declared.[33]

Wallace remained confident that democratic forces would ultimately prevail over the "inhuman concept" of Naziism. But the United States could hasten the defeat of Hitler by quickly expanding its industrial production beyond the expectation of foreign countries. If America rapidly increased its production, Wallace told Roosevelt, it could foil the dictators' plans to "destroy all resistance before adequate supplies can reach the allies." It would stiffen Britain's defiance of Germany, and discourage Japan and the Soviet Union from aligning themselves more closely with Hitler. By accelerating its production of munitions and other essential supplies, the Vice-President argued, the United States could end the war sooner and avoid belligerency. He denounced isolationists as "a loud minority who give aid and comfort to the enemies of civilization" and declared that the United States could hope to remain at peace only by strengthening its power and demonstrating its willingness "to go to war if necessary."[34]

Wallace disagreed with Roosevelt's advisors who wanted the President to ask Congress to declare war on Germany; he still hoped the United States could avoid belligerency. But throughout the spring and summer of 1941, he urged Roosevelt to take bolder action to stop Axis aggression. Wallace believed that the President overestimated the strength of the isolationists and was overcautious in his response to the world crisis. "I am confident the President has more backing in this country than he appreciates," he wrote. Wallace sent Roosevelt a poll taken by the *Des Moines Register* indicating that Iowa farmers were not imbued with a "Wheeler-Lindbergh mentality," and argued: "I believe the farm people of Iowa are ready for a more forceful and definite leadership than we have given them so far." In May 1941, the Vice-President suggested to Secretary Hull that he terminate all exports to Japan, including oil, because those materials would be used against the United States in event of war. Three months later, Wallace urged Roosevelt to "go to the absolute limit in your firmness in dealing with Japan." Asserting that an "appeasing stand" would produce unfortunate results in both the Far East and Europe, he argued that "if we take a strong stand, the entire Axis will be impressed and the psychology of the American people will be strengthened."[35]

The Japanese bombing of Pearl Harbor ended the great debate between isolationists and interventionists about American foreign policy. It resolved the dilemma of choosing between hatred of war and hatred of Axis aggression that had perplexed Wallace and other Americans for years. The Vice-President thought that the Japanese attack had "purchased for us a moral strength which has a value of perhaps a hundred or even a thousand times as great as the material losses we have sustained." Armed with that moral strength, he prepared to do his utmost to win both the war and the peace that followed.[36]

NOTES

1. Wallace to John C. Brodhead, January 15, 1938, Wallace to William E. Dodd, April 5, 1937, Secretary's Personal File, RG 16, NA; Statement prepared for *The Forum,* October 12, 1936, Henry A. Wallace Papers, University of Iowa; *New York Times,* August 19, 1934.

2. Wallace to Franklin D. Roosevelt, October 6, 1937, Box 58, President's Secretary's File, Wallace to Roosevelt, March 25, 1938, President's Personal File 41, Franklin D. Roosevelt Papers, Roosevelt Library; Wallace to Roosevelt, March 22, 1938, Wallace Papers.

3. Carl Snyder to Wallace, October 7, 1936, Wallace to Snyder, November 27, 1936, L. G. Michael to Wallace, February 9, 1937, Wallace to Michael, February 27, 1937, Secretary's Personal File, RG 16, NA.

4. Wallace interview with Edward Stuntz, March 2, 1941, interview with Manuel Seoane, November 18, 1942, Wallace Papers; *New York Times,* December 10, 1936.

5. Wallace to Grant Smith, January 14, 1937, Secretary's Personal File, Wallace to James R. Weir, June 22, June 29, 1938, Wallace to Melvin McGovern, August 9, 1938, Latin America File, RG 16, NA.

6. Wallace to Roosevelt, June 5, 1936, in Edgar B. Nixon, ed., *Franklin D. Roosevelt and Foreign Affairs* (Cambridge: Harvard University Press, 1969), Vol. III, p. 315; Henry A. Wallace, *Democracy Reborn,* Russell Lord, ed., (New York: Reynal and Hitchcock, 1944), pp. 148-49.

7. Wallace to Hugh S. Johnson, September 22, 1938, Wallace Papers; Wallace, *Democracy Reborn,* p. 153; *New York Times,* February 23, 1938.

8. Memorandum of phone conversation recorded by Henry M. Kannee, April 14, 1939, Box 58, President's Secretary's File, Roosevelt Papers; Wallace to Will Riley, April, 1939, Wallace Papers; James MacGregor Burns, *Roosevelt: The Lion and the Fox* (New York: Harcourt, Brace, and World, 1956), pp. 390-91.

9. Wallace to Harvey Ingram, September 5, 1939, Secretary's Office-Letters Sent, Wallace to Howard Hill, November 10, 1939, Secretary's Personal File, RG 16, NA; Wallace statement, September 1, 1939, Henry A. Wallace File, Department of Agriculture, Washington, D.C.; *Report of the Secretary of Agriculture: 1939* (Washington: Government Printing Office, 1939), p. 1.

10. *New York Times,* October 1, 1939; Henry A. Wallace, "Toward

An Inter-American Culture,'' *New York Times Magazine,* July 9, 1939, pp. 3, 20; Wallace to Bernard Baruch, September 29, 1939, Wallace to Edgar Smith, October 12, 1939, Secretary's Office-Letters Sent, RG 16, NA.

11. Wallace speech, ''Pan-America—The Road of Our Destiny,'' October 27, 1939, Wallace File, Department of Agriculture.

12. Ibid.

13. Wallace speech, ''Cooperation or Chaos,'' September 5, 1939, Wallace Papers; Wallace to Charles Edison, September 26, 1939, Secretary's Office-Letters Sent, Wallace to Frank Boykin, November 13, 1939, Foreign Trade File, RG 16, NA.

14. U.S. Congress, House, Committee on Ways and Means, *Hearings on Extension of Reciprocal Trade Agreements Act,* 76th Cong., 3rd Sess., 1940, pp. 120-21, 144-48; U.S. Congress, Senate, Committee on Finance, *Hearings on Extension of Reciprocal Trade Agreements Act,* 76th Cong., 3rd Sess., 1940, pp. 47-52.

15. Henry A. Wallace, ''Veblen's 'Imperial Germany and the Industrial Revolution,''' *Political Science Quarterly,* 55 (September 1940): 435-45.

16. Ibid.

17. Wallace to Roosevelt, March 30, 1940, April 1, 1940, Box 58, President's Secretary's File, Roosevelt Papers; Wallace to H. C. Taylor, April 16, 1940, Secretary's Office-Letters Sent, RG 16, NA.

18. Wallace to Ferner Nuhn, March 12, 1940, Secretary's Office-Letters Sent, RG 16, NA; Wallace to Mrs. John Cowles, May 26, 1940, Wallace Papers.

19. Wallace to Roosevelt, April 25, 1940, Volume 257, Transcript of phone conversation between Wallace and Henry Morgenthau, Jr., May 29, 1940, Volume 267, Henry Morgenthau Diaries, Roosevelt Library; Wallace to Jesse Jones, May 24, 1940, Secretary's Office-Letters Sent, RG 16, NA.

20. Wallace to Roosevelt, June 26, 1940, Box 58, President's Secretary's File, Roosevelt Papers; Sumner Welles, Henry Morgenthau, Jr., Harry Hopkins, and Wallace to Roosevelt, June 20, 1940, Cordell Hull Papers, Library of Congress; Wallace speech, ''Toward New World Solidarity,'' June 30, 1940, Wallace Papers.

21. Henry A. Wallace, ''Judaism and Americanism,'' article reprinted in *Congressional Record,* 76th Cong., 3rd Sess., 1940, Vol. 86, Part 17, pp. 4840-42.

22. Wallace to Harry Hopkins, June 10, 1940, Wallace to Maury Maverick, June 14, 1940, Wallace to Addison Parker, June 17, 1940, Wallace to Will Riley, June 17, 1940, Wallace to R. M. Yerkes, August 21, 1940, Secretary's Office-Letters Sent, RG 16, NA; Roswell Garst to Wallace, May 14, 1940, Wallace to Garst, May 18, 1940, Wallace Papers.

23. *New York Times,* October 26, 27, 1939; Wallace to B. C. Sullivan, May 17, 1940, Secretary's Office-Letters Sent, RG 16, NA.

24. Frances Perkins, *The Roosevelt I Knew* (New York: Harper and Brothers, 1946), p. 130; Eleanor Roosevelt, *This I Remember* (New York: Harper and Brothers, 1949), p. 216; Samuel Rosenman, *Working with Roosevelt* (New York: Harper and Brothers, 1952), p. 206; Charles J. Errico, "Foreign Affairs and the Presidential Election of 1940," (Unpublished Ph.D. Dissertation, University of Maryland, 1973), pp. 161-70.

25. *New York Times,* August 30, 1940.

26. Ibid., August 31, 1940; Roosevelt to Wallace, August 29, 1940, President's Personal File 41, Roosevelt Papers; *Congressional Record,* 76th Cong., 3rd Sess., 1940, Vol. 86, Part 17, pp. 5609, 5671.

27. *New York Times,* September 7, 10, 1940; *Washington Post,* September 7, 10, 1940; *Washington Star,* September 6, 1940; Wallace speech, "Appeasement," October 25, 1940, Wallace Papers.

28. Henry A. Wallace, *The American Choice* (New York: Reynal and Hitchcock, 1940); Wallace, "Pan American Defense," *International Conciliation* (Documents, 1941), pp. 89-94; "Appeasement," Wallace Papers; *New York Times,* September 4, 1940; *Baltimore Sun,* September 4, 1940.

29. Wallace to Grover Hill, August 15, 1940, Secretary's Office-Letters Sent, RG 16, NA; Wallace to Roosevelt, October 15, 1940, Wallace Papers; Hugh S. Johnson, "Heir Apparent," *Saturday Evening Post,* 213 (November 2, 1940): 18-19; Errico, "Election of 1940," pp. 363-64; *New York Times,* November 2, 1940.

30. *New York Times,* November 13, 1940; Bryce Wood, *The Making of the Good Neighbor Policy* (New York: Columbia University Press, 1961), p. 155; T. R. Fehrenbach, *Fire and Blood: A History of Mexico* (New York: Macmillan Co., 1973), pp. 602-05.

31. *New York Times,* November 27, December 2, 5, 1940; "New President, Old Job," *Time,* 36 (December 9, 1940): 28-30; "Next Vice President of U.S. Goes to Mexico," *Life,* 9 (December 16, 1940): 17-23.

32. Wallace to Nelson Rockefeller, December 26, 1940, Wallace to Sumner Welles, December 26, 1940, Wallace to Manuel Avila Camacho, January 10, 1941, Wallace Papers; Roosevelt to Wallace, January 10, 1941, Official File 4104, Roosevelt Papers.

33. Wallace, *Democracy Reborn,* pp. 176-79; Wallace speeches, "Democracy's Road Ahead in the World Crisis," February 22, 1941, "Democracy and the Dignity of Man," March 30, 1941, *Congressional Record,* 77th Cong., 1st Sess., 1941, Vol. 87, Parts 10, 11, pp. A810-11, A1565-66; Wallace to Francis P. Miller, May 7, 1941, Henry A. Wallace Papers, Library of Congress. There are large collections of Wallace Papers at the Library of

Congress and the Franklin D. Roosevelt Library as well as at the University of Iowa for the vice-presidential years, 1941-1945.

34. Wallace to Roosevelt, April 11, 1941, Wallace Papers, Roosevelt Library; Wallace to W. W. Waymack, April 11, 1941, Wallace Papers, Iowa; Wallace to James Crutchfield, June 13, 1941, Wallace Papers, Library of Congress; *New York Times,* April 13, 1941; *Des Moines Register,* August 1, 1941; Wallace speech, "Democracy's Road Ahead in the World Crisis."

35. Wallace to Marguerite LeHand, April 24, 1941, Wallace to Hull, May 10, 1941, Wallace to Roosevelt, May 26, 1941, August 29, 1941, W. W. Waymack to Wallace, May 17, 1941, Wallace Papers, Roosevelt Library.

36. Wallace to Maurice Sheehy, December 16, 1941, Wallace Papers, Library of Congress.

7

The Century of the Common Man

After the United States entered World War II, Henry Wallace's first priority was to contribute all he could to a quick and complete victory over the Axis. But he firmly believed that winning the war was only the initial step in building a peaceful and stable world. The Vice-President was driven by his deep conviction that the United States must begin to plan for the postwar era and lay the foundations for a just and lasting peace. "There are a number of things which can be done to prevent disaster after World War No. 2," he wrote in December 1941, "but the effort required will perhaps be even greater than that of the war itself." Wallace won wide attention, stirred controversy, and thrilled millions of Americans with his vision of a "century of the common man" that he hoped would produce permanent peace and global prosperity after the war.[1]

Wallace had begun to think about the postwar soon after hostilities broke out in Europe. Since he was convinced that American policies during the 1920s had played a major role in causing the world depression and the war, he focused his attention on the economic bases of the peace. In a letter to Roosevelt in April 1940, Wallace outlined his ideas for postwar economic programs that would contribute to stability and improve "conditions of life among the common people of the world." The measures he suggested included: (1) continuation of the reciprocal trade program to ensure a freer flow of goods and services between nations, (2) international commodity agreements and a world ever-normal granary to stabilize prices and encourage increased consumption, and (3) extension of credit by the United States to rebuild wartorn countries and promote world trade, accomplished in a way to allow borrowing nations to repay their debts.[2]

Postwar adjustments after World War II would be even more difficult than after World War I, Wallace believed, and he did not want the United States to repeat its earlier mistakes. "I would hate to see us again commit the various errors that we committed during the twenties and early thirties," he wrote. "We have greater wisdom now and would be more to blame if we should fall into some of the same traps." In a major address delivered before the Foreign Policy Association on April 8, 1941, the Vice-President asked Americans to accept their international obligations and adopt responsible foreign economic policies. He rebuked the apostles of isolation, protection, and normalcy, declaring that the United States must strive to counteract the disruptions and chaos the war inevitably would create.[3]

In an article written shortly before Pearl Harbor, Wallace asserted that "the overthrow of Hitler is only half the battle" and urged Americans to "think hard and often about the future peace." Arguing that determining national boundaries and setting up a new league of nations would not be enough to guarantee a durable peace, he called for careful economic planning on a world basis. He also advocated a concerted effort to promote industrialization and improved living standards throughout the world. Proper postwar preparation could help build a world "where security, stability, efficiency, and widely distributed abundance would prevail." If the United States shirked its world responsibilities, however, the consequences would be catastrophic.[4]

After the United States entered the war, Wallace became more fervid in his pleas that America take the lead to construct a peaceful and prosperous postwar world. He outlined his vision of a century of the common man in his most famous address of the wartime period, delivered before the Free World Association on May 8, 1942. Calling for complete victory over the enemies of democracy and forces of Satan, he declared that the United States was fighting for its belief in freedom and individual dignity. For 150 years, he exclaimed, the world had witnessed "a long-drawn-out people's revolution," characterized by an irrepressible march toward freedom for the common man that the "Nazi counterrevolution" could not stop. The United States and Western Europe had led the people's revolution by providing universal education, industrial progress, and self-government. Russia and China were taking strides in the same direction. But the revolution continued unabated; it would not be fulfilled until the dignity of the individual had been affirmed and the Four Freedoms implemented all over the world.[5]

Wallace contended that the most basic of the Four Freedoms was freedom from want. If that were achieved, he thought, the developing nations of the world would be more likely to create democratic institutions that would carry out the other freedoms. He urged Americans to help build a century of the common man by working to improve living standards, encourage education, and promote industrialization in underdeveloped countries. Pointing out that modern technology provided abundance so that people in all parts of the world could have enough to eat, Wallace suggested that one main objective of the war was to make certain "that everybody in the world has the privilege of drinking a quart of milk a day." He ended the speech with a religious affirmation: "The people's revolution is on the march, and the devil and all his angels cannot prevail against it. They cannot prevail, for on the side of the people is the Lord."[6]

A month after his May 8 address, Wallace gave a radio speech entitled "Why Did God Make America?" He concluded that God made America to lead the way toward a peaceful world based on justice, freedom, and abundance. "America will not have made her contribution," he stated, "until nine out of ten of the adults of the world can read and write, until all of the children of the world can have at least a pint of milk a day, until education brings with it such a sense of responsibility that all the people of the world can be trusted to take part in democratic government."[7]

Wallace's vision of the postwar world and his ideal of a century of the common man had evolved from his thoughts and experiences during two decades of depression and war. They reflected his belief in the economic interdependence and spiritual unity of the world. He insisted that the United States must strive to improve living standards in other parts of the world because it could not prosper if other countries remained impoverished. America must assert leadership by acting as a mature creditor state and promoting world trade and international economic cooperation. The Vice-President expressed confidence that the American people had learned from the recent past that another retreat to isolation would inevitably result in depression, upheaval, and a third world war. Wallace's fervent internationalism also derived from his long-standing conviction that a true millennium could be achieved if men everywhere would recognize their essential oneness, renounce selfish exploitation and greed, and join together in a spirit of cooperation. The message of the Sermon on the Mount could be implemented and the fruits of abundance widely distributed if industrialized nations would collaborate and apply modern technology to eradicate poverty, misery, and ignorance throughout the world.[8]

Wallace's ideas for the postwar were further shaped by his Pan-Americanism, anti-European biases, and Anglophobia. His interest in Latin America had alerted him to the needs and problems of developing nations. After his 1940 Mexican trip, he had stressed the importance of promoting industrialization to raise living standards in Latin America, and he had broadened his perspective to include other underdeveloped areas of the world. Since he still regarded Europe as a center of imperialism, colonialism, and war, he thought it was America's sacred mission to assume leadership in building a peaceful and prosperous world that was "not based on imperialistic intervention." God had made America, he believed, to utilize its resources and democratic traditions to break the patterns of European diplomacy and usher in an era of freedom and abundance. Wallace opposed British ambitions to maintain their empire and hoped that India would obtain its independence after the war. When Prime Minister Winston Churchill visited the United States in May 1943, Wallace was disturbed by his broad hints that an Anglo-American partnership should run the postwar world. At a White House luncheon honoring the Prime Minister, he challenged Churchill's claims of Anglo-American superiority, declaring that those views were repugnant to other countries and to many Americans.[9]

Wallace believed that his plan for the postwar world appealed to both altruistic and selfish impulses. In addition to its moral obligation to the millions of hungry and illiterate people in Asia and Latin America, he reasoned, the United States should strive to improve the lives of those people to advance its own interests. He argued that American economic and technical assistance to industrialize and increase prosperity in underdeveloped nations would provide important new markets for U.S. exports. Such a program would be more likely to prevent world depression and reduce the chances of war than would "high-tariff, penny-pinching, isolationist policies." The Vice-President feared that unless the United States took action to promote stability, prosperity, and hopefully democracy among "so-called backward peoples," those regions would remain chaotic and susceptible to the allurements of fascism and communism. He was particularly concerned about fascism securing a foothold in Argentina and spreading throughout Latin America, and about communism gaining strength in China and other parts of Asia.[10]

One important step toward achieving a century of the common man, Wallace maintained, was the establishment of a viable world organization. It would provide the mechanism for collective action against future aggression and for international economic cooperation to combat depression and modernize underdeveloped nations. He did not envision the international league as a supranational body, but contended that the United States and other nations must yield enough of their sovereignty to make the world organization effective. In a national radio speech delivered in December 1942, he advocated an arrangement in which regional councils would deal with problems arising in their particular areas, while the world organization would concern itself with issues "involving broad principles and those practical matters which affect countries of different regions or which affect the whole world." Wallace did not specify what powers he thought should be retained by individual nations, what powers should be assigned to regional councils, and what powers should be exercised by the entire world organization. Neither did he delineate the relative powers of large countries and small countries in the international body. But in 1944 he did express support for Sumner Welles' proposal for a United Nations Executive Council composed of the United States, Russia, China, and England and representatives of various regional organizations. Under Welles' plan, the Executive Council would deal with matters relating to the peace and welfare of the entire world.[11]

Although Wallace remained uncertain of exactly how the world organization should operate, he did suggest some specific functions it should perform. In order to maintain peace, it should have a military force equipped with air power capable of bombing aggressors "mercilessly" if necessary. In order to promote global prosperity, it should take action to curb international cartels that discouraged new industry, suppressed competition, and raised prices by creating artificial scarcity. The Vice-President called for an international commodity agency to insure equitable distribution of raw materials, stabilize prices, and expand world consumption. Since he anticipated a sharp reduction in government spending by all countries after the war, he favored the establishment of a United Nations investment corporation. It would utilize both public and private capital to forestall worldwide unemployment by undertaking postwar reconstruction projects as well as flood control, irrigation, soil reclamation, and rural electrification. Wallace thought the world organization could sponsor some form of an international TVA, and also suggested a combined highway and airway from Buenos Aires to Moscow. He was vitally concerned about assuring freedom of the air in the postwar world, and proposed that the United Nations construct and administer large international airports. He feared that the alternative would be a race for air supremacy that could lead to a third world war.[12]

In February 1943, Wallace wrote to Roosevelt, suggesting that a "United Nations Organization" be set up immediately to discuss ways to control international cartels that threatened "the true peace aims of the common peoples of the world." Even more importantly, it should consider plans to internationalize the world's airports. If the United Nations handled those tasks satisfactorily it could then be trusted to take on other projects. "In this way, international administration of international problems could grow and develop naturally," he stated.[13]

In addition to urging responsible American leadership and a strong United Nations, Wallace emerged as a leading spokesman for harmonious relations and closer ties between the United States and the Soviet Union. His call for Soviet-American friendship derived from a number of considerations. Like Roosevelt, he feared that Russia might sign a separate peace with Germany and withdraw from the war. Because he wanted to do whatever he could to keep that from happening, the Vice-President agreed to speak at a meeting of the Congress of American-Soviet Friendship in New York in November 1942. The address he delivered reflected his belief that the Soviets were making progress toward implementing "economic democracy" and ensuring a better life for their people. He declared that both the

United States and Russia were "striving for education, the productivity and the enduring happiness of the common man." Wallace's views on the Soviet system were excessively charitable. But he was not blind to some of the more unsavory aspects of Soviet society, and he held American Communists, many of whom had cheered his New York speech, in contempt. "A typical American communist is the contentious sort of individual that would probably be shot in Russia without any ceremony," he recorded in his diary. Nevertheless, he thought that the common goal of both America and Russia in trying to achieve "the democracy of the common man" provided a basis for mutual understanding. A conversation with Soviet Foreign Minister Vyacheslav Molotov persuaded him that the Russians were willing to cooperate with other nations to industrialize and raise living standards in underdeveloped areas throughout the world.[14]

Wallace's appeals for friendship between the United States and the Soviet Union stemmed above all from his conviction that it was an essential requisite for fulfilling his vision of the postwar world. He told publisher Roy Howard that "item No. 1 in world peace was a satisfactory understanding between Russia and the United States." The Vice-President maintained that the Soviets wanted peace and security after the war and were much more interested in developing their own country than in inciting world revolution. His views on Soviet intentions arose in part from his conversations with Molotov, Soviet Ambassador Maxim Litvinov, and others. But essentially they represented an expression of faith rooted in Wallace's belief that postwar tensions between America and Russia would destroy his hopes for a century of the common man. He thought that the United States must work to win the trust and confidence of the Soviets. He worried that some groups in England and America wanted to "gang up" against Russia, and that certain elements in the Army, the State Department, and the Catholic Church regarded the Soviet Union as a future enemy. The Vice-President told Henry Luce that the best way to achieve mutual understanding between America and Russia was to ensure prosperity and full employment at home to forestall any possibility of communist subversion, and to cooperate with the Soviet Union to develop Siberia and eastern Asia.[15]

On March 8, 1943, at a Conference on Christian Bases of World Order in Delaware, Ohio, Wallace publicly enunciated his hopes and fears about postwar relations between the United States and the Soviet Union. He compared Russia favorably to Nazi Germany, explaining that the Soviet Union had "never preached war as an instrument of national policy" and that many of its actions during the 1930s had been prompted by its fear of Hitler. The Vice-President pointed out that Russia did not expound theories of racial superiority, and contended that it was making some progress toward religious freedom. Western democracies had no reason to fear communism, he argued, as long as they provided jobs for their people and served the interests of the common man. But if the United States failed to sustain full employment after the war, or if it "double-crossed" Russia, or if "fascist interests motivated largely by anti-Russian bias," came to power, the seeds for another war would be sown. The Soviet Union, on the other hand, could cause a war by adopting "the Trotskyist idea of fomenting worldwide revolution." Wallace urged Americans to foster lasting peace by dealing "honestly and fairly with Russia" and by recognizing "that all men are brothers, and that God is their Father."[16]

Although Wallace focused his attention on the international aspects of postwar policy, he remained committed to the planned middle course. He supported a variety of domestic measures designed to prevent depression and raise living standards in the United States, including tax reform, extension of social security, rural electrification, and programs to improve health, education, and transportation systems. He thought it imperative that government, business, labor, and agriculture cooperate to provide jobs in a mixed economy. In January 1944, he stated privately that guaranteeing full employment in the United States was more important for promoting general prosperity than was reducing tariffs. He was uncertain that Congress would consent to lower trade barriers after the war, but he suggested that if the country attained full employment, it could import over tariff walls.[17]

Wallace's ideas about the postwar world elicited the admiration of many Americans, and he became the leading spokesman for liberals who shared his views. He was, said the *New Republic,* "the one outstanding American exponent of a good settlement and a permanent peace."[18] Only Wendell Willkie commanded as much attention as Wallace in outlining proposals for a lasting peace. The two former adversaries in the 1940 election campaign took remarkably similar positions. Both stressed the dynamic forces the war would set loose in underdeveloped nations, and the need to help those areas combat poverty and build democratic institutions. Both rebuked America's retreat to isolationism after World War I and called on America now to assert positive, constructive leadership. Wallace and Willkie opposed colonialism, detested power politics, and favored the establishment of an effective world organization. Each wanted freer international trade patterns and emphasized the economic interdependence of the world. Both believed that friendship and understanding between the United States and the Soviet Union was not only possible, but essential for maintaining peace after the war. Wallace differed from Willkie primarily in placing greater importance on the government's role in promoting global prosperity. He had less confidence than the former Wall Street lawyer in the ability of unrestrained private enterprise to provide economic justice throughout the world.[19]

The Vice-President's pronouncements about the postwar world provoked sharp criticism. Harry Beardsley of the *Chicago News* faulted him for raising false hopes that had no chance of being fulfilled and could only lead to disillusion. Referring to Wallace's assertion that modern technology made it possible for everyone to have enough milk, he commented that "many of the common peoples of the world . . . would resist any attempt to make them drink a quart of milk more violently than they would resist a quart of castor oil." The *Chicago Tribune* remarked that "the mystic Mr. Wallace . . . is now engaged in dreams which should invite more skepticism than admiration." Acid-tongued Congresswoman Clare Boothe Luce dismissed his proposals as "globaloney." W. P. Witherow, president of the National Association of Manufacturers, declared that he was "not fighting for a quart of milk for every Hottentot, or for a TVA on the Danube, or for governmental handouts of free Utopia."[20]

Wallace struck back at his critics, who, he complained, had purposely distorted his statements. He explained that his reference to providing a quart of milk for children was a figure of speech, and that he had no intention of forcing people who did not like milk to drink it. He denied that he had ever called for a TVA on the Danube, but reiterated his belief that the United States should provide technical assistance and self-liquidating loans to countries that wanted to build their own TVA's.[21]

Wallace told *New York Times* correspondent Arthur Krock that he did not want the United States to "play the role of Santa Claus to the rest of the world," but he thought that America should help other countries to industrialize so that they could begin to help themselves. Krock responded that Wallace's speeches seemed to describe as "this nation's accepted obligation, a postwar Utopia, paid for entirely by the United States and handed out to any that may ask for it." Wallace replied that since the United States possessed advanced technology, it should "provide leadership and guidance, and perhaps extend credit" to underdeveloped nations. He asserted that his program was "the only practical one in the world as we find it," because if the United States "let the rest of the world stew in its own misery," the inevitable result would be another war.[22]

Wallace faced difficulties in presenting his ideas for the postwar. If he sketched broad outlines without precise details, he was accused of being fuzzy-minded. If he formulated more specific proposals, however, his statements were often quoted out of context or dismissed as hopelessly impractical. Some parts of his program doubtlessly were unworkable, but he never regarded his specific schemes as inviolable and was willing to modify his thinking within his internationalist framework. At the least, he was performing an important service in trying to deal with problems that were likely to arise after the war, and educating the American people about the need to plan for those problems.

Wallace's proposals for the postwar world aroused anger and dismay in the State Department. Assistant Secretary Breckinridge Long called him one of the "Post War Dream Boys," and Secretary Hull agreed. On July 23, 1942, Hull delivered a nationwide radio address in which he advanced a more modest internationalist program than Wallace's. The speech was correctly viewed by many observers as a rebuttal to Wallace's and Sumner Welles' bolder statements. Hull worried that Wallace's pronouncements would alienate Congress and arouse opposition to his policies. The Vice-President reciprocated the State Department's animosity. He thought it was "probably the weakest department in our entire government," and regarded it as a bastion of stand-pat conservatism and anti-Soviet sentiment.[23]

Wallace hoped that President Roosevelt would be the agent for implementing his postwar plans. In some respects, Roosevelt's goals paralleled the Vice-President's. Both were anxious to make certain that the United States did not repeat its past errors by adopting isolationist policies after the war. Both wanted to combat economic nationalism and expand the volume of world trade. Each favored the establishment of a world organization to maintain peace. Although Roosevelt did not share Wallace's Anglophobia, he did share his anti-colonialism. President and Vice-President alike believed that achieving understanding with Russia was essential for ensuring lasting peace.[24]

In other respects, however, Roosevelt's thinking about the postwar diverged markedly from Wallace's. Whereas the Vice-President thought it imperative to begin preparations immediately, Roosevelt concentrated on the war effort and deferred detailed consideration of the problems of peace. "The slogan is 'Win the war before we give too much thought to post-war plans,'" he declared shortly after Pearl Harbor. In January 1943, a few days after the Vice-President delivered a radio address outlining his views on the world organization, Roosevelt remarked to aide Jonathan Daniels that "where Wallace went wrong was in discussing the mechanism of world peace at this time." Wallace was disappointed that the President refused to exert more leadership in formulating programs for the postwar. The two leaders also differed sharply on the role of the United Nations. Roosevelt opposed an international air force and preferred the concept of the "Four Policemen," in which the major powers would enforce the peace. In general, the President envisioned far more limited responsibilities for the United Nations than did Wallace. He also expressed doubts about Wallace's proposals for promoting world prosperity and his talk of "continuing revolution." Despite those differences of opinion, Wallace deeply admired the President, and thought that as long as Roosevelt occupied the White House, his own vision of the postwar could be fulfilled.[25]

Relations between Roosevelt and Wallace were cordial and mutually respectful, though never intimate. The President assigned Wallace important tasks to supplement his largely ceremonial vice-presidential duties, including the role of good will ambassador. In March and April of 1943, the Vice-President took an extended—and successful—trip through Latin America, where he enjoyed enthusiastic receptions. He was a popular figure in Latin America, and as he had done earlier in Mexico, won the affection of his hosts by his concern for their problems and his fluency in Spanish. Throughout the visit, Wallace preached the gospel of the common man. He told 40,000 Chileans that "stronger nations will have the privilege to help the younger ones to begin their industrialization, but without the slightest economic or military imperialism." The American ambassadors in the eight countries the Vice-President visited unanimously hailed the salutary effect of his trip and agreed that he had vigorously promoted the Good Neighbor policy.[26]

Wallace also discharged administrative duties in his capacity as chairman of the Board of Economic Warfare (BEW). In July 1941, Roosevelt had selected him to head the agency (then called the Economic Defense Board) to coordinate the activities of the numerous departments involved in economic defense, procure from abroad and stockpile strategic materials, and block Axis countries from obtaining essential war supplies. He also wanted the Board to investigate and advise him on matters relating to postwar economic planning. Wallace viewed his position not only as an instrument for defeating the Axis, but also for advancing his postwar ideas. He secured the appointment of Milo Perkins, an ardent New Dealer who had served under him in the Department of Agriculture, as executive director of the agency. Wallace and Perkins suggested to Roosevelt that the State Department be deprived of any significant role in postwar planning and that the Economic Defense Board be primarily responsible for formulating blueprints for the peace. The President refused. Shortly after Pearl Harbor, he changed the name of the agency to the Board of Economic Warfare and directed it to concentrate on the war effort and "defer or eliminate all postwar planning work."[27]

Despite Roosevelt's instruction, Wallace told him in February 1942 of his desire to utilize the BEW to prepare for the postwar. Contending that "we are writing the postwar world as we go along," he informed the President that BEW was thinking ahead to the peace and hoped to set up a functioning international ever-normal granary even before the war ended. The Vice-President also requested that BEW be granted financial authority to purchase strategic supplies. He argued that Jesse Jones, who served as Secretary of Commerce and administrator of the Reconstruction Finance Corporation and who had broad jurisdiction in buying vital commodities, had failed to acquire adequate supplies of essential goods because he quibbled about price rather than taking decisive action to procure essential war materials. Finally, he asked for greater independence from the State Department, which he thought deliberately impeded the BEW's foreign activities. Both Jones and Hull vigorously protested Wallace's effort to emasculate their power. Eventually, Roosevelt temporarily ended the bickering by denying the Vice-President's request for independent funds but directing Jones to accept and implement BEW's decisions on foreign purchasing. He placated Hull by refusing to allow the Board to deal directly with foreign governments.[28]

Roosevelt told Wallace in May 1942 that the BEW could proceed with some postwar planning as long as it did not "get caught by the State Department." Wallace and Perkins inaugurated a program that combined both altruistic and selfish motives. The BEW was vitally concerned with obtaining South American rubber that was desperately needed for the war effort. But labor conditions in the Amazon jungles were deplorable, making it difficult to attract workers to tap the rubber plants. So the BEW began to impose labor contracts on rubber producers; minimum standards of wages, hours, health, sanitation, and safety were required. Under the agreements, the United States underwrote the additional costs involved in improving living and working conditions of laborers. Wallace and Perkins defended the labor clauses as necessary to increase rubber production, but they also regarded the contracts as a modest step toward raising standards of living in underdeveloped nations. Once again, the BEW's policies aroused the opposition of the State and Commerce Departments, which contended that the labor clauses represented interference in the internal affairs of other countries. Jesse Jones and his top lieutenant, Assistant Secretary of Commerce William L. Clayton, objected to financing the costs of the contracts because they feared that Wallace and Perkins intended "to revolutionize social and working conditions" in Latin America.[29]

In the summer of 1943, Wallace's feud with Jones—which had smoldered for a year and a half—burst into headlines. Jones regarded Wallace as a financially irresponsible visionary who surrounded himself with "socialist-minded uplifters." Therefore, despite Roosevelt's instructions of April 1942, the Commerce Secretary moved slowly and cautiously in implementing the directives of the Board of Economic Warfare on foreign procurement. Jones' lassitude incensed Wallace. He viewed the Commerce Secretary as an overly

conservative, power-hungry banker whose failure to carry out promptly the BEW's mandates impeded the war effort. Moreover, Jones
embodied the kind of thinking that Wallace believed would lead to
disaster if it predominated after the war.[30]

Disturbed by comments Jones made about the BEW in a congressional hearing and unkind remarks about the agency by Senator
Kenneth McKellar, Wallace thrust his dispute with the Commerce
Secretary into a public forum on June 29, 1943. He issued a long,
contentious statement that was essentially accurate but decidedly
tactless. The Vice-President condemned Jones for failing to stockpile vital war materials before Pearl Harbor because of his "timid,
business-as-usual procedure." He outlined in detail the efforts of
the BEW to obtain essential supplies, and denounced Jones for his
"obstructionist tactics." The statement enraged the Commerce
Secretary and upset President Roosevelt, who had no advance warning
of Wallace's action. He ordered James F. Byrnes, director of the
Office of War Mobilization, to mediate between Wallace and Jones
and attempt to resolve their differences. A sullen Jones accused
Wallace of calling him a traitor, and Byrnes persuaded Wallace to
issue a statement making it clear that he did not question the Commerce Secretary's patriotism.[31]

Jones, however, was still not satisfied. On July 5, he released a
thirty-page letter to Senator Carter Glass, asserting that Wallace's
charges were "filled with malice, innuendo, half-truths, and no
truths at all." The Vice-President was out of town, but Milo Perkins
replied to Jones by labeling his statements as "false" or "purposely
misleading." Byrnes wrote to Jones and Wallace and demanded
they quit their public quarrelling. The public debate might have
ended at that point. But Milo Perkins reignited the controversy in a
talk to BEW employees that was intended to be off the record. Unaware that a reporter was present, Perkins delivered a scathing attack on Jones, and the next day the feud again made headlines.
Roosevelt's patience ran out. On July 15, he wrote sharply worded
letters to Wallace and Jones, abolishing the Board of Economic
Warfare and stripping the Commerce Secretary of some of his financial authority. Declaring that there was no time to investigate
the various charges of the adversaries, the President thought the
best course of action was to make "a fresh start with new men, un-
encumbered by interagency dissension and bitterness." He replaced

the BEW with the Office of Economic Warfare, and granted it most of the powers Wallace had struggled to obtain. Leo Crowley, a conservative friend of Jesse Jones, headed the new agency.[32]

The President's action clearly was a setback to Wallace. It deprived him of policy-making responsibilities and eliminated the agency he had hoped would help lay the foundations for the peace. Stunned by the reprimand, he noted after seeing Roosevelt on July 20 that the President seemed to be employing "his usual technique of being very nice to a person he has just gotten through hitting." But he retained his deep personal faith in Roosevelt, and blamed his defeat more on the White House "palace guard." Wallace believed that the abolition of the BEW represented a betrayal of liberalism and a victory for the opponents of his vision of the postwar world. The country, he feared, was moving in the direction of American fascism.[33]

NOTES

1. Henry A. Wallace to Lewis Morris, December 30, 1941, Henry A. Wallace Papers, University of Iowa.

2. Wallace to Roosevelt, April 25, 1940, Volume 257, Henry Morgenthau, Jr., Diaries, Roosevelt Library.

3. Henry A. Wallace, *Democracy Reborn,* Russell Lord, ed., (New York: Reynal and Hitchcock, 1944), pp. 176-79; Wallace to Robert M. Clark, January 14, 1941, Wallace to John Cowles, January 18, 1941, Wallace Papers, Library of Congress.

4. Wallace, "Foundations of the Peace," *Atlantic Monthly,* 169 (January 1942): 34-41.

5. Wallace, *Democracy Reborn,* pp. 190-96.

6. Ibid.

7. Wallace speech, "Why Did God Make America?" June 8, 1942, Wallace Papers, Iowa.

8. Entries for May 26, June 1, December 18, 1942 in John Morton Blum, ed., *The Price of Vision: The Diary of Henry A. Wallace, 1942-1946* (Boston: Houghton Mifflin Co., 1973), pp. 82, 84, 149 (hereafter cited as *Diary,* with date and page number); Wallace interview with Austin Wehrwein, December 10, 1942, Raymond Clapper Papers, Library of Congress; Wallace, *Democracy Reborn,* p. 193.

9. Wallace interview with Edward Stuntz, March 2, 1941, Wallace speech, "Why Did God Make America?" Wallace Papers, Iowa; *Washing-*

ton Post, February 23, 1941; Wallace, "Day of the New World," *New York Times Magazine,* October 11, 1942, pp. 3, 27; *Diary,* September 1, October 12, 21, 1942, May 22, 25, 1943, pp. 113, 119, 123-24, 202, 208, 212-13.

10. *Diary,* August 26, 1942, January 7, 18, March 24, 29, June 29, 1944, pp. 110-11, 290, 294, 318, 320, 357; Wallace, *Democracy Reborn,* p. 205; Wallace interview with Frank S. Mead for article published in *Christian Herald,* January 1943, Wallace Papers, Iowa.

11. Wallace, *Democracy Reborn,* pp. 200-204; *Diary,* June 4, 1943, January 25, 1944, pp. 203-205, 295; *Washington Post,* January 26, 1944.

12. Wallace, "What We Will Get Out of the War," *American Magazine,* 135 (March 1943): 22-23; Wallace to Isaiah Bowman, November 3, 1942, Wallace Papers, Iowa; Wallace interview with Raymond Clapper, December 31, 1942, Clapper Papers; *Diary,* August 13, 1942, February 26, 1943, pp. 106, 197.

13. Wallace to Roosevelt, February 5, 1943, Wallace Papers, Roosevelt Library.

14. Wallace, *Democracy Reborn,* pp. 196-200; *Diary,* June 3, October 14, November 7, 1942, pp. 85-86, 121-22, 131.

15. *Diary,* November 20, December 11, 29, 1942, January 28, 31, February 1, 1943, pp. 136, 143-44, 157, 174-77.

16. *New York Times,* March 9, 1943.

17. Wallace, *Democracy Reborn,* pp. 17-40; Wallace, "What We Will Get Out of the War"; *Diary,* January 7, 1944, p. 291.

18. Norman D. Markowitz, *The Rise and Fall of the People's Century: Henry A. Wallace and American Liberalism, 1941-1948* (New York: Free Press, 1973), p. 45; Alonzo L. Hamby, *Beyond the New Deal: Harry S. Truman and American Liberalism* (New York: Columbia University Press, 1973), p. 22; "Who Shall Make the Peace?" *New Republic,* 107 (December 14, 1942): 780.

19. On Willkie's views, see his *One World* (New York: Simon and Schuster, 1943).

20. *New York Times,* December 3, 1942, February 10, 1943; *Chicago Tribune,* June 11, 1942; *Chicago News,* June 5, 1942.

21. Wallace interview with Austin Wehrwein, Clapper Papers; Wallace, *Democracy Reborn,* p. 258.

22. Wallace to Arthur Krock, n.d., Krock to Wallace, December 8, 1942, Cordell Hull Papers, Library of Congress; Wallace to Krock, December 19, 1942, Wallace Papers, Iowa.

23. Fred L. Israel, ed., *The War Diary of Breckinridge Long* (Lincoln: University of Nebraska Press, 1966), pp. 271, 291, 294; Robert A. Divine, *Second Chance: The Triumph of Internationalism in America During World War II* (New York: Atheneum, 1967), pp. 67-68, 80; *Diary,* May 10, December 11, 1942, pp. 77, 143-44.

24. On Roosevelt's postwar views, see John Lewis Gaddis, *The United States and the Origins of the Cold War, 1941-1947* (New York: Columbia University Press, 1972), Chap. 1; and Robert A. Divine, *Roosevelt and World War II* (Baltimore: Penguin Books, 1969), Chaps. 3, 4.

25. Roosevelt to Attorney General, December 12, 1941, Official File 4226, Franklin D. Roosevelt Papers, Roosevelt Library; Jonathan Daniels, *White House Witness, 1942-1945* (Garden City, N.Y.: Doubleday and Co., 1975), p. 112; *Diary,* March 4, 1943, p. 199; Divine, *Second Chance,* p. 115.

26. *Foreign Relations: 1943,* Vol. V, pp. 62-75; *New York Times,* March 21, 1943, March 31, 1943.

27. Lillian Buller, "Chronological History of the Economic Defense Board," (Unpublished manuscript, 1943), Unit 184, Notes of Bernard L. Gladieux, November 19, 1941, Unit 181, Series 41.3, RG 51 (Records of the Bureau of the Budget), NA; Roosevelt to Attorney General, December 12, 1941, Official File 4226, Roosevelt Papers.

28. Wallace to Roosevelt, February 24, March 18, 20, 26, 1942, Wallace Papers, Roosevelt Library; Lillian Buller, "Administrative History of the Board of Economic Warfare," (Unpublished manuscript, 1944), Unit 183, Gladieux notes, April 9, May 20, 21, 1942, Unit 181, Series 41.3, RG 51, NA; *Department of State Bulletin,* 6 (May 23, 1942): 475-76.

29. *Diary,* May 28, December 28, 31, 1942, pp. 83, 156, 158-59; U.S. Congress, Senate, Committee on Banking and Currency, *Hearings on a Bill to Increase the Borrowing Authority of the Reconstruction Finance Corporation,* 77th Cong., 2nd Sess., 1942, pp. 62-92; Buller, "Board of Economic Warfare."

30. Jesse H. Jones with Edward Angly, *Fifty Billion Dollars: My Thirteen Years with RFC, 1932-1945* (New York: Macmillan Co., 1951), p. 491; *Diary,* December 28, 1942, October 17, December 18, 1943, pp. 155, 264, 287.

31. Wallace to Roosevelt, June 10, 1943, Wallace Papers, Roosevelt Library; *Diary,* June 30, 1943, pp. 219-22; *New York Times,* June 30, July 1, 1943.

32. *Diary,* July 6, 14, 1943, pp. 223-27; James F. Byrnes to Jesse Jones, July 6, 1943, Jesse Jones Papers, Library of Congress; Roosevelt to Wallace, July 15, 1943, Wallace Papers, Roosevelt Library; *New York Times,* July 6, 1943; *New York Herald Tribune,* July 18, 1943; Russell Lord, *The Wallaces of Iowa* (Boston: Houghton Mifflin Co., 1947), p. 512.

33. *Diary,* July 14, 20, 1943, pp. 226n, 227.

8

The Fight Against Fascism at Home and Abroad

Henry Wallace believed the war presented at the same time great opportunities and grave dangers. On the one hand, he thought it accorded the country a chance to rectify the errors of the 1920s and 1930s, to assume its proper role of world leadership and to usher in an era of universal peace and prosperity. If America adopted responsible, generous, and farsighted policies, the century of the common man would triumph and a brave new world would emerge from the ashes of war. But Wallace's millennial hopes were juxtaposed with apocalyptic fears of what would happen if the United States failed to act wisely after the war. His anxieties about the nature of the postwar world were no less passionate than his hopes. If the country retreated to isolationism, pursued narrow, shortsighted policies, and repeated its earlier mistakes, the aftermath of war would produce greater maladjustments, greater misery, and greater depression than had the first World War. The ultimate result would be a third world war. Those disasters were likely to occur, he reasoned, if "small but powerful groups" pursuing selfish goals guided U.S. policies. Those interests, Wallace believed, would lead the country toward fascism. Many liberals shared his fear of incipient American fascism, but the prominence of his position assured that his attacks on "midget Hitlers" would gain wide attention.[1]

During the early years of the war, Wallace was optimistic that his vision of the postwar world would be implemented. "I . . . have faith," he wrote in 1942, "that the American people have learned some lessons from the peace that was made after World War No. 1 and that they will be willing to do a better job this time." On June 6, 1943, speaking to the graduating class of the Connecticut College for Women, Wallace delivered a poignant eulogy to Milo Perkins' son George, a Marine flier who recently had died when his plane crashed. He related conversations in which the younger Perkins had expressed doubt that the older generation could erect a system that guaranteed permanent peace. The death of George Perkins and millions like him, the Vice-President intoned, bequeathed a sacred obligation to build a postwar world that assured peace and justice by realizing the ideals of the Sermon on the Mount. "May it so be that my George, your George, and all those who have sacrificed their lives will so inspire us to effective action that they will not have died in vain. . . . The world has never had such an opportunity. We must make the dead live. We must make them live in the world's commencement of abiding peace based on justice and charity."[2]

Accompanying Wallace's vision was the apprehension that it would remain unfulfilled. He worried that if "fascist interests motivated largely by anti-Russian bias" gained control of the American government, they would incite a war with the Soviet Union. He feared that reactionaries who opposed his vision of the peacetime world would undermine the ideals for which the war was being fought. "If this sacrifice of blood and strength again brings a concentration of riches in the hands of a few—great fortunes for the privileged and misery and poverty for the people in general—then democracy will have failed and all this sacrifice will have been in vain," he declared.[3]

Although Wallace was a gentle, compassionate man, he also felt intense hatred for those whom he believed pursued selfish ends at the expense of the general welfare. He had always harbored a particularly deep-seated antipathy for big business. Stemming from his agrarian background, it had surfaced during the 1920s in his condemnation of eastern manufacturers and financiers, and during the 1930s in his denunciations of conservative opponents of the New Deal. As early as 1935, Wallace had voiced concern that powerful industrialists might institute a form of American fascism, and that concern had extended into the war years. Moreover, Wallace had frequently displayed a strain of self-righteousness. It had emerged,

for example, in his ferocious attacks on the Republican party during
the 1940 election campaign. The urgency of the wartime crisis and
the vital importance he attached to proper postwar planning made
that tendency more pronounced. The Vice-President's conviction
that his cause was just and right had reinforced his impatience and
frustration with Jesse Jones' obduracy, and had prodded his ill-
advised decision to issue a public statement castigating the Commerce Secretary.[4]

Wallace's defeat in the dispute with Jones had clouded his optimism and intensified his anxieties about the nature of the postwar
world. His heightened fears that America would betray the legacy
of George Perkins and others who had died in the fight against
fascism, combined with his long-standing animosity toward big
business and his bristling self-righteousness, prompted him to initiate
a series of blistering attacks against those whom he labeled as American fascists.

In July 1943, a few days after Roosevelt abolished the Board of
Economic Warfare, Wallace journeyed to Detroit to speak before
a mass labor meeting. Shortly before the speech, he held a press
conference at which he repeatedly denounced American fascists
without specifying who they were. "Certain American Fascists
claim I'm an idealist," the Vice-President said. "I ask them to look
to themselves and ask if they have done as much to put their ideals
into practice." He continued his assault when he addressed the
labor meeting on July 25. He began with a warm tribute to Roosevelt, designed to silence speculation that he had lost faith in the
President. Then he launched into an attack on "isolationists, . . .
reactionaries, . . . and American fascists." Wallace still did not
specifically identify his targets, but he decried "small but powerful
groups which put money and power first and people last." He made
vague allusions to "power-crazed, money-mad imperialists," selfish
corporate interests, and international cartelists. Rebuking "those
twisters of fact who shriek that your Vice-President is a wild-eyed
dreamer trying to set up T.V.A.'s on the Danube and deliver a bottle of milk to every Hottentot," Wallace asserted that "no business
prospers without prosperous customers." He reiterated his standard
plea that the United States assume world leadership and strive to
bring about the century of the common man.[5]

The speech attracted wide attention and generated many favorable comments. The *New Republic* called it the "finest utterance" of Wallace's career, and "the finest expression by any American public official in many years." Other observers, however, were more critical. The *Baltimore Sun* regretted that the Vice-President had "worked up a complete assortment of epithets to discredit those who disagree with him." *Christian Century* noted the sharpened edge in Wallace's rhetoric, and asserted that by assuming the "posture of a barnstormer and rabble-rouser," he had reduced the effectiveness of his appeal.[6]

Wallace sought to clarify his charges a short time after the Detroit speech. His remarks had been misinterpreted, he said; his indictments did not apply to 99 percent of American corporations. He affirmed his belief that the corporate form of organization was an integral part of the democratic system in the United States. Wallace explained that "the difficulty with corporations comes when certain of the larger ones try to control the agencies of public opinion, including even the schools, and then go on to dominate elections, control State legislatures, the national Congress, and even the President himself."[7]

Wallace told Rexford Tugwell in November 1943 that "the forces of Anglo-Saxon Fascism are gathering themselves for a mighty effort in the period immediately following the war." The final defeat of fascism, he believed, entailed much more than crushing Germany. It could be obliterated only by ending poverty, misery, and disease all over the world, and improving the living standards of the common man. During a West Coast speaking tour in February 1944, Wallace emphasized the need for cooperation between labor, agriculture, and business to promote the general welfare and produce unprecedented prosperity in the United States and the world. He berated the "selfish, narrow-visioned branch of big business" that placed "Wall Street first and the nation second." He maintained that "to work together without slipping into an American fascism will be the central problem of postwar democracy." In Seattle, the Vice-President attacked "Wall Street and Wall Street stooges" who wanted to perpetuate scarcity economics, and who opposed the democratic planning that was necessary to accomplish a wide distribution of abundant riches. He warned that American fascists were "willing to go to any length . . . to keep Wall Street sitting on top of the country," and were "desperately striving to gain control of both political parties."[8]

The *New York Times* deplored Wallace's "vague, reckless" indictments and asked him to write an article to clarify his charges and identify his targets. The Vice-President responded that a fascist was "one whose lust for money or power is combined with such intolerance toward those of other races, parties, classes, religions, cultures, regions or nations as to make him ruthless in his use of deceit or violence to attain his ends." There were "several million" American fascists if the term were defined broadly to include those who placed "money and power ahead of human beings." In a more narrow sense, there were "probably several hundred thousand . . . who in their search for money and power are ruthless and deceitful." Wallace contended that American fascists deliberately distorted truth to delude the public and secure money and power. They employed propaganda techniques to malign democracy, promote isolationism, preach bigotry, and undermine constitutional liberties. They sought to obtain political power in order to "keep the common man in eternal subjection." After the war, they would undoubtedly "push steadily for Anglo-Saxon imperialism and eventually for war with Russia."[9]

Wallace warned that the real danger did not come from obvious kinds of fascists who received attention from the news media, but from the insidious types who wanted "to do in the United States in an American way what Hitler did in Germany in a Prussian way." He was gratified that fascist inclinations did not dominate any section or class in the country, but was troubled that evidence of the "infectious disease" could be perceived on "Wall Street, Main Street, or Tobacco Road." Wallace believed that fascism could overtake the United States either directly through domestic subversion or indirectly by first gaining a foothold in Latin America. His dread of the ultimate triumph of fascism in the United States remained ill-defined and imprecisely articulated, but it played a prominent role in his thinking in the closing years of the war. Although the Vice-President continued to hope that a century of the common man would emerge from the war, he also was gravely concerned that it would be undermined by the forces of American fascism.[10]

After a cabinet meeting on March 4, 1944, Wallace asked Roosevelt if he could make a trip to Russia. The President was dubious because he thought Wallace would be attacked during the upcoming election campaign "for being too far to the left," and that a journey to Moscow would therefore be inadvisable. He suggested that the Vice-President go to China instead, stopping along the way to visit towns in Siberia. When the forthcoming trip was announced publicly in April, it stirred speculation in the press that Roosevelt was sending Wallace abroad so that he would miss the Democratic convention and could be eased out of the vice-presidential nomination. The President, however, told Wallace to arrange his trip so that he would return in time for the convention, and the Vice-President informed friends that he definitely would be there.[11]

The official purpose for Wallace's trip to China was to reassure Generalissimo Chiang Kai-shek that as soon as conditions in Europe permitted, the United States would send full-scale assistance to China. Roosevelt, who confided that he was "apprehensive for the first time as to China holding together for the duration of the war," wanted Wallace to discuss several urgent matters with Chiang and thought his mission "could perform a very important function." In addition to his official role as the President's emissary, Wallace hoped that his visit would help build closer U.S.-Asian ties. He had a deep personal interest in the future of Siberia and East Asia and believed that those areas, along with Latin America, comprised a vast new frontier with enormous potential for growth. He thought the United States should play a key role in assisting their development and hoped the trip would promote that idea.[12]

"The peoples of the East are on the march," Wallace declared in a pamphlet written shortly before he left for Asia. The war had unleashed dynamic forces of change and aroused expectations so that the people of Asia would never be content to continue living in misery, poverty, and ignorance. "The genie has been let out of the bottle," he observed, and the United States must act wisely by promoting industrialization and improving agricultural efficiency to assure that the genie would be benevolent rather than "something utterly evil." Wallace urged Americans to extend private and public loans and technical assistance to the emerging countries of Asia. Not only would such policies fulfill America's moral responsibilities to less advanced peoples, they would also create jobs and help sustain prosperity at home. As always, Wallace pointed out that eventually the United States must be willing to accept goods and services from the countries in which it invested. He called for "orderly emancipation in colonial areas" of the Far East, insisting that it was not

America's duty "to underwrite other people's declarations of continuing empire." He recommended a system of trusteeships to prepare colonial states for self-government, but stipulated that a "definite date" should be determined for granting those countries independence. Convinced that any attempt to play power politics in Asia would result in war, he believed that the political stability of that region should be guaranteed by international cooperation through the world organization.[13]

Wallace departed on his journey on May 20, 1944. Accompanying him were China experts John Carter Vincent of the State Department and Owen Lattimore of the Office of War Information, and Soviet expert John Hazard of the Foreign Economic Administration. The entourage flew first to Siberia, where they spent over three weeks and visited numerous cities and towns. The Vice-President was greatly impressed with the modern development, cultural achievements, and throbbing vitality he encountered in Soviet Asia. He admired advances in agriculture, noting that despite an inhospitable climate, the Siberians raised a wide variety of crops, produce, and livestock. He commented enthusiastically on the burgeoning industry in Soviet Asia, and was deeply impressed by plays, operas, and concerts in the Siberian hinterlands. He had begun to take lessons in the Russian language in 1942, and speaking in Russian to the citizens of Novosibirsk, stated: "During the past fifteen years, all has been changed as if by magic. In a resurgence of pioneering the Siberian people founded great mills and factories, opened new roads, rail, and airways, sunk new mines into mineral rich earth. . . . The climate of Siberia has not changed, it is true. But the spirit of its people has changed."[14]

The spirit and the progress of the people of Siberia suggested parallels with the American frontier experience to Wallace. "The history of Siberia and her heroic population reminds one of the history of the Far West of the United States," he told the citizens of Irkutsk. The Vice-President believed the Russians would develop political democracy out of their frontier in the same way Americans had done. "Men born in wide, free spaces will not brook injustice and tyranny," he declared. Wallace was convinced that Americans and Russians could understand one another because their frontier experiences had been similar. Conversations with Soviet officials who talked of building new towns in the wilderness reminded Wallace of the spirit of pioneer America, further persuading him that two such kindred spirits could continue to cooperate in the postwar world. "The trans-Ural peoples of Soviet Asia are on the move in a way that is easy for Americans to understand," he asserted.[15]

The Soviet people and government officials accorded Wallace and his party a friendly reception wherever they went. The audiences who heard him speak in Irkutsk, Novosibirsk, and Tashkent greeted him warmly and enthusiastically. In towns the Americans visited, crowds often gathered around them in the streets and applauded. In Ulan-Ude, local officials presented Wallace with "a beautiful Buryat costume of a type given only to a high representative of a powerful, friendly nation." He interpreted those gestures as proof that the Soviets desired to continue cordial relations with the United States after the war. He was convinced that direct contacts between the people of America and the Soviet Union would dispel their mutual suspicions and promote understanding. Wallace later told Andrei Gromyko that his trip "was a journey I shall never forget—and one which I feel gave me a much greater understanding of your problems than I had been able to gain from secondhand reports."[16]

Not until many years later did Wallace become aware of how artfully the Soviets had staged his tour of Siberia. He remarked favorably on the industrial progress of the city of Magadan, not realizing that it was the site of one of the most notorious slave labor camps in Siberia. Just before the Americans arrived in Magadan, the Soviets dismantled incriminating wooden guard towers. To make certain that no prisoners were seen, the Russians relieved them of their work duties and kept them occupied by showing movies for three consecutive days. Citizens of the town were astonished to discover that an abundance of Russian-made consumer goods suddenly appeared in shop windows. A huge meat-packing plant near Semipalatinsk normally took stringent security precautions to assure that workers did not steal food. It utilized guards and dogs and thoroughly frisked laborers as they left the plant. About a week before Wallace arrived, however, the guards and dogs disappeared, and the frisking of workers ceased. Meat suddenly became available in the town's market place, and beggars were removed from public view. Wallace's visit to Siberia reinforced his belief that the Soviet Union was progressing toward economic democracy, that the American and Soviet systems were gradually growing closer together, and that the Russian people were anxious to continue friendly relations with the United States after the war.[17]

After his lengthy tour of Soviet Asia, Wallace moved on to China for a much briefer stay. Conditions in that troubled land were chaotic. The Japanese had recently launched an offensive in eastern China, routing Chiang's inferior armies and threatening the existence of the Kuomintang regime. Inflation ran rampant, inefficiency and corruption pervaded the government, and signs of domestic discontent became increasingly obvious. Distrust, suspicion, and mutual hostility between Chiang's government and the Chinese Communists precluded a unified effort against the Japanese. A border incident in which Soviet planes had fired on Kuomintang troops had heightened tensions between Russia and China and underscored Chiang's conviction that the Soviets were conspiring with the Chinese Communists to overthrow his government.[18]

Roosevelt was troubled by China's state of affairs. He had asked Wallace to determine ways to control inflation there and reduce tensions between China and the Soviet Union. He also wanted him to relay an offer to mediate differences between Chiang and the Chinese Communists, and tell the Generalissimo that it might be wise if "he would call in a friend." Wallace's views on the Communists had been influenced by a conversation he had with Martel Hall, former manager of the Peking branch of the National City Bank of New York, shortly before leaving on his trip. Hall had been prejudiced against the Communists until he had lived with them for eight months after the Japanese attack on Pearl Harbor. He had grown to admire and respect them, and described them as "agrarian reformers" rather than Communists. In Siberia, Wallace had talked at length with Averell Harriman, American Ambassador to the Soviet Union, about Chinese-Russian relations. Harriman related a recent discussion with Premier Joseph Stalin in which the Soviet leader had complained of the Kuomintang's feeble war effort, but affirmed his support for Chiang and derided the Chinese Communists as "margarine communists." A short time later, the Vice-President had flown to China to meet with Chiang Kai-shek.[19]

Wallace arrived in Chungking on June 20, 1944. After chatting briefly with Chiang, he observed that the Generalissimo had "an almost feminine charm." The following afternoon, the two men began their formal discussions, which extended over a period of three days. Wallace communicated Roosevelt's offer to arbitrate between the Kuomintang and the Chinese Communists, but Chiang asked that the President mediate between his government and the Soviet Union. Wallace firmly refused that suggestion, stating that the United States would be willing to bring China and Russia together, but would not act as a guarantor of an agreement between the two countries. When he remarked that the Chinese army had made a "poor showing" against the Japanese, Chiang bewailed America's failure to fulfill its promises of military aid for China. "The Chinese people felt they had been deserted," he said. The Generalissimo also complained bitterly about General Joseph Stilwell, commander of the American forces in the Far Eastern theater and Chiang's Chief of Staff. He told Wallace that he "lacked confidence" in Stilwell, and that criticism in the American press, and the attitude of the American military toward his army, "had adverse effects on Chinese morale."[20]

When Wallace again broached the subject of Chiang's relations with the Communists, the Generalissimo launched into a tirade. He stated that Americans did not understand the problem, that the Communists "refused to obey his orders," and that they took their instructions from the Communist International. Wallace reminded him that the Third International had been dissolved, but Chiang replied that the situation had not changed. The Vice-President mentioned Martel Hall's views, but Chiang responded that Hall, like many Americans, "was under the influence of Communist propaganda." He also contended "that the Communists desired a breakdown of Chinese resistance against the Japanese because this would strengthen their own position." Wallace "expressed amazement" at that assertion. Although Chiang reacted negatively to Wallace's suggestion that American military observers be allowed to visit Communist controlled areas of China to gather intelligence, he eventually relented. That was the only concrete agreement that came out of the discussions. Wallace repeatedly admonished Chiang that he must avoid conflict with the Soviet Union, and the Generalissimo agreed. But they did not devise a formula for settling Russian-Chinese differences. The Vice-President also pointed out that the Bolsheviks had triumphed in Russia because of economic chaos, and warned "that when the war was over it would take much energy and foresight for the Chinese government to avoid the fate of the

Kerensky Government in Russia." Privately, Wallace noted that he was saddened by his talks with Chiang, who was "headed straight toward being a Kerensky. I like him but I do not give him one chance in five to save himself."[21]

Wallace left Chungking on June 24, and made brief stops in other parts of China. At Chengtu, he declared that with a concerted effort and American aid, China could improve its agricultural efficiency, expand industry, and rapidly raise its standard of living. But Wallace's hopes for a prosperous China were marred by the conditions he observed. In Kunming, he visited an artillery school where Americans trained Chinese soldiers. Wallace remarked in his diary that Chiang and his advisors did not like Americans to operate military schools because the men who went there would "prove very superior to the Chinese trained." He contended that the Generalissimo feared that those men eventually would challenge his leadership and the status quo in China. Wallace admired the Chinese soldiers he saw in Kunming. "But the damned smiling grafters above? They stand for mediocrity forever continued."[22]

Wallace's reports to President Roosevelt reflected his pessimism about the plight of China. "I have found economic, political, and military situations in China extremely discouraging," he wrote. A "general collapse" did not appear "imminent," but conditions were "unstable and tense with rising lack of confidence in the G-mo [Generalissimo] and his reactionary entourage." Chiang seemed "bewildered" by the economic instability of China and incapable of repulsing the Japanese; his attitude toward the Communists, the Vice-President stated, "is so imbued with prejudice that I perceive little prospect of a satisfactory long-term settlement." But Wallace did not believe the situation was entirely hopeless. Chiang was so worried about his predicament that if "wisely approached," he might be amenable to making far-reaching, constructive changes. Wallace suggested that General Stilwell be replaced by an American who could win the Generalissimo's confidence and persuade him to make effective political and military reforms.[23]

Wallace argued that American policy toward China "should not be limited to support of Chiang." He recommended alignment with liberal, non-Communist elements of Chinese society (such as progressive bankers and businessmen), western-educated individuals who were not committed to the status quo, and a "considerable group of generals and other officers who are neither subservient to the landlords nor afraid of the peasantry." Although for the moment Wallace saw no viable alternative to Chiang, he believed that the Generalissimo was, at best, "a short-term investment." He lacked either "the intelligence or political strength" to govern post-war China, and therefore, the United States should be flexible enough to shift its support if a more promising leader appeared. "The leaders of post-war China will be brought forward by evolution or revolution," the Vice-President warned, "and now it seems more like the latter."[24]

After completing his Asian journey, Wallace returned home to tend to his political fortunes. His standing in the Democratic party remained precarious and his chances for renomination as Roosevelt's running mate were highly uncertain. Never adept at nor much interested in political infighting and intrigue, he had done nothing during his vice-presidency to enhance his position in the party or to cultivate the backing of the Democratic regulars who had protested his selection in 1940. Southern conservatives, city bosses, and party professionals such as Edwin Pauley and George E. Allen of the Democratic National Committee and Postmaster Frank Walker were particularly adamant in their opposition to Wallace. They sought to persuade Roosevelt that if Wallace ran as his vice-presidential candidate in 1944, he would cost the ticket millions of votes and jeopardize the President's bid for a fourth term.[25]

Roosevelt regretted that Wallace had not made his peace with party leaders, and he was disturbed by their reports that the Vice-President would be a major liability in the election. He had not lost faith in Wallace and personally preferred him for the nomination. On June 27, 1944, he told a group of aides: "Of course, everybody knows I am for Henry Wallace." But the President added that although he had believed that the opposition to Wallace came largely from the politicians, he was beginning to think that it also existed at the grass roots level. As the Democratic convention approached, Roosevelt remained undecided about the vice-presidency. He was certain, however, that he would not force Wallace's name on the party as he had done in 1940.[26]

Wallace met with Roosevelt on July 10, 1944, immediately after his return to Washington from Asia. The President assured him that he was his personal choice for vice-president, and accepted

Wallace's suggestion that he issue a statement saying: "If I were a delegate to the convention I would vote for Henry Wallace." When the President declared that he would not dictate Wallace's nomination, the Vice-President replied that he did not want "to be pushed down anybody's throat." He only wished to make certain, he said, that Roosevelt wanted him for his running mate and would agree to say so publicly. Roosevelt then reiterated his support for Wallace.[27]

The next evening, however, a group of party leaders met with Roosevelt, urging him to abandon Wallace. Their arguments were convincing enough that after the session ended, Roosevelt scrawled a letter indicating that he would be happy to have either Senator Harry S. Truman or Supreme Court Justice William O. Douglas as a running mate. When Roosevelt again conferred with Wallace on July 13, he told him about the meeting, but denied that he had agreed to submit an alternative name to the convention. As the Vice-President prepared to leave, Roosevelt drew him close and said: "While I cannot put it just that way in public, I hope it will be the same old team." But the President's endorsement of Truman or Douglas and his lukewarm support for Wallace crippled Wallace's candidacy. After a tumultuous floor battle at the convention, Truman secured the nomination on the second ballot.

Wallace was stunned and shocked by Roosevelt's duplicity, concluding that "he wanted to ditch me as noiselessly as possible." For the first time, he privately expressed reservations about the President's liberalism, but decided that he would campaign for Roosevelt because he feared the consequences of a Republican victory. Wallace still believed, as he had stated a few months before, that a fourth term for Roosevelt was necessary because he was "our best insurance against American fascism" and "against an Anglo-American imperialism which would get [us] into war with Russia."[28]

Harry Truman called on Wallace shortly after the convention. He was apologetic and obsequious, assuring Wallace that he had neither sought nor wanted the vice-presidential nomination. Wallace was cordial but rather patronizing, and noted after their discussion that Truman impressed him as "a small man of limited background who wants to do the right thing." Remembering that Truman had once endorsed his bid for renomination, while at other times expressing support for Speaker of the House Sam Rayburn and James Byrnes for vice-president, Wallace added: "This kind of action convinces me beyond doubt that he is a small opportunistic man, a man of good instincts, but, therefore, probably all the more dangerous. As he moves more in the public eye, he will get caught in webs of his own making.''[29]

Wallace did not see Roosevelt until August 29, over a month after the convention. By that time, he had already begun to campaign for the Democratic ticket. Roosevelt expressed appreciation for those efforts, and remarked that although Wallace's ideas were a few years ahead of their time, they would inevitably prevail. He sought to soothe the Vice-President's disappointment with the convention results by saying that if the Democrats won in November, Wallace could have any government post he wanted except the State Department. Roosevelt explained that ''Cordell Hull was such an old dear and he could not bear to break his heart.'' When the President mentioned that he planned to remove Jesse Jones from the cabinet, Wallace asked that he be appointed Secretary of Commerce. ''There would be poetic justice in that,'' he remarked. Roosevelt neither granted nor denied the request, but told Wallace that he would like him to attend some of the upcoming international conferences that would discuss plans for the postwar world.[30]

Wallace was not a vindictive person, and he had more compelling reasons for wanting the Commerce slot than simply to wreak vengeance on Jesse Jones. Herbert Hoover had exercised enormous influence on foreign and domestic policies as Secretary of Commerce, and Wallace hoped to use that same position to make certain the United States did not repeat the errors of the 1920s. He believed that expansion of American exports after the war was necessary to underwrite domestic prosperity, but he was anxious to make certain that the United States eventually be prepared to import more goods than it exported. He also wanted to avoid indiscriminate exporting that might cause unemployment in other countries. Moreover, Wallace envisioned the Commerce post as an opportunity to aid small business and exercise some control over monopolies and cartels. It would also enable him to promote programs to guarantee full employment and higher living standards in the United States.[31]

After Roosevelt's victory in the election of 1944, he considered appointing Wallace as U. S. ambassador to China, or as Secretary of State to replace Hull, who had recently resigned in poor health. But he decided against offering him either of those positions because he thought Wallace would not find the ambassadorship particularly attractive and feared that naming him Secretary of State "would have killed" Hull. So he submitted Wallace's nomination for Secretary of Commerce. Although the former Vice-President had presided over the Senate for four years, his confirmation by that body was problematical. A hostile Commerce Committee subjected him to grueling interrogation, questioning his ability to handle vast sums of money. The Senate finally approved Wallace's nomination on March 1, 1945, but only after removing important lending agencies from his jurisdiction. Ironically, Wallace might have been defeated without the timely assistance of Vice-President Harry Truman.[32]

NOTES

1. Henry A. Wallace, *Democracy Reborn,* Russell Lord, ed., (New York: Reynal and Hitchcock, 1944), pp. 179-89, 231-45; Alonzo L. Hamby, *Beyond the New Deal: Harry S. Truman and American Liberalism* (New York: Columbia University Press, 1973), pp. 5-7.

2. Wallace to Esther Skow, June 30, 1942, Henry A. Wallace Papers, Library of Congress; Wallace, *Democracy Reborn,* pp. 231-38.

3. *New York Times,* April 20, 1943; Wallace, *Democracy Reborn,* p. 225.

4. Henry A. Wallace, "In Search of New Frontiers," *Vital Speeches,* 1 (July 29, 1935): 706; Wallace to William Allen White, November 22, 1938, William Allen White Papers, Library of Congress.

5. Wallace to Roosevelt, July 21, 1943, Wallace Papers, Roosevelt Library; *New York Times,* July 25, 1943; Wallace, *Democracy Reborn,* pp. 238-45.

6. *Baltimore Sun,* July 27, 1943; "Wallace Speaks Out," *New Republic,* 109 (August 2, 1943): 127; "Steady, Mr. Wallace," *Christian Century,* 60 (August 11, 1943): 912.

7. *New York Times,* August 20, 1943.

8. Wallace to Rexford Tugwell, November 4, 1943, Wallace Papers, Roosevelt Library; *Diary,* November 13, 1943, p. 268; *New York Times,* November 18, 1943; Wallace, *Democracy Reborn,* pp. 17-40.

9. *New York Times,* February 11, 1944; Henry A. Wallace, "Wallace Defines 'American Fascism,'" *New York Times Magazine,* April 9, 1944, pp. 7, 34-35.

10. Wallace, "Wallace Defines 'American Fascism,'" pp. 7, 34-35; Wallace to Josephus Daniels, January 28, 1944, Wallace to Nelson Rockefeller, February 1, 1944, Wallace Papers, Iowa.

11. *Diary,* March 3, 6, 1944, pp. 308, 310; *Foreign Relations: 1944,* Vol. VI, p. 216; Wallace to Jake More, April 25, 1944, Wallace Papers, Iowa; *Washington Star,* April 12, 1944; *New York Herald Tribune,* April 13, 1944; *Indianapolis News,* April 13, 1944.

12. *Diary,* March 6, 1944, p. 310; *Foreign Relations: 1944,* Vol. VI, p. 230; *New York Times,* April 12, 1944.

13. Henry A. Wallace, *Our Job in the Pacific* (New York: Institute of Pacific Relations, 1944).

14. Henry A. Wallace with the collaboration of Andrew J. Steiger, *Soviet Asia Mission* (New York: Reynal and Hitchcock, 1946), pp. 130-35, 140, 222-23; Wallace to Jo Davidson, December 10, 1942, Wallace Papers, Iowa.

15. Wallace, *Soviet Asia Mission,* pp. 108, 136-38.

16. Ibid., pp. 56, 241-42; *Foreign Relations: 1944,* Vol. IV, pp. 968, 970; Wallace to Andrei Gromyko, July 2, 1946, Box 1055, File 104251, RG 40 (General Records of the Commerce Department), NA; *Chicago News,* June 21, 1944.

17. Wallace, *Soviet Asia Mission,* pp. 40, 88-89; Henry A. Wallace, "Where I Was Wrong," *This Week Magazine,* September 7, 1952, p. 30; U.S. Congress, Senate, Judiciary Committee Subcommittee on Internal Security, *Hearings on Institute of Pacific Relations,* 82nd Cong., 1st Sess., 1951, p. 1323; Interview with Michael Gleiberman, a former resident of Semipalatinsk, March 13, 1973.

18. Herbert Feis, *The China Tangle: The American Effort in China from Pearl Harbor to the Marshall Mission* (Princeton: Princeton University Press, 1953) pp. 136-40; Barbara W. Tuchman, *Stilwell and the American Experience in China, 1911-45* (New York: Macmillan Co., 1970), pp. 455-64.

19. Feis, *China Tangle,* pp. 140-41, 144; *Diary,* May 9, 18, 1944, pp. 329-30, 332n, 333.

20. *Diary,* June 20, 1944, p. 349; "Notes on the Vice President's Conversation with President Chiang," June 21-24, 1944, Box 130, President's Secretary's File, Franklin D. Roosevelt Papers, Roosevelt Library. A slightly abridged text of the conversations between Wallace and Chiang appears in *United States Relations With China* (Washington: Government Printing Office, 1949), pp. 549-60.

21. "Notes on Conversation with Chiang," Roosevelt Papers; *Diary,* June 22, 24, 1944, pp. 351-52.

22. *Diary,* June 26, 1944, p. 355; Wallace speech at Chengtu, June 29, 1944, Wallace Papers, Iowa.

23. *Foreign Relations: 1944,* Vol. VI, pp. 234-47.

24. Wallace to Roosevelt, July 10, 1944, Box 130, President's Secretary's File, Roosevelt Papers.

25. Norman D. Markowitz, *The Rise and Fall of the People's Century: Henry A. Wallace and American Liberalism, 1941-1948* (New York: Free

Press, 1973), pp. 91-97; James MacGregor Burns, *Roosevelt: The Soldier of Freedom* (New York: Harcourt, Brace, Jovanovich, 1970), p. 503.

26. Jonathan Daniels, *White House Witness, 1942-1945* (Garden City, N.Y.: Doubleday and Co., 1975), pp. 231-32; Eleanor Roosevelt, *This I Remember* (New York: Harper and Brothers, 1949), p. 220.

27. *Diary,* "Summary of Political Maneuvering," pp. 361-62.

28. Ibid., July 31, August 8, 1944, pp. 366-67, 370-71, 375; Markowitz, *People's Century,* pp. 102-14; Louis Bean interview, Columbia Oral History Collection; Wallace Diary (typescript), March 2, 1944, Book 27, Wallace Papers, Iowa.

29. *Diary,* January 22, August 3, 1944, pp. 295, 373-74.

30. Ibid., August 29, 1944, pp. 381-82.

31. Ibid., December 20, 1944, pp. 406-10; *New York Times,* January 26, 1945; Wallace, *Democracy Reborn,* pp. 273-74.

32. Markowitz, *People's Century,* pp. 130-35; U.S. Congress, Senate, Committee on Commerce, *Hearings on Administration of Certain Lending Agencies of the Federal Government,* 79th Cong., 1st Sess., 1945, pp. 71-134; Thomas M. Campbell and George C. Herring, ed., *The Diaries of Edward R. Stettinius, Jr., 1943-1946* (New York: New Viewpoints, 1975), pp. 170, 184.

9

One World or None

At his first press conference as Secretary of Commerce, Henry Wallace emphasized a familiar theme: the United States must avoid the mistakes of the 1920s and establish trade on a sound basis. "This idea of pushing out a large volume of exports without effective methods of payment is like using one hand to pull a fellow toward you and using the other hand to push him away," he declared. In the spring of 1945, Wallace vigorously supported extension of the Reciprocal Trade Agreements Act. The trade agreements promoted peace, he told the House Ways and Means Committee, "by eliminating or minimizing friction in international economic relationships." If the United States failed to provide world leadership by adopting liberal trade policies, other countries would resort to discriminatory practices and gravitate toward economic self-sufficiency. Not only would those methods create tensions between countries and threaten peace, Wallace asserted, but they would undermine free enterprise by necessitating greater government supervision of America's foreign trade. He also pointed out that extension of the reciprocal trade acts would ease reconversion to a peacetime economy by creating jobs through the expansion of exports. The United States stood at "the fork in the road," and the Commerce Secretary strongly urged that it take the path of international cooperation rather than that of "tariff walls, discrimination, economic isolation, government trading, economic warfare, and international misunderstanding."[1]

The European conflict ended in May 1945, but the continent remained afflicted by the unprecedented wreckage and desolation that the war produced. Pointing out that the United States was the only major country to escape the devastation of war, Wallace advocated both government programs and private investment to help finance the reconstruction of Europe. He also urged public and private loans to encourage industrialization and improve living standards in underdeveloped areas of the world. As he had done during World War II, the Commerce Secretary contended that economic assistance to wartorn and backward countries served both altruistic and selfish ends. In addition to "following our higher impulses and aspirations," he asserted, "we shall find that by helping others we have also helped ourselves." Foreign aid and investment would expand exports, promote domestic prosperity, help prevent depression, and most importantly, contribute to lasting peace. But Wallace warned that in order to sustain a healthy foreign trade, the United States must be willing to accept goods from abroad to provide other countries with the means to repay loans and buy American exports. "To escape a repetition of the disasters of the twenties and thirties, we must build up the national policies and business arrangements that will make foreign trade a permanent two-way street—not a temporary detour to a precipice," he wrote.[2]

Although Wallace favored expanding America's foreign trade and encouraged businessmen to invest abroad, he denounced "selfish and ruinous exploitation so common to the days of dollar diplomacy." American capital should be used to modernize and industrialize backward countries, he argued, rather than to plunder the natural resources of those areas and keep them "in a colonial stage of development." Wallace thought the United States should employ its vast economic power to improve the lives of the underprivileged throughout the world, not to "exercise sovereignty over dependent peoples" or embark on a course of "economic imperialism." He was appalled by collusion between the State Department and International Telephone and Telegraph (ITT) in a transaction that was detrimental to Mexican consumers. ITT requested a loan from the Export-Import Bank to expand its operations in Mexico. With the cooperation of the State Department, the company secured the approval of the Mexican government to raise telephone rates in order to repay the money it borrowed. In effect, the State Department had helped arrange a deal whereby Mexican consumers would be assessed to enable an American corporation to repay a loan to the American government. "This kind of thing has been done again and again by the State Department working with private corporations," Wallace complained. His adamant opposition helped frustrate the plan and prevent its consummation.[3]

Although he believed that expanding foreign trade would contribute to domestic well-being, Wallace placed even greater emphasis on ensuring prosperity by developing the American economy. He urged cooperation between government, business, labor, and agriculture and a unified effort to guarantee full employment and a better distribution of income at home. "Higher standards of living in foreign countries would mean new markets; but so would higher standards of living, say, in Mississippi or North Dakota—or in the slums of New York and Chicago," he remarked. As always, Wallace called on Americans to forsake special interests and work for the general welfare. He proposed an ambitious program to improve the quality of life in the United States, including federal aid in housing, health, education, transportation, soil conservation, and rural electrification. The Commerce Secretary was convinced that if the United States implemented his programs at home and acted responsibly abroad, it could lead the world toward enduring peace and widespread prosperity.[4]

Wallace continued to envision an important and ever-increasing role for the United Nations organization in the postwar world. He believed that the international body should play a key role in ensuring peace, reducing trade barriers, providing higher standards of living, and controlling international cartels. But he realized that in order to be effective, the United Nations required the support and cooperation of the world's two most powerful countries. The Commerce Secretary was profoundly disturbed by the disputes between the United States and the Soviet Union that arose at the conference to draft the charter of the United Nations, convened in San Francisco in April 1945. Rather than laying the foundations for international peace and understanding, the San Francisco conference produced heated debates between American and Russian delegates, particularly over allowing Poland and Argentina to join the United Nations. The United States blocked admission of the Soviet-dominated Polish government but combined with Latin

American countries to vote Argentina into the UN, although that country had done nothing to help defeat the Axis. Wallace felt "very much depressed" by those events and feared they presaged "an era of power politics rather than world organization."[5]

The possibility of a U.S.-Soviet confrontation deeply troubled Wallace. Many Americans expressed outrage at Russian activities in Eastern Europe and denounced the Soviets for violating the Yalta agreement. Alarmed by anti-Russian sentiments he heard expressed at Washington social gatherings, the Commerce Secretary noted: "More and more it begins to look like the psychology is favorable toward our getting into war with Russia." He attacked "the rankest kind of un-Americans" who advocated war between the United States and the Soviet Union, and decried "irresponsible defeatist talk" about conflict between the two countries.[6]

Wallace did not specify what groups he thought were agitating for war with Russia. But he was highly critical of the State Department's attitude toward the Soviet Union, and commented that many of its personnel had "a great deal spirituaiiy in common with Nazis and fascists." The Commerce Secretary kept abreast of developments in Eastern Europe by reading State Department dispatches, including some sent by George F. Kennan of the American embassy in Moscow. He did not dispute Kennan's argument that Russians were distrustful and suspicious of American intentions, but he disagreed with the assertion that hopes for cooperation between the two countries were chimerical. The way to guarantee peace, Wallace believed, was to dispel Soviet fears and earn their confidence.[7]

Convinced that world peace and prosperity depended on harmonious relations between America and Russia, Wallace stated that "strengthening the ties of friendship" between the two countries "should be the foundation of our foreign policy." He had been stunned by the death of Franklin Roosevelt in April 1945, and thought that the increasing tensions between the United States and the Soviet Union betrayed the legacy of the late President. On June 4, he delivered an address eulogizing Roosevelt and assailing the "enemies of peace . . . who are deliberately trying to stir up trouble between the United States and Russia." Referring to the dispute over admission of Argentina to the United Nations, Wallace declared that although Roosevelt had promoted the Good Neighbor policy in Latin America, "he never looked on Pan-Americanism as a regional instrument of power politics." The Commerce Secretary urged Americans to fulfill the vision of the late President by winning the trust and friendship of Russia, and by cooperating with the Soviet Union to achieve lasting peace through the United Nations. Wallace lauded Roosevelt for acting "as though he really believed in the fatherhood of God and the brotherhood of man," and also hailed President Truman for carrying out his predecessor's policies "to the letter."[8]

Wallace still remained skeptical of President Truman's ability. But both he and the President endeavored to maintain a friendly working relationship. After seeing Truman shortly after Roosevelt's death, the Commerce Secretary noted that the President had been "exceedingly cordial" and "eager to agree with everything I said." Wallace told correspondents that Truman was "starting out in a fine way" as chief executive. But Wallace's letters and diary still reflected an air of condescension toward Truman. "The new President is exceedingly anxious to do the right thing and we all are going to do the best we can to help him," he wrote to an old friend.[9]

Wallace admired Truman's decisiveness, but worried that the President tended to make hasty judgments based on incomplete information. Above all, he was concerned about Truman's position toward Russia. Wallace believed that the President was predisposed against the Soviet Union because of a statement Truman had made shortly after Germany invaded Russia in June of 1941. At that time, Truman had remarked that the United States should help whichever side was losing so that the maximum number of Germans and Russians would be killed. "Neither of them think anything of their pledged word," the *New York Times* had quoted Truman as saying. Conversations with the President in the spring of 1945 deepened the Commerce Secretary's suspicion that Truman inclined toward "acting tough" with Russia. But he hoped that Truman was not irrevocably committed to that viewpoint and could be persuaded to adopt a conciliatory attitude toward the Soviets. Wallace's public assertion that the President intended to follow Roosevelt's policy toward Russia reflected that hope. Wallace was encouraged that Truman felt "much more kindly toward the Russians" after Harry Hopkins talked with Stalin in Moscow in May 1945.[10]

Wallace did not believe that there were any irreconcilable differences between the United States and the Soviet Union. He argued that the two countries shared many similar goals and attributes.

Both used modern technology to improve the lives of their common people, and both wanted to assist underdeveloped countries to raise their standards of living. Neither country possessed colonies nor desired to obtain them. Both America and Russia affirmed in principle the rights of smaller countries, but both "occasionally stepped over the line when . . . national defense is involved." Wallace admitted that the Soviet system lacked many of the liberties that Americans cherished, but he contended that the Russian government was gradually granting its people more freedom. "The Russians today have more of the political freedoms than they ever had," he wrote. "Undoubtedly, they still have a long way to go but they are moving in the right direction." The Commerce Secretary also was satisfied that the Soviet Union was demonstrating "increasing signs of religious toleration."[11]

Wallace took an overly indulgent view of the Soviet system of government, but his opinions on Soviet-American relations stemmed much more from his belief in the absolute need for understanding between the two powers than from his perceptions of domestic policies in Russia. He denied any fundamental ideological conflict between the United States and Russia. Each was attempting to serve the interests of the common man, and each should respect the other's determination to preserve its form of government. He believed that provocations of both countries had contributed to existing tensions, but he cautioned Americans against taking an aggressively anti-Russian position that would reinforce Soviet insecurity and mistrust. Wallace was convinced that the Russians were eager to maintain peace and were willing to do their share to build friendly relations with the United States. His trip to Soviet Asia had helped persuade him that the Soviets admired the American people and wanted to cooperate with them. He urged Americans to recognize "the basic lack of conflict between the United States and the the USSR" and to meet the Russians half-way to achieve mutual understanding. The peace of the world, he argued, depended on harmony and good will between the two powers.[12]

The atomic bomb explosion in August 1945 heightened the urgency of Wallace's plea for trust and understanding between the United States and the Soviet Union. As Vice-President, he had been among the first to know about the American effort to build an atomic bomb. Vannevar Bush, who played a key role in the Man-

hattan Project, had informed Wallace of progress in atomic research in July 1941. Bush realized that Wallace was one of few
administration officials who could comprehend the scientific com-
plexities of the undertaking. Throughout the war, Bush had reported intermittently to Wallace on the status of the Manhattan
Project. Wallace had not figured significantly in atomic policy
decisions during the war, however, and had no connection with
plans to develop and use the bomb after he left the vice-presidency
in January 1945. But he was keenly aware of both the potential
dangers and the potential blessings of atomic energy.[13]

The onset of the atomic age presented two fundamental and related
problems for American policy makers. One involved the issue of
domestic control of atomic energy, and the other concerned the
role of the bomb in American foreign policy. The international
implications of the awesome new weapon and the question of sharing
atomic information were the subject of discussion at a famous
cabinet meeting on September 21, 1945. Secretary of War Henry L.
Stimson, attending his last cabinet session, began by outlining his
views on the bomb and its meaning for American-Russian relations.
He reiterated the same argument he had presented a week earlier in
a long memorandum to President Truman. Stimson pointed out
that atomic scientists agreed that the United States could not maintain its atomic monopoly indefinitely, and that the Soviet Union
would be able to develop a bomb within a few years. He urged Truman not to use America's temporary advantage to intimidate Russia,
but to approach them directly and attempt to work out an agreement to control use of the bomb. If the United States flaunted its
atomic arsenal and failed to invite the Soviets into a "partnership
upon a basis of co-operation and trust," it would reinforce Soviet
suspicions of the United States and lead to an arms race "of a rather
desperate character." The Secretary of War recommended that
the United States take the initiative to win the confidence of the
Soviet Union and that it permit free exchange of basic scientific
information about atomic energy that could not be kept secret.[14]

Stimson's proposals evoked a mixed response from the cabinet.
Secretary of the Navy James V. Forrestal and Secretary of Agricul-
ture Clinton P. Anderson led the opposition, declaring that the
United States should not divulge the "secret" of the atomic bomb.
Dean Acheson of the State Department, Abe Fortas of Interior,

and Secretary of Labor Lewis B. Schwellenbach expressed agreement with Stimson's ideas. Henry Wallace also stood behind the
Secretary of War. He carefully distinguished between basic scientific
information about atomic energy, and details about the design and
manufacturing processes involved in building the bomb. Wallace
explained that basic knowledge about atomic energy already was
widely disseminated among scientists and would never remain the
exclusive property of the United States. He cautioned against adopting
a "Maginot line" mentality that would give Americans a false sense
of security while other countries surpassed the United States in
atomic achievements. He strongly advocated that America permit
unrestricted interchange of scientific data among members of the
United Nations. But the Commerce Secretary made it clear that he
did not favor sharing the secret of how to produce the atomic bomb
with any country.[15]

The day after the cabinet meeting, the *New York Times* printed
a distorted version of the discussion on atomic policy. It alleged
Wallace's "ardent advocacy" that the United States divulge its
atomic secrets to Russia. Although shocked by the violation of the
confidence of a cabinet meeting and dismayed by the total inaccuracy of the story, Wallace refused to discuss the matter with newsmen. President Truman denied the report at an impromptu press
conference, and stated that the Commerce Secretary had taken no
more active part in the meeting than any other cabinet member.
Wallace privately complained bitterly to Truman about the "lying
leaker" who had planted the story. He appreciated the President's
prompt disavowal of it and commented that Truman had done his
best to correct the garbled account of the meeting. But he regretted
that Truman did not make it clear that no member of the cabinet
had suggested that America share its atomic secrets with another
country. Even after the President's disclaimer, Arthur Krock continued to assert in the *New York Times* that Wallace favored di-
vulging the secret of the bomb. The "lying leaker," who probably
was James Forrestal, succeeded in discrediting Wallace. The widespread reports that the Commerce Secretary wanted to relinquish
atomic secrets to Russia contributed to his image of a misguided
idealist.[16]

Immediately after the September 21 cabinet meeting, Wallace attended a conference of atomic scientists in Chicago. His conversa-

tions with the scientists reinforced his commitment to the free exchange of scientific information regarding atomic energy. In a letter to Truman, he expanded on the remarks he made at the cabinet session. Wallace reemphasized his opposition to disclosing the engineering and industrial techniques involved in manufacturing the atomic bomb. But he reminded the President that enough scientific information had already been published to enable any country that so desired to build the bomb within five or six years. Therefore, it would be foolish and dangerous for the United States to continue its policy "of maintaining useless secrecy and at the same time building up a stock-pile of atomic bombs."[17]

The proper course for the United States, Wallace argued, was to share basic scientific knowledge with other countries in order to promote world cooperation. That gesture would "lay the foundation for sound international agreements that would assure the control and development of atomic energy for peaceful use rather than destruction." If the United States, Britain, and Canada refused to permit free exchange of information, they would arouse the animosity of other countries, divide the world into hostile camps, and engender "hate and fear [of] all Anglo-Saxons without having gained anything." Therefore, Wallace asserted, achieving international collaboration on atomic energy matters was vital to American security. "Far from being a substitute for international cooperation," he wrote, "the atomic bomb makes such cooperation essential to the preservation of civilization." He warned a group of Senators that the United States would be vulnerable to an atomic attack no matter how many bombs it possessed, and called for international supervision of atomic energy through the United Nations. "So far as this particular field is concerned," he stated, "it is one world or no world."[18]

On October 3, 1945, Truman sent an atomic energy message to Congress that endorsed the idea of sharing scientific knowledge with other countries. He declared his intention to conduct discussions with Britain and Canada, "and then with other nations, in an effort to effect agreement on the conditions under which cooperation might replace rivalry in the field of atomic power." A few days later, he told Wallace that after meeting with the British and Canadians, he planned to confer with the Russians. The President commented that Stalin "was a fine man who wanted to do the right thing." Wallace stated his opinion that the British wanted to cause an "unbreachable break" between the United States and the Soviet Union, and were engaged in their usual "intrigue" in international politics. Truman said he agreed and again commended Stalin as "an honest man who is easy to get along with."[19]

In mid-November, Prime Minister Clement Attlee of Britain and Prime Minister Mackenzie King of Canada met with Truman to discuss international control of atomic energy. After four exhausting days of negotiations, the three leaders agreed that in order to eliminate the threat of atomic power for "destructive purposes" and to employ it for "industrial and humanitarian purposes," a United Nations commission should be set up. It would formulate proposals for the free exchange of scientific information; for methods of international control that would insure that atomic energy was used only for peaceful purposes; for the elimination of atomic weapons; and for effective means of inspection to guarantee the compliance of all countries. The commission would implement its plan in separate stages, "the successful completion of each one of which will develop the necessary confidence of the world before the next stage is undertaken."[20]

Wallace was generally satisfied with the agreement, but he was dubious about the stipulation that the work of the UN commission proceed in stages. He thought it implied "that Russia would have to pass the first grade in moral aptitude before she would be allowed to enter the second grade in moral aptitude." Soviet approval of the agreement, he believed, depended largely on how far they had progressed in their atomic program. "If they have made a really great advance they may not care to accept England, the United States, and Canada as their teachers in international morality."[21]

Wallace considered the regulation and peaceful application of atomic power the most urgent issue of the time. He publicly stated his views before the Independent Citizens Committee of the Arts, Sciences, and Professions on December 4, 1945. He called for agreement between the United States, Britain, and Russia to effectively sheathe the atomic bomb through the United Nations. "The bomb, uncontrolled, can be the greatest evil which ever plagued man," he warned. But Wallace emphasized the wondrous positive applications that proper use of atomic energy could effect. It could usher in a new age of abundance, help raise the living standards of people throughout the world, and ensure the triumph of the century of the common man. Atomic energy offered unlimited possibilities in producing power, aiding biology, agriculture, and medicine, and enabling underdeveloped countries to leap into modernity. "We have been given, through the fantastic discovery of atomic energy, the unique opportunity to build one, single, human community, on the highest spiritual level, accompanied by unlimited material facilities," the Commerce Secretary exclaimed. He urged both international control and a sensible program of domestic regulation so that rapid progress could be made toward safe and constructive application of atomic energy.[22]

The question of domestic regulation of atomic energy directly related to the problem of international atomic supervision and also greatly concerned Wallace. He was anxious that the military be deprived of the broad power it had exercised over atomic research during the Manhattan Project, and that civilians assume the management of matters relating to atomic energy. He was, therefore, dissatisfied with a plan for an atomic power commission introduced in Congress on October 4, 1945 by Senator Edwin C. Johnson and Representative Andrew J. May. Drafted in the War Department, the May-Johnson bill proposed an agency that enabled members of the armed services to play a significant role in atomic policy decisions. It called for close scrutiny of atomic research and imposed severe penalties for security violations as defined by the commission. While it neither prohibited nor approved the sharing of basic atomic information with other countries, it emphasized the military aspects of atomic energy.[23]

The May-Johnson bill alarmed atomic scientists because of its strictures on research, stress on military applications and possible control of atomic energy, and failure to permit explicitly the exchange of scientific knowledge. They organized an impressive campaign in opposition to the proposal. Wallace shared the misgivings of the scientists, and assisted them in their efforts to defeat the bill. He arranged for scientists to talk with government officials and personally voiced his objections to Truman. He was gravely concerned by the vast power invested in the atomic commission, and particularly troubled that its administrator would exercise broad independent authority because he was neither appointed nor easily removed by the President.[24]

The Commerce Secretary feared that the May-Johnson bill would allow a cabal of military leaders and industrialists to acquire con trol of atomic policy and institute a "Fascist dictatorship" in the United States. He warned the President that the bill would make it "easily possible for certain groups that definitely do not stand for what you and I stand for to gain an astonishing amount of control in an amazingly short time." He urged Truman to make the administrator subservient to the President and see that no active member of the armed forces be permitted to act as chief or deputy administrator. The clamorous protests of the atomic scientists, Wallace, Budget Director Harold Smith, and others effectively untracked the May-Johnson bill. Truman withdrew his support, and in December 1945, Congress shelved the proposal.[25]

In the same month, Senator Brien McMahon of Connecticut introduced a new proposal for domestic control of atomic energy. The McMahon bill provided for a five member, full-time atomic commission appointed by and directly responsible to the President. Although it did not specifically delineate the relative roles of military and civilian personnel on the commission, it clearly aimed to assure civilian management of atomic energy. In contrast to the May-Johnson bill, the McMahon measure encouraged development of nonmilitary uses of atomic power and explicitly permitted free exchange of basic scientific information between countries. It emphasized the need for international agreement on atomic energy.[26]

Henry Wallace and the atomic scientists endorsed the McMahon bill. In an appearance before the Senate Special Committee on Atomic Energy, the Commerce Secretary strongly urged approval of the measure. It would guarantee "civilian control of military matters," he declared, and "prevent undesirable forms of authoritarianism of military dictatorship." By promoting peaceful application of atomic energy and underwriting scientific freedom, it could lead toward "a new and undreamed-of mastery of the secrets of the universe in the interest of a better life for all." Most importantly, Wallace pointed out, enactment of the McMahon bill would indicate willingness to join with other countries to achieve international agreement on control and inspection of atomic energy. If the United States simply talked grandly about international cooperation while consigning atomic policy to the military, it would arouse the suspicions of other countries about its motives. Domestic legislation must be framed to enable America to participate in international efforts to limit atomic power to peaceful purposes. Otherwise, he feared, "civilization as we know it will be destroyed."[27]

Wallace was uneasy about the status of relations between the United States, Britain, and Russia. He remained convinced that the British were trying to incite suspicion and misunderstanding between America and Russia. "British policy clearly is to provoke distrust between the United States and Russia and thus prepare the groundwork for World War III," he wrote in his diary. Wallace thought that Secretary of State James F. Byrnes was biased against the Soviet Union and unabashedly pro-British. But he defended Byrnes when Anatola Gromov, First Secretary of the Soviet embassy in Washington, complained about the Secretary of State's Anglophilia. Wallace explained that Byrnes was a Southerner and that people from that section of the country traditionally favored England. Gromov informed the Commerce Secretary that the Soviet Union was "deeply hurt" by U.S. policies regarding the atomic bomb, Eastern Europe, Great Britain, and Argentina. He lamented that America appeared ready to loan money to Britain for postwar reconstruction but had made no similar gesture to Russia.[28]

Shortly after Wallace's conversation with Gromov, he spoke to the President about Soviet-American relations. He warned Truman against showing partiality toward the British, and urged a loan to Russia of similar proportions to that being contemplated for Britain. He compared Russian machinations in the Balkan states to American maneuvers in Cuba and Mexico. The Commerce Secretary referred to his trip to Mexico in December of 1940, when he had gone "to serve as a front for the United States to help prevent what otherwise might have been a revolution." He also argued that unless friendly relations with Russia were achieved, the fear of pending war would undermine business confidence and keep millions of people unemployed in the United States. Truman said he agreed, and indicated to Wallace that "the thing he most wanted in the world was an understanding with Russia."[29]

Wallace continued to be cautiously optimistic that Truman would adopt a conciliatory attitude toward Russia. Relations between the two men remained cordial, largely because of Truman's lack of candor with the Commerce Secretary. Although Truman had not irreversibly committed himself to a firm stand toward Russia, his position was stiffening throughout the fall of 1945. But he was careful not to reveal his feelings to Wallace. He told Byrnes that he needed two persons on his "political team"—Wallace and Eleanor Roosevelt. The Commerce Secretary was a popular figure with many Americans, and Truman assured Byrnes that he could "take care of Henry." His method of handling Wallace was to agree eagerly with practically everything the Commerce Secretary said. At first, Wallace was pleased with Truman's apparent endorsement of his ideas, but he gradually grew more suspicious of the President's dissembling tactics. "He does *so* like to agree with whoever is with him at the moment," Wallace observed. But he still hoped that Truman would accept his point of view.[30]

The Commerce Secretary remained convinced that certain interests in the United States and other countries were actively seeking to promote war between the United States and the Soviet Union. By the end of 1945, he was much more specific than he had been earlier in the year. The war agitators included, he believed, small groups among British Tories, the American armed forces, American businessmen, and the hierarchy of the Roman Catholic Church; "a substantial group" of Chinese Nationalists, London Poles, and wealthy people who lived in countries near Russia; and "a very strong element in the Republican Party." "All of these people feel that it is only by the United States whipping Russia that they have a chance to maintain their positions in life," he commented. Wallace was grateful that peace-loving common people everywhere, including Britain and the Catholic Church, far outnumbered the war-mongers. But he worried that the latter group would eventually organize and unite to instigate a third world war. "This is the great danger of the future," he noted.[31]

In the months following the end of World War II, Henry Wallace was deeply troubled by the growing discord between the United States and the Soviet Union. He privately sought to persuade Truman to act in a conciliatory manner toward Russia, but his arguments had little effect. Although the President had not settled on a policy of firmness toward the Soviets, he was losing patience with them. In early 1946, as differences between the United States and the Soviet Union hardened into cold war, Wallace became increasingly outspoken, both privately and publicly, in pleading for understanding and mutual trust between the two countries.

NOTES

1. *New York Times,* March 13, 1945; Statement on Extension of Reciprocal Trade Agreements Act, April 23, 1945, Alfred Schindler Papers,

Harry S. Truman Library, Independence, Missouri; Wallace to Blaine S. Hollimon, May 2, 1945, Henry A. Wallace Papers, University of Iowa.

2. Henry A. Wallace, *Sixty Million Jobs* (New York: Reynal and Hitchcock, 1945), p. 142; Wallace speeches, "Reconversion and Foreign Trade," May 24, 1945, Wallace Papers; "The United States and the Industrialization of the World," May 24, 1945, Schindler Papers.

3. Wallace, *Sixty Million Jobs,* pp. 134-39; "The United States and the Industrialization of the World," Schindler Papers; *Diary,* June 12, August 9, 1945, pp. 460-61, 473.

4. Wallace, *Sixty Million Jobs, passim.*

5. Ibid., pp. 6, 143-47; *Diary,* May 3, 1945, pp. 439-40.

6. *Diary,* May 6, 10, 1945, pp. 443, 446-47; Wallace to Anna T. Davis, May 5, 1945, Wallace Papers; Wallace, *Sixty Million Jobs,* pp. 6-7.

7. *Diary,* May 17, 18, July 24, 1945, pp. 448, 450, 470; Mildred Eaton to Mrs. I. B. Noden, June 1, 1945, Box 1033, File 104251, RG 40 (General Records of the Commerce Department), NA.

8. *Diary,* May 10, 1945, p. 446; Wallace to Adolph J. Sabath, August 21, 1945, Wallace to Dwight D. Eisenhower, August 14, 1945, Box 1038, Wallace speech, "In Memorium of Franklin D. Roosevelt," June 4, 1945, Box 1058, File 104251, RG 40, NA.

9. *Diary,* April 27, 1945, pp. 435-37; Wallace to Jake More, April 18, 1945, Box 1031, Wallace to Frederick Hammet, April 23, 1945, Box 1032, File 104251, RG 40, NA.

10. *Diary,* May 4, 18, 29, 1945, pp. 440-41, 450-51, 454-55; Wallace to Zoe L. Treguboff, May 31, 1945, Box 1070, File 104251/6, RG 40, NA; *New York Times,* June 24, 1941.

11. Henry A. Wallace, "America, Russia and the World," *New Republic,* 112 (June 11, 1945): 808-809; Wallace to Bertram Weaver, June 27, 1945, Box 1036, File 104251, Wallace to Edgar R. Smothers, June 13, 1945, Box 1070, File 104251/6, RG 40, NA.

12. Wallace to Anna T. Davis, June 2, 1945, Wallace Papers; Wallace to Marcel H. Stieglitz, June 8, 1945, Wallace to Edgar R. Smothers, June 13, 1945, Box 1070, File 104251/6, RG 40, NA; Wallace, *Sixty Million Jobs,* pp. 6-8.

13. *Diary,* June 6, December 21, 1942, pp. 92, 152; Wallace to John Gosfield, August 23, 1945, Box 1038, File 104251, RG 40, NA; Henry L. Stimson interview, Columbia Oral History Collection; Richard G. Hewlett and Oscar E. Anderson, *The New World, 1939-1946: A History of the United States Atomic Energy Commission* (University Park: Pennsylvania State University Press, 1962), p. 45.

14. *Diary,* September 21, 1945, p. 482; Henry L. Stimson and McGeorge Bundy, *On Active Service in Peace and War* (New York: Harper and Brothers, 1948), pp. 642-46; Hewlett and Anderson, *The New World,* p. 420.

15. *Diary,* September 21, 1945, pp. 483-84; Wallace to Arthur Krock,

October 23, 1951, Wallace to Eugene Rabinowitch, January 27, 1952, Wallace Papers; Hewlett and Anderson, *The New World,* p. 421.

16. *Diary,* September 23, October 1, 15, 16, 1945, pp. 485, 487, 491-92; Wallace to *New York Herald Tribune,* October, 1951, Wallace Papers; *New York Times,* September 22, 24, 1945.

17. Wallace to Harry S. Truman, September 24, 1945, Wallace to Eugene Rabinowitch, January 27, 1952, Wallace Papers.

18. Wallace to Truman, September 24, 1945, Wallace Papers; Wallace to Jack MacMichael, October 26, 1945, Box 1041, File 104251, RG 40, NA; U.S. Congress, Senate, Subcommittee of the Committee on Military Affairs, *Hearings on Science Legislation,* 79th Cong., 1st Sess., 1945, pp. 158-59.

19. Harry S. Truman, *Memoirs: Year of Decisions* (Garden City, N.Y.: Doubleday and Co., 1955), Vol. I, p. 531; *Diary,* October 15, 1945, p. 490.

20. Truman, *Year of Decisions,* pp. 538-44; Hewlett and Anderson, *The New World,* p. 465.

21. *Diary,* November 16, 1945, p. 516; Wallace phone conversation with Philip Hauser, November 16, 1945, Wallace Papers.

22. Wallace speech, "Wallace Hails New Atomic Age of Abundance," December 4, 1945, Wallace Papers.

23. Wallace to Truman, September 12, 1945, Wallace phone conversation with Creekmore Fath, September 5, 1945, Wallace Papers; Alice Kimball Smith, *A Peril and A Hope: The Scientists' Movement in America, 1945-47* (Chicago: University of Chicago Press, 1965), pp. 129-31.

24. Wallace to Truman, October 17, 1945, Box 1041, File 104251, RG 40, NA; Smith, *Peril and Hope,* Chap. 3.

25. *Diary,* November 7, 1945, p. 508; Wallace to Truman, November 9, 1945, Box 1042, File 104251, RG 40, NA; Wallace phone conversation with Harold Smith, November 7, 1945, Wallace Papers; Hewlett and Anderson, *The New World,* pp. 433, 438; Smith, *Peril and Hope,* p. 197.

26. Smith, *Peril and Hope,* pp. 273-75; Hewlett and Anderson, *The New World,* pp. 482-90.

27. Wallace statement before Senate Special Committee on Atomic Energy, January 31, 1946, Wallace Papers.

28. *Diary,* October 17, 24, November 13, 28, 1945, pp. 492-93, 499, 513, 523.

29. Ibid., October 26, 1945, pp. 501-503.

30. Ibid., October 15, November 28, December 11, 1945, pp. 491, 525, 528; James F. Byrnes, *All in One Lifetime* (New York: Harper and Brothers, 1958), p. 373; John Lewis Gaddis, *The United States and the Origins of the Cold War, 1941-1947* (New York: Columbia University Press, 1972), Chap. 8.

31. *Diary,* December 29, 1945, pp. 535-36.

10

Outsider in the Cabinet

During the early months of 1946, world tensions increased as both America and Russia pursued policies that aroused mutual suspicion and hostility. The United States became committed to a firm stand toward the Soviet Union. Although President Truman had leaned in that direction throughout 1945, he had at the same time sincerely attempted to achieve understanding with Russia through accommodation and compromise. By January 1946, however, he had decided that he was "tired of babying the Soviets." Outraged by the presence of Russian troops in Iran and the Soviets' heavy-handed interference in Bulgaria and Rumania, the President concluded that "unless Russia is faced with an iron fist and strong language another war is in the making."[1]

Congressional leaders had been pressuring Truman to stiffen his position toward the Soviets for some time. Arthur H. Vandenberg won a rousing ovation from his Senate colleagues when he delivered a speech in late February calling for stout resistance to Russian expansion. Secretary Byrnes echoed the same sentiments in an address given to the Overseas Press Club in New York the following day. The exposure of a Soviet atomic spy ring in Canada and Russia's refusal to remove its forces from northern Iran reinforced the growing conviction in the United States that the Soviet Union was an ideological enemy bent on aggressive expansion. A public opinion poll taken in late February 1946 revealed that only 35 percent of the

American people thought Russia would cooperate with the United States in world affairs.[2]

George F. Kennan, the American chargé d'affaires in Moscow, intellectualized the Truman administration's emerging firm stand toward Russia. He argued that Soviet leaders viewed the world as irrevocably split between capitalism and communism and "were committed fanatically to the belief that . . . there could be no permanent modus vivendi" with the United States. They constantly strived to increase the strength of the Soviet Union and to weaken the capitalist world in preparation for the coming conflict. They did not base their foreign policy on external circumstances, Kennan wrote, but depicted "the outside world as evil, hostile and menacing" in order to justify their suppression of the Russian people and perpetuate their rùle. Therefore, gestures of good will and attempts to win the friendship of the Soviet Union were doomed to failure. He recommended that the United States act firmly and resolutely to frustrate Soviet expansion, which was "highly sensitive to [the] logic of force." Kennan's analysis of Soviet behavior circulated throughout the higher echelons of the government and exerted a major impact on the thinking of many administration officials.[3]

On February 9, 1946, Joseph Stalin delivered an election speech to the Russian people that underscored and contributed to the increasing polarization between America and Russia. He stated that permanent peace was "impossible" under the "capitalist system of world economy." He hailed the success of the Five Year Plans in preparing his country for World War II, and contended that Russia's triumph in the war had proven the viability of its system and the indisputable strength of the Red Army. Stalin announced that new Five Year Plans would be necessary so that in the future Russia would be "insured against any eventuality." Some Americans viewed Stalin's address as an attempt to win popular support for unrelenting exertion and sacrifice. Most commentators, however, regarded it as a belligerent call for world revolution. It was, said William O. Douglas, "The Declaration of World War III."[4]

Less than a month later, Winston Churchill delivered his famous "Iron Curtain" speech in Fulton, Missouri. With Truman sitting on the platform, the former Prime Minister condemned Soviet expansion and domination of Eastern Europe. "This is certainly not the liberated Europe we fought to build up," he declared. Churchill also assailed "Communist fifth columns" throughout the world that represented "a growing challenge and peril to Christian civilization." Asserting that the Russians respected only strength, he called for collaboration between the United States and Britain to present a solid front that would thwart Soviet expansion. Stalin denounced the speech as "a call for war against the Soviet Union." Churchill, he said, was a "firebrand of war" who had supporters in both Britain and America. The Soviets were also embittered that not only had the United States failed to grant them economic assistance for postwar reconstruction, but it had tried to prevent them from securing oil concessions in Iran comparable to those received by American and British interests.[5]

The ominous tide of events deeply troubled Henry Wallace. He attacked individuals and groups who were "talking up war with Russia." Stalin's February 9 speech, he contended, was a "friendly challenge" to the American economy to prove that it could provide increasingly higher standards of living during peacetime. The Commerce Secretary believed that the Soviet leader's address was an understandable response to "the various challenges which we have been making all the way from the President on down." American air bases in Greenland, Iceland, Alaska, and Okinawa threatened Soviet security and made it "obvious to Stalin that our military was getting ready for war with Russia."[6]

Wallace deplored Churchill's speech, and publicly described it as "shocking." At a private dinner he stated firmly that America should not join an alliance with Britain against Russia because "it was not a primary objective of the United States to save the British Empire." He argued that the Soviet Union feared encirclement by the United States and England, and that it was imperative to dispel those fears and win the trust of the Russians. Otherwise, an atomic armaments race would occur, and the Soviets "would not scruple fifteen years hence to drop bombs on us without warning." Wallace told Truman that Churchill had "insulted" him by calling for an Anglo-American partnership with him on the platform. The President disclaimed foreknowledge of the speech and assured the Commerce Secretary that the country would not join an alliance with Britain. Wallace declared that the United States should "serve as an intermediary between Britain and Russia and not as a defender of England." As always, Truman agreed. Wallace was troubled but not convinced by reports that the President had seen Churchill's speech before it was given.[7]

At a dinner honoring the retiring Ambassador to the Soviet Union, Averell Harriman, Wallace publicly enunciated his views on international affairs. The Soviets were determined to secure their borders, he pointed out, and were wary of "capitalist encirclement." As the most powerful country in the world and the one whose motives were least suspect, the United States must allay Russian fears and lead the world toward lasting peace. Wallace admitted that "the anti-Russian press has plenty of material to use for its own ends," but he added: "I still say that the U.S. has nothing to gain but on the contrary everything to lose by beating the tom-toms against Russia." He called for friendly competition between the United States and Russia to determine which system could provide a better life for its people. Wallace hoped the Soviets would make it clear that they had no plans for world conquest, and urged Americans to reject any idea of special arrangements with other countries. He emphasized the need to build a strong United Nations that would provide machinery for negotiation, cooperation, and compromise in which all countries would accept the will of the majority. "We must furnish leadership in cultivating this method of international discussion and adjustment as the only hope of escaping from the horrors and miseries of war."[8]

The proper policy for the United States, Wallace believed, was to assume an even-handed position toward the Soviet Union and Great Britain. His opposition to collaboration with England reflected in part his long-standing Anglophobia, but it also stemmed from his conviction that America must stand between Russia and Britain to guarantee the preservation of peace. Wallace accused both the British and the Soviets of establishing competing power blocs and of violating "the letter and spirit of Potsdam and Yalta." The United States, he told Truman, must reject Churchill's appeal for a Western partnership, because it was the only nation "capable of making the spirit of the UNO come alive in some other form than an Anglo-American alliance versus the Russians." Wallace wrote to one correspondent that it would be a "serious mistake to give Russia the impression that we are ganging up with England against her." Although it would be "equally serious" to side with Russia against England, he thought that was highly improbable.[9]

In an atmosphere of increasing hostility toward the Soviet Union, Wallace's position made him appear pro-Russian. Unlike a growing number of Americans, he did not view the Soviet Union as an implacable ideological foe that intended to spread communism throughout Europe. He contended that the best way to check communism was by demonstrating that capitalism worked better, not by adopting a belligerent posture toward Russia that aggravated tensions and caused misunderstandings. The Commerce Secretary was not an abject apologist for Soviet behavior, but he denied that the Soviet Union was solely responsible for cold war frictions.

In keeping with his hopes that the United States would employ a balanced approach in international affairs, Wallace advocated economic assistance for both Britain and the Soviet Union. He urged Congress to approve a $3.75 billion loan to Britain in order to foster unfettered world trade and multilateral economic cooperation. He argued that it would help maintain peace, promote world recovery, and discourage the British from entering special arrangements within the Imperial Preference System. Failure to extend the loan, Wallace asserted, would hurt American export trade because Britain had always been the country's largest importer. By refusing to grant credit, the United States would divide the world into competing economic blocs that endangered peace. The Commerce Secretary emphatically denied that the loan to Britain was a step toward an Anglo-American military alliance. He stated that loans to other countries were "equally necessary" to cultivate international cooperation. "I am just as much opposed to an Anglo-American bloc as to a British bloc that excludes us," he declared. "It must be our foreign economic policy to promote recovery in the east of Europe as well as in the United Kingdom."[10]

Wallace opposed the use of economic leverage for political purposes, and was disturbed that the United States was extending loans to France, China, and other countries with political considerations in mind. He favored foreign trade and economic aid as means to ensure peace and promote international prosperity, not to influence the internal affairs of other countries. "We cannot make a foreign system of government our business and be true to our democratic principles," he wrote. In a letter of March 15, 1946, Wallace suggested to Truman that the recently appointed Ambassador to the Soviet Union, Walter Bedell Smith, initiate discussions on economic matters when he arrived in Moscow. He argued that "much of the recent Soviet behavior . . . has been the result of their dire economic needs and of their disturbed sense of security." In order to soothe Soviet fears of "capitalist encirclement," the United States should make it clear "that we want to trade with them and to cement our economic relations with them." The Commerce Secretary recommended that the two countries discuss Russia's long-range economic needs and the basis for "future economic collaboration" rather than "immediate proposals such as a loan." He believed that closer economic ties between the United States and the Soviet Union would help foster mutual understanding and peace.[11]

Truman read the letter and indicated that he would give it to Smith, but then decided to ignore it because he saw "little to be gained from the Wallace proposal." Wallace was surprised and disappointed, and wondered whether Truman had made an "oversight" or if he thought it "unwise" to give Smith the letter. Wallace failed to realize how much Truman's views were diverging from his own. He told the President that the Commerce Department should know "exactly what your attitude is with regard to promoting the maximum of foreign trade with Russia. We don't want to get out of line with over-all policy."[12]

Wallace's position on American-Soviet relations made him an increasingly isolated cabinet figure. An incident involving the deployment of American military forces in Iceland further estranged him from other administration members. On March 21, 1946, Ruben Karlsted of the Associated Press told Wallace that the Scandinavian countries were gratified that the Soviet Union had withdrawn its troops from the Danish island of Bornholm, and that the Scandinavians wondered when the United States intended to evacuate its forces from Iceland. The Commerce Secretary replied that he thought those countries wanted the United States to stay in Iceland as a deterrent to the Soviets. When Karlsted said that was not true, Wallace remarked that, personally, he believed American troops should leave Iceland because the Russians regarded them as a "direct threat." He reiterated that he was speaking as a private individual and not as a government official.[13]

The following day, the *New York Times* reported that in an "exclusive interview," Wallace had urged American withdrawal from Iceland. It quoted him as saying: "The only interpretation the Russians could place on continued occupancy of bases in Iceland by American troops would be that it was aimed at them.'' Wallace did not see the article and was puzzled when Joseph Alsop berated him for his views on the Iceland situation. Administration officials who did see the article were incensed. The State Department had been conducting discussions with the government of Iceland to secure a lease on air bases, but Wallace's statement, along with a similar one by Senator Claude Pepper, undercut the negotiations by making the question of American bases an explosive political issue in Iceland. Secretary Byrnes complained bitterly at a cabinet meeting from which Wallace was absent, declaring that his efforts ''had been aborted to a considerable extent by the statements and speeches of Secretary Wallace and Senator Pepper.'' James Forrestal and Arthur Vandenberg were equally indignant.[14]

Wallace remained unaware of the controversy until Joseph and Stewart Alsop published an article in *Life* magazine, condemning his ''irresponsible intervention in a matter of great delicacy and seriousness.'' He immediately wrote to the editor of *Life,* protesting that the Alsops had printed a distorted version of his off-the-record remarks to Ruben Karlsted. A short time later, columnist Bert Andrews reported that Truman, Byrnes, and Vandenberg were ''upset'' with Wallace's statement on Iceland. ''All three have as much as said that their task of dealing with Russia would be made much easier if Wallace and Pepper would support them or keep quiet,'' he disclosed. Wallace then explained the situation to Truman, who responded with a friendly note that belied his anger. The President still sought to avoid a politically embarrassing rift with his Commerce Secretary.[15]

Wallace still hoped that Truman would adopt a conciliatory attitude toward the Soviet Union. On March 23, 1946, only two days after discovering that the President had not acted on his proposal for building economic ties with Russia, Wallace publicly lauded Truman for perpetuating the legacy of Franklin Roosevelt. Two months later, he assured Henry Morgenthau that ''Truman was definitely sold on the Roosevelt policies and wanted to do everything he could to carry them out.'' Truman carefully cultivated the Commerce Secretary's misconception. He told Wallace that ''we don't have any aggression whatever in our plans against Russia,'' and that ''he was sure that war with Russia was not inevitable.''[16]

Truman's comments were disingenuous, though not untruthful. He did not want to alienate Wallace and risk losing the support of the left wing of the Democratic party. Therefore, he sought to give Wallace the impression that he concurred in his analysis of Soviet-American relations. But even though the President disagreed with the Commerce Secretary on the means to attain understanding with the Soviets, he shared the desire to maintain peace with them. Truman and Byrnes thought that their policy of "patience and firmness" was most likely to preserve peace, and that it stood between the ideas held by Wallace and the opinions of those who were calling for a more rigorous "get tough with Russia" posture. The President seemed to have little awareness of how his policies appeared in Soviet eyes. He told Wallace that the United States "could be a great deal of help to Russia if Russia would only let us help her," but he failed to understand why the Soviet Union was "continuously suspicious of us." The Commerce Secretary was rather perplexed by Truman's attitude toward Russia. But he still hoped that the President would accept his point of view and resolved to remain in the cabinet as long as Truman did not demand "blind acquiescence" from his advisors.[17]

The most critical issue of the day, Wallace believed, was domestic and international regulation of atomic energy. He continued his ardent support for the McMahon bill, designed to assure "civilian control of military matters." His appeal for limiting the power of the military struck a responsive chord with the American people, and helped convince Truman to endorse the measure in early February 1946. The War Department, the Navy Department, and many congressmen disliked the McMahon bill because they feared it would exclude the armed services from participating in atomic energy decisions. Wallace and the atomic scientists opposed the efforts of the military to secure an influential position on the proposed atomic commission. The Commerce Secretary warned Truman "that this would lead toward a military dictatorship and the domination of our foreign policies by the military."[18]

Senator Vandenberg attempted to resolve the controversy over military versus civilian control of atomic energy by drafting an amendment to the McMahon bill. It proposed a military liaison board that would "advise and consult" with the atomic commission on "all atomic energy matters which the board deems to relate to national defense." The board would review matters before the commission and make recommendations on policy. If it believed that a decision of the commission was harmful to the "common defense and security," it could appeal to the President, whose authority was final. When the Senate Committee on Atomic Energy approved the Vandenberg amendment in March 1946, Wallace attacked it as "an exceedingly unfortunate development." The revised bill, he exclaimed, "now has the potential of delivering us into the hands of military fascism in this country." Vandenberg, who was committed to civilian control but believed that the military should not be "totally excluded from consultation" on atomic policy, thought Wallace's charge was "fantastic nonsense."[19]

The Commerce Secretary explained his position in a long letter to Truman. Although he conceded that the War and Navy Departments had "legitimate interest" in the military uses of atomic energy, he was gravely concerned about consigning them broad responsibility in atomic matters relating to the "common defense and security." He feared that such a sweeping definition would impose "no limit" on military power because "almost no aspect of national life" was unrelated to defense and security. Arguing that the Vandenberg amendment would lead to "military supremacy" of atomic energy, Wallace urged that the influence of the armed forces be restricted to "military applications." He sent a copy of the letter to Eleanor Roosevelt, who did not share his deep anxiety about the Vandenberg amendment. "In the main it seems to me reasonable," she wrote.[20]

Many Americans, however, were more alarmed by the amendment than was the former First Lady. The objections voiced by Wallace, Senator McMahon, atomic scientists, and other critics provoked a public uproar. Besieged with protests, Vandenberg attributed the popular outcry to "the grossest misrepresentations through persistent and hysterical propaganda that I have ever seen in my entire Senatorial career." But he worked out a revised amendment that curtailed the power of the armed forces. It limited the authority of the military liaison board on atomic energy matters to "military applications" rather than "common defense and security," and made the board responsible to the Secretaries of War and Navy rather than directly to the President. The compromise wording ended the dispute, and the new amendment was incorporated into the McMahon bill.[21]

Although the major questions relating to domestic control of atomic energy were resolved, international aspects of the problem remained unsettled. In addition to his fear of military fascism, Wallace opposed a dominant role in atomic policy for the armed services because it would arouse the suspicions of other countries. "If we place the direction and control of atomic energy in the hands of military people," he declared, "we are in effect serving notice on the world that we look on this great power as a weapon." If the United States adopted "an attitude of hostility and antagonism," it would be responsible for inciting an atomic armaments race. Wallace denied that an arms race with the Soviet Union was inevitable, but confided that he was "afraid of Russia if we develop a spirit of competitive rearmament." An aggressive stand toward the Soviet Union would transform that country into "a wild beast." In May 1946, Wallace told newsman Richard Wilson that "if the present trend of events continued, Russia would, when she had an adequate supply, use the atomic bomb without warning." Therefore, it was of paramount importance that an effective international agreement on control and inspection of atomic energy be achieved through the United Nations.[22]

On June 14, 1946, Bernard M. Baruch presented the American proposal for international regulation of atomic energy to the United Nations. Baruch promised that the United States would stop producing atomic bombs, destroy existing stockpiles, and reveal all atomic information when a satisfactory system of control was set up. His plan called for a United Nations atomic development authority to assume control over raw materials and supervise licensing, inspection, and management of atomic energy operations throughout the world. To make sure no country conducted illegal activities outside the auspices of the authority, Baruch emphasized that "the matter of punishment" was essential to a workable agreement. He argued that the veto power must be denied Security Council members on atomic energy questions. Baruch also pointed out that it would require some time for the UN authority "to become fully organized and effective." Therefore, implementation of international control should proceed by separate stages. The United States would disclose atomic information gradually as the successive stages were reached.[23]

Andrei Gromyko responded for the Soviet Union five days later. He proposed a treaty that would prohibit production and use of atomic weapons. Within three months after the agreement was finalized, signatory nations would destroy existing supplies of atomic armaments. Within another three months, those countries would enact legislation to punish violators. The Soviet plan contemplated United Nations committees to recommend practical methods for exchanging scientific information and insuring compliance with the ban on atomic weapons. Gromyko made it clear that Russia would not consent to abolishing the veto on issues relating to atomic energy. Americans generally disapproved and distrusted the Soviet proposal, and many liberals sympathetic to the Soviet Union were keenly disappointed with it. Wallace, however, commented that the Soviet reaction to the Baruch plan indicated "that the Russians simply don't trust us." He added that they "had some very real and very well-founded reasons for not trusting us."[24]

The impasse over international control of atomic energy further heightened Wallace's anxiety about the course of American-Soviet relations. For some time, he had been drafting a comprehensive statement concerning world tensions, and on July 23, 1946, handed Truman a twelve page, single-spaced letter that soberly and thoughtfully outlined his position. "How do American actions since V-J Day appear to other nations?" he asked in the letter. Citing the country's large military budget, the continued production of atomic bombs and long-range bombers to deliver them, and "the effort to secure air bases spread over half the globe," Wallace argued that it looked as if the United States were preparing "to win the war which we regard as inevitable," or it was "trying to build up a predominance of force to intimidate the rest of mankind." Then he queried: "How would it look to us if Russia had the atomic bomb and we did not, if Russia had 10,000 mile bombers and air bases within a thousand miles of our coast lines and we did not?"[25]

In his letter, the Commerce Secretary attacked those who believed that the best way to maintain peace was to "build up a predominance of force." He contended that atomic weapons made such reasoning obsolete because there was no advantage in possessing more atomic bombs than a rival country. "If another nation had enough bombs to eliminate all of our principal cities and our heavy industry, it wouldn't help us very much if we had 10 times as many bombs as we needed to do the same to them." Moreover, the proliferation of atomic weapons would inevitably engender "a neurotic, fear-ridden, itching-trigger psychology in all the peoples of the world'' that could easily set off a cataclysmic war. Wallace asserted that some military leaders, recognizing those realities, favored a "preventive war" against the Soviet Union before it acquired atomic weapons. Such a maneuver would be "not only immoral but stupid," because the Soviets would simply move the Red Army into Western Europe, where America would not dare attack. Therefore, since "predominance of force" and "preventive war" were unfeasible, the United States had no alternative but to achieve an international accord on atomic energy.[26]

Wallace then launched into a critique of the Baruch plan. Its "fatal defect," he wrote, was the stipulation that international control would be implemented in stages. That meant that while other countries were required to divulge information about their uranium and thorium supplies and cease atomic research for military applications, the United States could withhold technical knowledge until some unspecified time when international regulation was functioning to its satisfaction. "In other words, we are telling the Russians that if they are 'good boys' we may eventually turn over our knowledge of atomic energy to them and to the other nations." The Commerce Secretary was not surprised that the Soviets had reacted as they did to the Baruch plan, and maintained that the United States would act the same way in Russia's position. An international accord must be "wrapped up in a single package," he argued, and the United States "must be prepared to reach an agreement which will commit us to disclosing information and destroying our bombs at a specified time or in terms of specified actions by other countries, rather than at our unfettered discretion." Wallace also objected to Baruch's insistence on abolishing the veto on atomic energy matters. The issue was "irrelevant," he declared, because in case of a treaty violation "the remaining signatory nations are free to take what action they feel is necessary, including the ultimate step of declaring war." He suggested that Gromyko's proposal indicated that the Soviets "may be willing to negotiate seriously if we are."[27]

As always, Wallace contended that the way to ease world tensions and secure peace was to "allay any reasonable Russian grounds for fear, suspicion, and distrust." The United States should recognize valid Soviet security requirements, "even at the expense of risking epithets of appeasement." He affirmed that communism and capitalism could exist together peacefully, pointing out that many different religions, "all claiming to be the true gospel," had managed to live in the same world for centuries "with a reasonable degree of tolerance." Urging a loan to Russia and discussions about its long-range economic needs, he renewed his appeal for increased trade and closer economic ties with the Soviet Union. Wallace admitted that his program would arouse criticism, but insisted that attaining world unity was more important than domestic harmony. "I think there is some reason to fear that in our earnest desire to achieve bipartisan unity in this country we may have given way too much to isolationism masquerading as tough realism in international affairs," he commented. Although winning the confidence of the Soviet Union would be difficult, it was a necessary requisite to ensuring peace and preventing "a disastrous atomic world war."[28]

Wallace's letter was a lucid, well-argued summation of his position, but it failed to move Truman, who replied with a perfunctory, noncommittal note. Public opinion surveys revealed how far Wallace's views departed from those of most Americans. A poll taken on June 7, 1946, indicated that while 58 percent of those questioned thought Russia was "trying to build herself up to be the ruling power of the world," only 29 percent thought it was "just building up protection against being attacked in another war." Yet the Commerce Secretary was not despondent about the prospects for peace. He reminded a war veteran that "when the odds against you were the greatest you fought your hardest. . . . The outlook is not entirely black." He told one correspondent who feared that Soviet expansion would lead to war that he was "not so pessimistic about the immediate situation with regard to Soviet-American relations."[29]

Wallace's continuing optimism about world affairs reflected his belief that the Soviets wanted peace and would cooperate with the United States. His position on Soviet-American relations stemmed from his analysis of the historical roots of Russian insecurity, from his conviction that the fundamental goals of the United States and the Soviet Union were not incompatible, from his experiences in Soviet Asia in 1944, and from his conversations with respected observers, including Walter Lippmann. But above all, it was an expression of faith in the good will of the Soviets and the ability of the United States to win their confidence. The United States could and must develop friendship with Russia, he believed, or his dream of a century of the common man would be shattered. If all nations would follow the Golden Rule and learn to "look at things from the other fellow's point of view," Wallace declared in a radio speech in July 1946, the world could achieve lasting peace through international trust and understanding.[30]

But Truman and his closest advisors had lost faith in Russia. They had concluded that the Soviets were unwilling to cooperate with the West and that they were trying to strengthen themselves for an inevitable clash between capitalism and communism. In a confidential report to Truman prepared in the summer of 1946, presidential assistant Clark Clifford argued that the Soviets were unmoved by "good will gestures or acts of appeasement." He dismissed the Soviets' fear of "capitalistic encirclement" as "absurd." The best way to maintain peace, he contended, was to deal firmly with Russia and make it clear that "we are too strong to be beaten and too determined to be frightened." Only then would the Soviets modify their principles and "work out with us a fair and equitable settlement." Clifford's memorandum reflected the predominant thinking in the Truman administration about the Soviet Union. The inevitable confrontation between Truman's policy of firmness and Wallace's appeal for conciliation came in September 1946.[31]

NOTES

1. John Lewis Gaddis, *The United States and the Origins of the Cold War, 1941-1947* (New York: Columbia University Press, 1972), Chap. 9; Lisle A. Rose, *After Yalta: America and the Origins of the Cold War* (New York: Charles Scribner's Sons, 1973), Chap. 6; Harry S. Truman, *Memoirs: Year of Decisions* (Garden City, N.Y.: Doubleday and Co., 1955), Vol. I, pp. 551-52.

2. Arthur H. Vandenberg, Jr., ed., *The Private Papers of Senator Vandenberg* (Boston: Houghton Mifflin Co., 1952), pp. 247-51; Hadley Cantril and Mildred Strunk, *Public Opinion, 1935-1946* (Princeton: Princeton University Press, 1951), p. 371; Gaddis, *Cold War,* Chap. 9.

3. George F. Kennan, *Memoirs (1925-1950)* (Boston: Little, Brown, and Co., 1967), pp. 547-59; Gaddis, *Cold War,* pp. 302-304; Rose, *After Yalta,* pp. 166-67.

4. Gaddis, *Cold War,* pp. 299-301; Walter Millis, ed., *The Forrestal Diaries* (New York: Viking Press, 1951), p. 134; *New York Times,* February 10, 1946.

5. *New York Times,* March 6, 1946; Herbert Feis, *From Trust to Terror: The Onset of the Cold War 1945-1950* (New York: W. W. Norton,

1970), p. 79; Thomas G. Paterson, *Soviet-American Confrontation* (Baltimore: Johns Hopkins University Press, 1973), pp. 50-53, 179-80; Frederick L. Schuman, *Russia Since 1917: Four Decades of Soviet Politics* (New York: Alfred A. Knopf, 1962), p. 353.

6. *Diary,* February 12, 13, 1946, pp. 547, 550; Wallace to Daniel A. Reed, April 5, 1946, Box 1074, File 104251/6, RG 40, NA; *New York Times,* February 20, 1946.

7. *New York Times,* March 8, 1946; *Diary,* March 5, 12, 1946, pp. 556-60; Wallace to Manuel Avila Camacho, March 21, 1946, Henry A. Wallace Papers, University of Iowa.

8. Wallace speech at dinner in honor of W. Averell Harriman, March 19, 1946, Alfred Schindler Papers, Truman Library.

9. *Diary,* February 12, March 12, 22, April 5, 1946, pp. 547-49, 558-59, 567-68, 570; Wallace to Frank W. Sterrett, April 26, 1946, Box 1051, File 104251, RG 40, NA; "Memorandum given to Truman," March 20, 1946, Wallace Diary (typescript), Book 39, Wallace Papers.

10. U.S. Congress, Senate, Committee on Banking and Currency, *Hearings on Anglo-American Financial Agreement,* 79th Cong., 2nd Sess., 1946, pp. 265-67, 303; U.S. Congress, House, Committee on Banking and Currency, *Hearings on Anglo-American Financial Agreement,* 79th Cong., 2nd Sess., 1946, pp. 399-405; Wallace speech to National Foreign Trade Convention, November 12, 1945, Schindler Papers.

11. Wallace to Truman, March 15, 1946, Wallace Papers; Wallace to Leo H. O'Hare, May 29, 1946, Box 523, File 82220/1, RG 40, NA; *Foreign Relations: 1946,* Vol. I, pp. 1433-34; *Diary,* March 14, 15, 1946, pp. 561-63.

12. Wallace to Truman, March 21, 1946, Box 522, File 82220/1, RG 40, NA; *Diary,* March 15, 1946, p. 563; Truman, *Year of Decisions,* p. 556.

13. *Diary,* March 21, 1946, pp. 565-66.

14. Ibid., March 22, 1946, p. 567; *New York Times,* March 22, 1946; Millis, ed., *Forrestal Diaries,* pp. 154-55; Vandenberg, ed., *Private Papers of Senator Vandenberg,* p. 266; Wallace to Wilson Hicks, July 8, 1946, Box 1055, File 104251, RG 40, NA.

15. Wallace to Wilson Hicks, May 21, 1946, Truman to Wallace, June 7, 1946, Box 1053, File 104251, RG 40, NA; *Washington Post,* June 2, 1946; Joseph and Stewart Alsop, "Tragedy of Liberalism," *Life,* 20 (May 20, 1946): 68.

16. *Diary,* May 28, July 18, 23, 1946, pp. 577, 586, 588; *New York Times,* March 24, 1946.

17. *Diary,* July 18, 24, 1946, pp. 587, 602-03; George Curry, *James F. Byrnes* (New York: Cooper Square Publishers, 1965), pp. 210, 258; Russell Lord, *The Wallaces of Iowa* (Boston: Houghton Mifflin Co., 1947), p. 574.

18. *Diary,* February 28, 1946, p. 552; Alice Kimball Smith, *A Peril and A Hope: The Scientists' Movement in America, 1945-47* (Chicago: University of Chicago Press, 1965), pp. 366-72; Richard G. Hewlett and Oscar E.

Anderson, *The New World, 1939-1946: A History of the United States Atomic Energy Commission* (University Park: Pennsylvania State University Press, 1962), pp. 490-91; Arnold Rogow, *James Forrestal: A Study in Personality, Politics, and Policy* (New York: Macmillan Co., 1963), pp. 167-70.

19. *New York Times,* March 13, 1946; Vandenberg, ed., *Private Papers of Senator Vandenberg,* pp. 254-57; Hewlett and Anderson, *The New World,* pp. 504-506; Smith, *Peril and Hope,* pp. 388-89.

20. Wallace to Truman, March 15, 1946, Wallace to Eleanor Roosevelt, March 21, 1946, Eleanor Roosevelt Papers, Roosevelt Library; Eleanor Roosevelt to Wallace, April 1, 1946, Box 1050, File 104251, RG 40, NA.

21. Vandenberg, ed., *Private Papers of Senator Vandenberg,* pp. 258-61; Hewlett and Anderson, *The New World,* pp. 507-13; Smith, *Peril and Hope,* pp. 388-409.

22. *Diary,* March 5, 1946, p. 557; Wallace to Brien McMahon, April 2, 1946, Box 1084, File 104406, Wallace to Edmund H. Stinnes, April 3, 1946, Box 1050, File 104251, RG 40, NA; Wallace radio interview, March 15, 1946, Schindler Papers; *Des Moines Register,* September 22, 1946.

23. Hewlett and Anderson, *The New World,* pp. 574-82; Barton J. Bernstein and Allen J. Matusow, eds., *The Truman Administration: A Documentary History* (New York: Harper and Row, 1966), pp. 225-27; Barton J. Bernstein, "The Quest for Security: American Foreign Policy and International Control of Atomic Energy, 1942-1946," *Journal of American History,* 60 (March 1974): 1032-37.

24. Hewlett and Anderson, *The New World,* pp. 583-84; Bernstein and Matusow, *Truman Administration,* pp. 228-32; Bernstein, "Quest for Security," p. 1038; Alonzo L. Hamby, *Beyond the New Deal: Harry S. Truman and American Liberalism* (New York: Columbia University Press, 1973), p. 106; *Diary,* June 25, 1946, p. 582.

25. Richard Hippelheuser to Philip Hauser, July 17, 1946, Wallace Papers; Wallace to Truman, July 23, 1946, Schindler Papers.

26. Wallace to Truman, July 23, 1946, Schindler Papers.

27. Ibid.

28. Ibid.

29. Truman to Wallace, August 8, 1946, Clark Clifford Papers, Truman Library; Wallace to Jane O'Connor, July 24, 1946, Box 1056, File 104251, Wallace to Norman Mackie, August 1, 1946, Box 1075, File 104251/6, RG 40, NA; *Public Opinion Quarterly,* 10 (Summer 1946): 265.

30. Wallace radio speech, July 31, 1946, *Congressional Record,* 79th Cong., 2nd Sess., 1946, Vol. 92, Part 12, pp. A4790-91.

31. Clifford's report is printed in Arthur Krock, *Memoirs: Sixty Years on the Firing Line* (New York: Funk and Wagnalls, 1968), pp. 419-82.

11

Dissent
and
Dismissal

Although the majority of Americans rejected Henry Wallace's views on international relations, he remained the foremost spokesman for American liberals, who were an influential force within the Democratic party. Many liberals were disgruntled with Truman's leadership and looked to Wallace, the only New Dealer left in the cabinet, to uphold and sustain the legacy of Franklin Roosevelt on both foreign and domestic issues. In mid-summer 1946, Wallace accepted an invitation from two liberal organizations, the Independent Citizens Committee for the Arts, Sciences, and Professions and the National Citizens Political Action Committee, to speak at a political rally scheduled for September in New York City. The Commerce Secretary initially planned to concentrate on denouncing Republicans and endorsing the Democratic candidates for governor and U.S. senator from New York. But when C. B. (Beanie) Baldwin, former director of the Farm Security Administration and a leader of the Political Action Committee, obtained a copy of Wallace's July 23 letter to Truman, he was so impressed that he persuaded the Commerce Secretary to enunciate his views on foreign policy in the upcoming address. Wallace still hoped Truman would adopt his ideas, but was disturbed enough by the lack of response to his previous appeals to force the issue publicly.[1]

On September 10, 1946, two days before he was scheduled to appear in New York, Wallace met with Truman and showed him a

copy of his address. The President read through the speech carefully, frequently commenting: "That's right," or "Yes, that is what
I believe." He suggested no changes and expressed his appreciation
to Wallace for showing him the speech in advance. The Commerce
Secretary was astounded that Truman "apparently saw no incon-
sistency" between his address and the policies being followed by
Secretary Byrnes. Truman approved the speech partly because
Wallace was a political asset and the President did not want a rift
with him before the upcoming November elections. He also endorsed it because evidently he did not view it as being glaringly
inconsistent with his own position. Wallace's address was moderate
in tone and included a number of critical comments about Soviet
conduct. Although at one point the Commerce Secretary rebuked
advocates of "getting tough" with Russia, the President did not believe that he was following such a course. He regarded his stance as
one of "patience and firmness" and did not construe Wallace's
statements as a reproach to the administration's foreign policies.[2]

After the meeting with the President, Wallace told colleagues at
the Commerce Department that Truman had read his speech "word
for word," but that he was uncertain "that the President understood
the full implications of what he intended to say." Presidential Press
Secretary Charles Ross privately disclosed that Truman had "been
over" Wallace's speech and that "he liked it very much." On September 12, the day of the rally, newsmen received advance copies of
the speech. When they asked Truman about it at a press conference,
he replied that he had approved "the whole speech" and asserted
that it was "exactly in line" with Byrnes' policies. The same day,
Wallace wrote that his address would "probably make everybody
sore but it is the way I think and perhaps it will help clear the air."[3]

A predominantly left-wing, pro-Russian crowd of twenty thousand jammed Madison Square Garden the evening of September
12. Before Wallace rose to speak, they passed a resolution assailing
American foreign policy and loudly cheered Claude Pepper's fervid
denunciation of the diplomacy of the Truman administration. But
if they expected a one-sided and impassioned attack from Henry
Wallace, they were soon disappointed.[4]

Wallace began his discourse on how to attain peace by issuing his
standard plea for unfettered world trade and assistance to underdeveloped countries. The United States should invest in the ad-

vancement of undeveloped areas, he declared, to underwrite "the long-term stability that comes from an ever increasing standard of living." The Republican party stood for "economic nationalism and political isolation" that could lead only to "world wide depression, ruthless economic warfare, and eventual war." The Commerce Secretary warned that the Republicans wanted the United States to align itself with Great Britain, which would be "the height of folly." The United States must act independently, he said, and not allow its policies to be determined by the British Foreign Office or by pro-British newspapers. "I want one thing clearly understood," he stated. "I am neither anti-British, nor pro-British; neither anti-Russian, nor pro-Russian." Then he added: "And two days ago, when President Truman read these words, he said they represented the policy of his administration." The mention of Truman's name brought jeers and hisses from the restless crowd.[5]

Wallace assailed "numerous reactionary elements" in all parts of the world that were trying to stir up a war between America and Russia. The United States must disdain those forces and build friendly relations with the Soviets. "The real peace treaty we now need is between the United States and Russia," he observed. Americans must realize that a firm posture toward the Soviets aggravated world tensions, because: "The tougher we get, the tougher the Russians will get." But the Commerce Secretary insisted that the Soviets meet the United States "half way" by "cooperating with the United Nations in a spirit of openminded and flexible give-and-take." When he pointed out that Soviet activities in Eastern Europe angered a majority of Americans, the audience responded with more hissing and heckling.[6]

Wallace contended that Americans should recognize that "we have no more business in the political affairs of Eastern Europe than Russia has in the political affairs of Latin America, Western Europe, and the United States." The Soviets were determined "to socialize their sphere of influence," just as the United States intended to "democratize" its sphere of influence. Although the Russians should not encourage Communist activities in foreign countries, neither should the United States intrude in the domestic political affairs of Eastern Europe and the Soviet Union. But the Commerce Secretary insisted that the United States could not "permit the door to be closed against our trade in Eastern Europe." He believed economic matters could be separated from political ones, and maintained that the Soviets would permit economic penetration of their sphere of influence.[7]

Wallace's references to American and Russian spheres of influence seemed inconsistent with his universalist views. But he was not resigned to the idea of a divided world. He believed that the current differences and misunderstandings between the United States and the Soviet Union made spheres of influence an inevitable, though unfortunate, reality. Eventually, Wallace asserted, both countries would realize that communism and capitalism could exist together peacefully, although they would continue to engage in "peaceful competition" to demonstrate which system could "deliver the most satisfaction to the common man in their respective areas of political dominance." Gradually, as the Russians granted their people more personal liberties and the United States concentrated more on "problems of social-economic justice," the two systems would grow closer together and the world would become more unified.[8]

In order to build a strong United Nations, Wallace believed, the United States must show it was not planning a war against the Soviet Union, and Russia must show that it was not intent on territorial expansion and world conquest. Once mutual fears and suspicions had been mollified, and a practical regional arrangement within the United Nations worked out, the veto power would assume much less importance. Wallace still favored a system of regionalism within the United Nations, but he remained convinced that the world organization should have supreme power "in those areas that are truly international and not regional." Only the United Nations should possess atomic bombs, and it should operate the air bases "with which the United States and Britain have encircled the world." In addition, the countries of the world should agree to a code of international law, "based on moral principles, and not on Machiavellian principles of deceit, force, and distrust."[9]

Wallace's speech was an attempt to deal with the existing international situation. He thought world tensions would be eased and mutual suspicions soothed if the United States and Russia each refrained from interfering in areas of vital concern to the other. Then the two countries could begin to cooperate to ensure peace and build a century of the common man. Wallace's suggestion of recognizing spheres of influence stirred a great deal of adverse reaction. Several newspapers condemned him for wanting to abandon Eastern Europe to communism and interpreted the address as a call for isolationism for America. David Lawrence attacked it as a "Machiavellian thrust" that dealt "a shattering blow to the ideals of Woodrow Wilson and Cordell Hull." Wallace was disturbed by the misconception that he had renounced his one world views, and he retained his deep aversion to power politics. But he believed that any American efforts to undermine Soviet influence in Eastern Europe would intensify Russian distrust of the West, heighten Soviet-American discord, and imperil his dream of an ultimately peaceful, unified world.[10]

As Wallace had anticipated, his statements about Soviet-American relations caused a furor. The address was not an apologia for Soviet behavior or an extravagant condemnation of American diplomacy. Unnerved by the hostile crowd reaction, the Commerce Secretary had omitted some, but not all, of the critical remarks about the Soviet Union in his original text. As many commentators were quick to point out, however, the address departed from the course being followed by the Truman administration by appealing for a conciliatory attitude toward the Soviet Union and denying that a policy of firmness could achieve peace. Some observers applauded Wallace's speech. The *New Republic* hailed him as a "world leader," and the *Nation* thought he had "many excellent things . . . to say." But most of the country's newspapers rallied behind Secretary Byrnes and many called for Wallace's dismissal from the cabinet.[11]

Despite the widespread controversy that Wallace's address provoked, the major issues he raised were hardly discussed. The *Des Moines Register* regretted that most commentators ignored the most important question: "Are we really making any progress in the direction of world peace by the 'get tough' approach?" James Reston of the *New York Times* noted that most people were not primarily concerned with assessing the validity of Wallace's position. The controversy focused instead on the question of whether or not the speech heralded a new foreign policy for the United States. "Mr. Truman seems to be the only person in the capital who thinks that Mr. Wallace's proposals are 'in line' with Mr. Truman's or Mr. Byrnes'," he wrote. The Secretary of State, Senator Vandenberg, and Senator Tom Connally, who were attending a meeting of the Council of Foreign Ministers in Paris, were profoundly distressed. Wallace's speech and Truman's endorsement of it undercut their negotiating position and aroused speculation among foreign diplomats that the United States was shifting its policy. Byrnes withheld public comment, but Vandenberg angrily announced that the Republican party could "only cooperate with one Secretary of State at a time."[12]

On September 14, in an attempt to end the controversy, Truman called in newsmen and read a short statement: "There has been a natural misunderstanding. . . . It was my intention to express the thought that I approved the right of the Secretary of Commerce to deliver the speech. I did not intend to indicate that I approved the speech as constituting a statement of the foreign policy of this country." He affirmed that "there has been no change in the established foreign policy of our government." Truman's contrived explanation elicited sharp criticism from many observers. *Time* magazine called it a "clumsy lie," and *PM* columnist Max Lerner wrote that Truman "took a lame and shabby way out of a difficulty he had put himself into." Wallace, however, phoned the President and told him he had done "exactly the right thing" by issuing the statement. He thought Truman "had given him a good out" by standing up "for his right to say what he wanted to say." In order to avoid alienating Wallace and his supporters, Truman thanked the Commerce Secretary and suggested they both meet with Byrnes to determine some way for Wallace to speak on foreign policy without undercutting the State Department.[13]

Aside from the misunderstanding about his spheres of influence proposal, Wallace was "delighted with the reception which the speech received." He remained convinced that the President was not irrevocably committed to a policy of firmness toward Russia. On September 16, shortly after his phone conversation with Truman, he released a statement of his own. "I stand upon my New York speech," he declared. "It is interesting to find that both the extreme right and the extreme left disagreed with the views I expressed." Truman had given no indication that he wanted Wallace to stop talking about foreign affairs, and the Commerce Secretary promised that he would speak out again in the near future. Aroused by Wallace's statement, Byrnes cabled Truman from Paris. His tone was moderate and respectful, but he asked the President either to keep Wallace from publicly discussing foreign affairs or to accept his resignation as Secretary of State.[14]

The following day, a new development aggravated the crisis. Press Secretary Charles Ross received information that columnist Drew Pearson had obtained a copy of Wallace's July 23 letter to Truman and intended to print it. Ross notified Wallace, who discovered that the State Department had been the source of the leak. When other reporters found out about the letter, they insisted that the White House release it to everybody. Without consulting Truman, Ross advised Wallace to distribute copies of the letter to prevent Pearson from getting an exclusive story. Wallace agreed. Meanwhile, presidential advisor Clark Clifford had persuaded Truman that he should not permit the letter to be released to the press, even though Pearson was going to publish it. Giving out the letter or allowing Wallace to do so, he argued, would indicate the President's "tacit approval" of it and cause a "stink . . . ten times worse than the New York speech." Ross immediately called Wallace to stop distribution of the letter, but the Commerce Department had already released it. The July 23 statement appeared in newspapers across the country on September 18, further embarrassing Truman because it proved that Wallace had made his views on Soviet-American relations clear to the President weeks before the New York speech.[15]

The same day that the letter was published, Wallace met personally with Truman for the first time since the controversy over the speech began. The conference lasted over two hours and was amicable throughout. Truman remarked that he had suffered "more sleepless nights than at any time" since the 1944 Democratic convention. He said that he was more to blame for the crisis than Wallace, and that Byrnes "had been giving him hell." The Commerce Secretary reported that his mail was running five to one in favor of his speech. "The people are afraid that the 'get tough with Russia' policy is leading us to war," he declared. Then he added: "You, yourself, as Harry Truman really believed in my speech." The President neither agreed nor disagreed, but responded: "Jimmie Byrnes says I am pulling the rug out from under him." He asked Wallace to refrain from making speeches dealing with foreign policy so that the United States could "present a united front abroad."[16]

Wallace was reluctant to agree to remain silent on foreign affairs. He was particularly anxious to correct the impression that he favored a divided world and to reaffirm his commitment to one world. He suggested that in future speeches he specifically state that he spoke only for himself and not for the administration. But Truman insisted that Wallace "quit talking on foreign affairs." He urged him to continue to make speeches on domestic issues, but Wallace refused unless he could also discuss foreign policy. Eventually, they agreed that Wallace would desist from any public statements until after the Paris Foreign Ministers Conference.[17]

Wallace warned the President that his policies were antagonizing Russia, and that in twenty or thirty years, when the Soviets were much stronger, they would not hesitate to use the atomic bomb against the United States. Truman denied that he was following a "get tough with Russia" approach. He said that "he had always liked Stalin" and that he intended to ask Congress for a loan to the Soviet Union. Wallace pointed out that Congress would never approve a Russian loan without demanding political concessions, but Truman insisted that "he could put it through." He contended that the United States lacked sufficient military strength to act aggressively toward the Soviet Union even if it so desired. But the President also remarked during the course of the meeting that the Washington Naval Conference of 1922 had been the main cause of World War II. Wallace disagreed, arguing that economic factors, not disarmament, had led to war. Privately, he noted that Truman was "a big Army and a big Navy man. . . . He believes in military force because of his experience with the Army in World War I."[18]

A throng of reporters waited impatiently for the meeting between Wallace and Truman to end, and a large crowd gathered outside the White House gates. When Wallace emerged, he read a short statement on which he and Truman had agreed. He announced that he had a "detailed and friendly discussion" with the President and that he would make no public statements of any kind until after the Paris conference. In response to questions, he declared that he "absolutely" stood on his Madison Square Garden speech and that the President was "very confident about peace with Russia." He disclosed that he did not intend to resign from the cabinet, and remarked: "Everything's lovely." When Wallace got back to the Commerce Department, he told a group of subordinates about his conference with Truman and praised the President's sincerity. Aides described Wallace as "utterly satisfied with the situation" and unperturbed by the continuing controversy.[19]

Truman, who was receiving angry reactions to Wallace's July 23 letter, was considerably less content. The morning the letter was published, Bernard Baruch protested bitterly to the President about its attack on the American plan for international control of atomic energy. He denounced Wallace's "irresponsible statements" and suggested that the Commerce Secretary had gotten his information "from somebody who was trying to preach Red doctrine." The same day, Secretary of War Robert Patterson and Secretary of the Navy James Forrestal heatedly denied that their departments or any military leaders had considered a "preventive war" against Russia, as Wallace had charged in the letter.[20]

The following day, September 19, Truman talked by teletype with Byrnes, who was dissatisfied that Wallace had agreed only to stop discussing foreign policy for a limited time. He told the President that when the Commerce Secretary began to speak out again, it would create confusion about America's foreign policy. Byrnes said that he would rather resign as Secretary of State than constantly "be confronted with statements of Mr. Wallace in conflict with views expressed by me." He issued no ultimatums, but commented: "I do not think that any man who professes loyalty to you would so seriously impair your prestige and the prestige of the government with the nations of the world." Truman assured Byrnes of his "wholehearted support" and promised that he would make his position clear the following morning. The President faced a difficult dilemma. With elections less than two months away, he hesitated to openly disavow Wallace's ideas and alienate the left wing of the Democratic party. Yet Wallace's foreign policy views and his insistence on expressing them posed a threat to the integrity and credibility of the Truman administration's diplomatic position. The vigorous complaints of his advisors, added to his own exasperation with Wallace for talking with newsmen and Commerce Department aides about the previous day's meeting, convinced the President to resolve the dilemma by dismissing Wallace from the cabinet, regardless of the political consequences.[21]

The earthy, practical Truman never had understood his idealistic, contemplative Secretary of Commerce. A week of strain and unmitigated controversy had not sharpened his perspicacity or disposed him to be charitable. Wallace was, he wrote in his diary on September 19, "a pacifist 100 per cent. He wants us to disband our armed forces, give Russia our atomic secrets and trust a bunch of adventurers in the Kremlin Politbureau." The President added: "I do not understand a 'dreamer' like that. The German-American Bund under Fritz Kuhn was not half so dangerous.'' Still in an overwrought state of mind the following morning, Truman dispatched an intemperate letter to Wallace, asking for his resignation. The Commerce Secretary, who had no reason to suspect he might be discharged, was stunned. Nevertheless, he complied graciously with the request. In order to spare the President unnecessary embarrassment, Wallace returned Truman's indiscreet letter to the White House, where it was destroyed. He also talked cordially with the President by telephone. Wallace was certain that Byrnes, either directly or indirectly, had persuaded Truman to dismiss him.[22]

Truman announced his decision on the morning of September 20, shortly after his telephone conversation with Wallace. He told newsmen that ''the government of the United States must stand as a unit in its relations with the rest of the world.'' He could not allow the ''fundamental conflict'' between Wallace's views and those of the administration ''to jeopardize our position in relation to other countries.'' The President reaffirmed his ''complete confidence'' in Secretary Byrnes. The same evening, Wallace read a statement carried by all major radio networks. ''Winning the peace is more important than high office,'' he declared. ''The success or failure of our foreign policy will mean the difference between life and death for our children and grandchildren.'' Although he did not want to undercut the American negotiators at Paris, he said, he no longer felt constrained to remain silent on foreign affairs. Wallace was anxious to clear up the ''widespread misunderstanding'' his New York speech had created. He reminded his listeners that he had begun ''talking about 'one world' more than fifteen years ago,'' and insisted that he still believed that ''we cannot have peace except in 'one world.''' He reiterated that he opposed ''all types of imperialism,'' whether American, British, or Russian, and affirmed his commitment to the rights of small countries. Wallace vowed to ''carry on the fight for peace'' as a private citizen, and hoped that, by presenting his opinions to the American people, he would stir a ''full and open debate'' about U.S. foreign policy.[23]

Most Americans applauded Truman's decision to dismiss Wallace. Senator Robert M. LaFollette was ''gratified,'' and Senator Robert A. Taft did not ''see how the President could do anything else.'' Harry Lundeberg, president of the Seafarers International Union, contended that Truman ''should have fired that Commy-loving Cabinet member long ago.'' George S. Messersmith, American

Ambassador to Argentina, denounced Wallace as "fanatic and ill-informed," and reported that his proposal for spheres of influence had aroused criticism in Latin America. George F. Kennan denied that the United States could win the trust of the Soviet Union. "If Mr. Wallace thinks . . . that the golden touch of his particular personality and the warmth of his sympathy for the cause of Russian communism would modify to some important degree the actions of the Soviet Government," Kennan argued, "he is . . . flying in the face of some of the most basic and unshakable Russian realities." A public opinion poll taken on September 25, 1946, showed that of those Americans who had followed the dispute between Byrnes and Wallace, 70 percent thought Truman was right to discharge the Commerce Secretary; only 22 percent thought he was wrong. While 78 percent of those surveyed believed the United States should follow Byrnes' approach in foreign affairs, only 16 percent favored Wallace's ideas.[24]

Wallace retained the support of the majority of liberals. In Max Lerner's opinion, he "emerged from the ordeal a more massive figure than he ever has been, with more distinctly Presidential stature than any man in public life today." The National Citizens Political Action Committee called Wallace's ouster "a blow to the progressive forces of the country and to the cause of peace." The *New Republic* commented that "Harry Truman has proved himself an even weaker leader than most people had estimated."[25]

Wallace did not regret leaving the administration. He confided to an old friend: "While I didn't plan it that way, the whole situation worked out miraculously. I don't see how I could have bought more for less. Therefore, I am very, very happy." He reported that he had received about 8000 letters, 85 percent of which supported his position. "To read this mail renews one's faith in the American people," he wrote. Wallace thought that the recent controversy had contributed to peace while reducing the possibility of war. He was, he said, "happy to rest on the verdict of history."[26]

One person who was not happy with the outcome of the Wallace controversy was Bernard Baruch. He was distressed that the administration had made no effort to refute Wallace's criticisms of the American plan for international control of atomic energy in the July 23 letter. On September 24, he wrote Truman a long letter, disputing Wallace's arguments point by point. Baruch denied Wallace's assertion that the transitional stages for implementing international control gave the United States an unfair advantage, and told Truman that Wallace's statement displayed "complete ignorance of the United States position." He denied that the Soviets had proposed a practical program for regulation of atomic energy or shown any inclination to negotiate seriously.[27]

Determined that Wallace correct his "various misstatements of fact," Baruch requested a meeting with him. Wallace and his former aide in the Commerce Department, Philip Hauser, conferred with Baruch and his assistants on September 27. Hauser, who had helped Wallace prepare the July 23 letter, admitted that most of it had been written before Baruch presented his plan to the United Nations, and that the criticisms of the American proposal had not been carefully considered. He contended, however, that the wording regarding the matter of stages was "ambiguous" and left it unclear that the United States did not intend to exercise "unfettered discretion" in revealing atomic information. Baruch and his assistants, after a lengthy discussion, convinced Hauser and Wallace that the American plan assured that the timing and sequence of the transitional stages would be a part of a "single package" in the final agreement, which would be "fair, equitable, and applicable" to all countries. After further discussion, Wallace also expressed "full accord" with Baruch's position on the veto issue. But he argued that the major problem of winning the trust of the Soviet Union remained unresolved, and suggested that the United States should stop manufacturing atomic bombs to induce the Soviets to accept the American proposal. As Wallace left the meeting, he conceded that he had not been "fully posted" on the Baruch plan. Hauser stayed behind to help draft a statement suitable to both Baruch and Wallace.[28]

When Wallace saw the statement that Hauser and Baruch's aides proposed, he declined to accept it. He was willing to admit his errors concerning some of the technical details of the Baruch plan, but he refused to give it a blanket endorsement. The "central issue" of his July 23 letter remained unsettled. Wallace argued that two fundamental questions prevented agreements on international control of atomic energy. The most important involved whether or not the United States should continue to build and stockpile atomic bombs "during the period of negotiation and the transition to full international control." The other related to Russia's refusal to accept internationally supervised inspection of atomic energy projects. Only when "mutual trust and confidence" between the United States and the Soviet Union was established could those issues be resolved. Wallace believed that since the United States possessed the atomic bomb, it should take the initiative, "by deed as well as by word," to forestall an atomic armaments race.[29]

Incensed by Wallace's intransigence, Baruch issued a public statement denouncing him for "creating confusion and division among our people." He rebuked Wallace for failing to admit his errors, deliberately ignoring a proposed letter of Wallace's that acknowledged the misconceptions of his July 23 letter. "You have disappointed me sorely," Baruch told the former Commerce Secretary. "You have no monopoly on the desire for peace. I have given thirty years of my life to the search for peace and there are many others whose aims have been the same." Wallace responded with an equally acrimonious statement, attacking Baruch for failing "to distinguish the fundamental, critical issues from their purely procedural aspects." He demanded: "When are you going to get down to business, Mr. Baruch?" He accused Baruch of trying to "intimidate" him "into issuing a statement that would be interpreted as full support of his position."[30]

The feud between Wallace and Baruch redounded to neither's credit. Baruch seemed more concerned with soothing his bruised ego than advancing the cause of international control of atomic energy. The *Washington Post* contended that Wallace's objections had forced Baruch to clarify the question of transitional stages and restate "the American position much more reasonably." It worried that if Baruch became "so zealous for self-vindication that he cannot yield on any aspect of the plan which he has proposed, then the prospect for an atomic development agreement is very slim indeed." Wallace's careless criticisms of the Baruch plan in his July 23 letter, made without fully checking the facts, weakened his position and undermined his credibility. The great majority of Americans continued to support the Baruch plan, and some people who had sympathized with Wallace in the dispute with Byrnes did not endorse his attack on the American proposal for regulating atomic energy.[31]

In October 1946, Wallace accepted a position as editor of the *New Republic*. It would, he wrote, give him "the opportunity of saying exactly what I think at a time when a bi-partisan bloc mouthing the phrase 'One World' is really dividing the world into two armed camps." He expressed confidence that "millions of progressive-minded Americans" would support his quest for a "peaceful century of the common man." Wallace was optimistic about the prospects for the future. He had experienced "some good fights in the past," he stated, "but the best are yet to come." He believed there were "great things in the offing," but first, "we have to go through some difficult times politically and otherwise."[32]

Before assuming his duties with the *New Republic,* Wallace embarked on a speaking tour to campaign for liberal Democratic candidates in the upcoming November elections. He urged America to quit manufacturing atomic bombs in order to dispel Russian fears and make an international agreement on atomic energy possible. "It's the old principle of parking your guns outside while talking it over inside," he declared. He hailed Soviet Foreign Minister Molotov's proposal for general disarmament of both conventional and atomic weapons as a "daring challenge." But he warned that such a plan would not be acceptable to the "Russia baiters" and those who favored immediate war with the Soviet Union. "Ever since Churchill spoke in Missouri last summer," Wallace complained, "there has been a veritable wave of Soviet-baiting in this country."[33]

The way to combat communism, Wallace maintained, was to ensure world peace and abundance. "Communism can thrive only on scarcity and inequity," he wrote. "Atomic energy properly applied can mean the disappearance of both." A war with Russia would make "the triumph of Communism inevitable" by creating the conditions on which communism flourished. Wallace feared that Truman was "too much in the hands of the military." But the large crowds that turned out during his speaking tour convinced him "that people . . . are deeply concerned about what is going on in the world. They do not want a third world war, and they do not believe that Secretary Byrnes and his aides will assure us of lasting peace." His faith in the American people reaffirmed, Wallace began his career as editor of the *New Republic* with a buoyant, hopeful spirit.[34]

NOTES

1. Alonzo L. Hamby, *Beyond the New Deal: Harry S. Truman and American Liberalism* (New York: Columbia University Press, 1973), pp. 121-29; Norman D. Markowitz, *The Rise and Fall of the People's Century: Henry A. Wallace and American Liberalism, 1941-1948* (New York:

Free Press, 1973), pp. 181-82; Curtis D. MacDougall, *Gideon's Army* (New York: Marzani and Munsell, 1965), Vol. I, pp. 59-60.

2. *Diary,* September 10, 1946 (misdated September 12), p. 612; Wallace diary note for September 10, 1946 in Wallace to Arthur Hays Sulzberger, October 1, 1955, Henry A. Wallace Papers, University of Iowa.

3. Wallace phone conversation with Dick Hippelheuser, September 10, 1946, Wallace Papers; "Conversations with Secretary Wallace," September 12, 1946, Bernard L. Gladieux Papers, Truman Library; Louis Bean interview, Columbia Oral History Collection; Wallace to Richard C. Patterson, September 12, 1946, Box 1058, File 104251, RG 40, NA; "Wallace to Truman to Trouble," *Newsweek,* 28 (September 23, 1946): 27.

The meeting between Wallace and Truman on September 10 has been a subject of controversy. Truman claimed in his *Memoirs* that he did not even look at the speech. See Truman, *Memoirs: Year of Decisions* (Garden City, N.Y.: Doubleday and Co., 1955), Vol. I, p. 557. His defenders have asserted that Truman glanced hastily at the speech but did not read it carefully. See, for example, Hamby, *Beyond the New Deal,* p. 128, and Cabell Phillips, *The Truman Presidency* (New York: Macmillan Co., 1966), p. 150. Wallace, on the other hand, insisted that Truman had read the speech page by page and expressed complete agreement with it. His diary notes for the day of the conference with the President, and his remarks to colleagues before he delivered the speech conclusively prove his case. Certainly he had no reason to prevaricate before the speech, while Truman had compelling reasons to do so after it caused an uproar and considerable embarrassment to him. For a well-argued defense of Wallace, see Markowitz, *People's Century,* pp. 182-83.

4. Hamby, *Beyond the New Deal,* p. 129; *New York Times,* September 13, 1946.

5. Wallace speech at Madison Square Garden rally, as delivered, September 12, 1946, Wallace Papers; *New York Times,* September 13, 1946.

6. Wallace speech, September 12, 1946, Wallace Papers.

7. Ibid.

8. Ibid.

9. Ibid.

10. David Lawrence, "Who Speaks for America?" *United States News,* 21 (September 20, 1946): 29; "Foreign Policy of Mr. Wallace," ibid., 21 (September 27, 1946): 32; "What I Meant to Say," *Time,* 48 (September 23, 1946): 22.

11. "Wallace—A World Leader," *New Republic,* 115 (September 23, 1946): 339; "The Wallace Speech," *Nation,* 163 (September 21, 1946): 312; "Foreign Policy of Mr. Wallace," *United States News,* p. 31.

12. *Des Moines Register,* September 16, 1946; *New York Times,* September 13, 1946; Arthur H. Vandenberg, Jr., ed., *The Private Papers of*

Senator Vandenberg (Boston: Houghton Mifflin Co., 1952), pp. 300-301; James F. Byrnes, *Speaking Frankly* (New York: Harper and Brothers, 1947), p. 239.

13. *Diary,* September 16, 1946, pp. 613-14; *New York Times,* September 15, 1946; *PM,* September 16, 1946; "What I Meant to Say," *Time,* p. 22.

14. Wallace to William F. Ogburn, September 17, 1946, Box 1058, File 104251, RG 40, NA; *New York Times,* September 17, 1946; *Baltimore Sun,* September 17, 1946; Byrnes, *Speaking Frankly,* p. 240; George Curry, *James F. Byrnes* (New York: Cooper Square Publishers, 1965), pp. 262-64.

15. *Diary,* September 16, 17, 1946, pp. 615, 617; Wallace phone conversation with Charles Ross, September 17, 1946, Wallace Papers; George M. Elsey memorandum, "L'Affaire Wallace," September 17, 1946, George M. Elsey Papers, Truman Library.

16. *Diary,* September 18, 1946, p. 618.

17. Ibid., pp. 620-25.

18. Ibid. Truman's recollection of the meeting differs from Wallace's record made at the time. Wallace, the President recalled, "talked about the beauty of peace" and Russia's desire for peace, prompting Truman's fears that he "would lend himself to the more sinister ends of the Reds." The President thought that by retaining Wallace in the cabinet, he could "put some check on his activities." Truman contended that Wallace agreed to make no statements to the press about the conference other than the brief announcement that he authorized. Wallace mentioned no such agreement. See Truman, *Year of Decisions,* p. 558.

19. "Conversations with Secretary Wallace," September 18, 1946, Gladieux Papers; *PM,* September 19, 1946; *New York Times,* September 19, 20, 1946.

20. *Foreign Relations: 1946,* Vol. I, pp. 932-34; *New York Times,* September 19, 1946.

21. James F. Byrnes, *All in One Lifetime* (New York: Harper and Brothers, 1958), pp. 374-76; Truman, *Year of Decisions,* pp. 558-60.

22. William Hillman, ed., *Mr. President* (New York: Farrar, Straus, and Young, 1952), p. 128; Truman, *Year of Decisions,* p. 560; "Conversations with Secretary Wallace," September 20, 1946, Gladieux Papers; *Diary,* p. 629; Phillips, *The Truman Presidency,* p. 153.

23. *Washington Post,* September 21, 1946.

24. *New York Times,* September 21, 1946; George S. Messersmith to James F. Byrnes, September 21, 1946, 811.002/9-2146, RG 59, NA; George F. Kennan speech, " 'Trust' As a Factor in International Relations," October 1, 1946, James V. Forrestal Papers, Princeton University Library, Princeton, N.J.; Hadley Cantril and Mildred Strunk, *Public Opinion, 1935-1946* (Princeton: Princeton University Press, 1951), p. 964.

25. *PM,* September 22, 23, 1946; "The Liberals and '46," *New Republic,* 115 (September 30, 1946), p. 396; Hamby, *Beyond the New Deal,* p. 134.

26. Wallace to Donald Murphy, September 28, 1946, Wallace to Max Lerner, September 28, 1946, Wallace to Buford Tynes, October 23, 1946, Wallace Papers.

27. Bernard M. Baruch to Truman, September 24, 1946, Bernard M. Baruch Papers, Princeton University Library.

28. *Foreign Relations: 1946,* Vol. I, pp. 937, 939-43.

29. "Statement Proposed by Mr. Hauser," September 27, 1946, "Alternate Statement Proposed by Mr. Wallace," September 30, 1946, "Proposed Wallace Letter," October 2, 1946, Baruch Papers.

30. Baruch to Wallace, October 2, 1946 (issued as a public statement), "Wallace's Reply to Baruch Charges," October 3, 1946, Baruch Papers.

31. *Washington Post,* October 4, 5, 1946; Albin E. Johnson to Baruch, October 28, 1946, Baruch Papers; Joseph P. Lash, *Eleanor: The Years Alone* (New York: W. W. Norton, 1972), p. 89.

32. Henry A. Wallace, "To Edit *New Republic,*" *New Republic,* 115 (October 21, 1946): 497-99; Wallace to William Thatcher, October 7, 1946, Wallace Papers; Wallace to Jo Davidson, October 11, 1946, Jo Davidson Papers, Library of Congress.

33. *New York Times,* October 29, November 5, 1946; *Chicago News,* November 2, 1946; *Seattle Times,* October 28, 1946.

34. Wallace to Gil Harrison, October 11, 1946, Wallace to Frank Thone, October 16, 1946, Wallace to Robert Stuart, November 13, 1946, Wallace to Anita McCormick Blaine, November 19, 1946, Wallace to Dan Wallace, December 28, 1946, Wallace Papers.

12

Year of Hope: 1947

Henry Wallace's first editorials in the *New Republic* reflected his optimism about world conditions. "The international situation today is unbelievably better than it seemed to be last summer," he declared. "My frank speaking of last September and the international clamor aroused thereby may have helped to force the extremists on both sides to modify their positions." He was convinced that the people of the United States, Great Britain, and the Soviet Union wanted peace, and he argued that the Soviets had shown their willingness to meet the United States halfway by advancing a proposal for general disarmament. If the United States reciprocated by ceasing to produce and stockpile atomic bombs, a UN disarmament agreement could be achieved. Once that was accomplished, the countries of the world could cooperate to eradicate the "fundamental causes of war." Lasting peace and security, Wallace maintained, depended on raising living standards throughout the world. He called on America, Russia, and Britain to work together to eliminate illiteracy, starvation, and disease, and to modernize the underdeveloped areas of the world. "Technologically, it can be done. Morally, it must be done," he wrote. "Practically, it is cheaper than war and the only alternative to war."[1]

Wallace hailed the selection of George C. Marshall to replace James Byrnes as Secretary of State. "The appointment of General Marshall," he wrote, "lends good hope in the field of foreign affairs." In an open letter to the new secretary, he argued that the "basic problem" in American foreign policy was "to adjust the attitude of our country to a world that is in full flood of change." Throughout the world, people were striving to build a new order "because the old order has brought upon them poverty, disaster and war." By attempting to uphold the status quo, the United States was permitting the Soviets to pose as the champions of anticolonialism and as the "only guarantors against hunger and war." Wallace hoped that Marshall would infuse a new dynamism in American policies. He also hoped the secretary could establish a close working relationship with Stalin so that differences between the United States and the Soviet Union could be settled. Wallace blamed both countries for existing tensions. He thought some Soviet official should explain to Stalin that large numbers of Americans, not just reactionaries, feared that the Soviet Union was "intent on dominating Europe and eventually the world." Wallace believed that if mutual misapprehensions and distrust were counteracted by friendly discussions, the upcoming Moscow Foreign Ministers Conference could take important strides toward enduring peace.[2]

Despite his optimism about the chances for peace, Wallace remained disturbed by "the dangerous drift toward war." He denounced Americans who favored war with the Soviet Union and attacked Churchill's pleas for Anglo-American collaboration against Russia as "a modern crusade as fantastic as any of those led by Richard the Lion-Hearted.'" He feared that the United States would "squander its greatness in propping up corrupt and reactionary regimes as supposed safeguards against communism." Wallace worried that the Republican Congress would raise tariffs, reject reciprocal trade, refuse to assist backward countries, and repeat the disasters of the 1920s. But above all, he was alarmed by the growing influence of the military. He acknowledged the need for adequate defense preparations, but he was gravely disturbed that military contracts awarded to universities and private industries would imperil freedom and lead toward a "police state." "American militarists are acting more determinedly to dominate our universities, our scientists, and our civilian affairs," Wallace wrote. He warned that an atomic arms race would give the military, and "their good friends among the larger corporations," unprecedented power. "Down this road lies American fascism—less brutal but infinitely more powerful in its ultimate compulsions than anything that Mussolini fostered."[3]

On March 12, 1947, President Truman appeared before Congress and enunciated what soon became known as the Truman Doctrine. He asked Congress to appropriate $400 million of economic and military aid for Greece and Turkey. Those countries, he said, were in dire need of American assistance to preserve their independence and repel the threat of totalitarianism being imposed from without. Truman made no specific references to the Soviet Union, but he denounced "coercion and intimidation, in violation of the Yalta Agreement," in Eastern Europe. He described a fundamental ideological conflict between two contrasting ways of life, and declared that "it must be the policy of the United States to support free peoples who are resisting attempted subjugation by armed minorities or by outside pressures." The President contended that the crisis in Greece and Turkey demanded immediate attention, and that the United Nations was "not in a position to extend help of the kind that is required."[4]

The Truman Doctrine represented the antithesis of Henry Wallace's vision of the postwar world. He bitterly attacked the President's speech in a nationally broadcast radio address on March 13. Instead of a century of the common man, he asserted, Truman envisioned "generations of want and war" and had "summoned in a century of fear." Wallace assailed Truman's proposed military aid program "as a down payment on an unlimited expenditure aimed at opposing communist expansion." He acknowledged that Greece badly needed assistance, but he contended that Truman's plan was ill-conceived and self-defeating. America should send technical assistance for reconstruction of wartorn, poverty-stricken countries—food and plows rather than tanks and guns. By supporting corrupt, undemocratic regimes in the name of anticommunism, the United States would be undertaking a futile effort to resist change and would become "the most hated nation in the world." The way to combat communism, Wallace argued, was to "give the common man all over the world something better." By offering "unconditional aid to King George of Greece," Truman was "acting as the best salesman communism ever had."[5]

Wallace also denounced Truman's program because it would bypass the United Nations and antagonize the Soviet Union. Instead of fostering cooperation and building one unified world, it would undercut the United Nations—"our great hope for peace"—and divide the world into hostile camps. If the administration were interested in economic aid to wartorn countries, Wallace asked his radio audience, why did it "allow the United Nations Relief and Rehabilitation Administration to die?" He pointed out that a UN commission was investigating conditions in Greece, and urged that the United States follow its recommendations rather than acting unilaterally. He upbraided Truman for "telling the Soviet leaders that we are preparing for eventual war." The President, Wallace said, had scuttled the Moscow conference by delivering his speech just two days after it opened. "That which I feared when I wrote President Truman last July has come upon us," he declared. "Only the American people fully aroused and promptly acting can prevent disaster."[6]

Wallace continued to assault the Truman Doctrine in editorials and speeches. He accused the President of creating a false atmosphere of impending crisis and "whipping up anti-Communist hysteria" to win backing for his proposal. He found Truman's March 12 message vague and unconvincing—"a mixture of unsupported assertions, sermonizing and exhortation." As an alternative to Truman's program, Wallace advocated a massive long-term program of economic assistance to Greece and Eastern Europe, administered by the United Nations. Speaking before a packed house at Madison Square Garden on March 31, 1947, he declared: "The world cries out, not for an American crusade in the name of hatred and fear of communism, but for a world crusade in the name of the brotherhood of man." The way to assure peace, Wallace asserted, was to build a strong United Nations. Pointing out that its budget was millions of dollars less than that of the New York City Sanitation Department, he pleaded for American economic support for a UN program of world reconstruction. "If the United Nations is untested, let us test it," he cried. "If the United Nations is weak, let us strengthen it. . . . If we reject this course, the United Nations will crumble and man's hope will perish."[7]

The optimism Wallace had displayed early in the year about the course of world events was shaken by the Truman Doctrine. Although he had been worried about "the dangerous drift toward war," he now talked of "the frightening march toward war." He decried the President's newly established loyalty program for government employees, and predicted that it would lead to a "witch hunt." "Hatred and violence abroad, hatred and fear at home will be the fruits of the Truman Doctrine," he exclaimed. Still, Wallace did not despair. Many liberals shared his reservations about the program, and he hoped that Americans would rise up in angry protest. "President Truman has not spoken for the American ideal. It is now the turn of the American people to speak," he wrote in the *New Republic.* "There is opportunity for great good as well as great evil in this hour."[8]

In January 1947, Wallace had accepted an invitation from Kingsley Martin, editor of the British journal *New Statesman and Nation,* to visit England. The former Vice-President flew to London on April 7. In a series of public speeches, he attacked the Truman Doctrine before large, enthusiastic audiences. Wallace denied that communism could be fought by military means. "Communism is an idea for ending poverty and exploitation," he stated. "It can only be made superfluous by a better idea." The problem with Truman's program was that it bore "no real relation to the needs of the world." The people of the world wanted technological assistance to raise their living standards rather than tanks and guns to undertake an anticommunist crusade. Moreover, Wallace argued that the United States lacked the power "to spread herself effectively over the entire world" in an effort to stop communism. He cautioned supporters of the Truman Doctrine that they were "undertaking an unlimited commitment without recognizing the responsibilities it involves." An attempt to prevent the spread of communism by military measures would be tremendously costly and ultimately futile. Wallace pointed to the "great national awakening" taking place in Asia and other former colonial states, and warned: "This new nationalism will turn to communism and look to the Soviet Union as its ally if the United States declares that this is a century of power politics rather than the century of the common man." Throughout his tour of Britain, he reiterated his plea for a strong United Nations and a massive program for world reconstruction financed through the International Bank. Wallace denounced Truman for betraying the legacy of Roosevelt, but he affirmed that the spirit of the late President was "alive in millions of Americans" and would "rise again."[9]

Wallace's speeches in Britain caused an uproar in the United States. Senator J. William Fulbright thought one speech sounded as if it "were written in the Kremlin," while Representative Mendel Rivers contended that Wallace spoke for only "a small bunch of pinks" and suggested that his passport be revoked. The *New York Times* denounced Wallace's "extravagant and excited charges," and the *Philadelphia Inquirer* described him as the "loud-mouthed No. 1 propagandist for Communist Russia in America." Walter Lippmann wrote that Wallace had been a "good and faithful public servant" so long as he was "protected, led, guided, and disciplined. . . . But when he had to face the realities of our time directly, . . . the reality was too much for him." Senator Vandenberg said it was "a shocking thing when an American citizen goes abroad to speak against his own government," and asked Truman to rebuke him publicly. The President withheld public comment, but privately he described Wallace's speeches as "wild statements." Attorney General Tom Clark spoke for the administration by declaring that Wallace was perpetrating "a most cruel falsehood" that displayed "an utter lack of understanding or appreciation of the American way of life."[10]

Some people spoke out in defense of Wallace, but their voices generally were drowned by the tumult. Eleanor Roosevelt pointed out in her newspaper column that he was trying to prevent "a two-world catastrophe" and that Britons had not "jumped on Winston Churchill" for his Iron Curtain speech, "which certainly was not exactly in line with what his government was saying at the time." Privately, however, she did not think it "wise for Mr. Wallace to be making the kind of speeches he is making . . . in foreign countries." She believed that her husband would have tried to strengthen the United Nations, but doubted "if he would want to do it in just the way that Mr. Wallace has found necessary." *Christian Century* regretted that hardly anybody seemed interested in evaluating the merits of Wallace's arguments. It contended that although Wallace did "not have *all* the truth," he did "have *some* of the truth." It noted that Congress was "seething mad" at the former Vice-President, and feared that it was rushing to approve Truman's request for aid to Greece and Turkey to spite Wallace. "To commit the United States to the heaviest political, economic and military commitments in its history as a means of spanking one private individual looks like an astonishingly childish performance," the magazine editorialized. Yet many observers asserted that Wallace's opposition had rallied congressional support for Truman's proposal. Representative Kenneth Keating stated that "Wallace has done more to advance that cause than perhaps anyone else," and an unnamed Democrat remarked: "The sooner we pass this bill, the sooner we will answer Mr. Wallace."[11]

Wallace had often been sharply criticized throughout his public career, but the attacks on his speeches in Britain exhibited a new level of ferocity. He publicly admitted that he was surprised at the intensity of the protests, and friends told newsmen that he was "jolted." Wallace replied to his critics by stating that they displayed "a hysterical state of mind" and that their indictments would be legitimate only if the United States were at war. Wallace was indiscreet in attacking American foreign policy in another country, but his criticisms were generally moderate and reasonable, and hardly seemed to justify the virulence of the denunciation he suffered. It underscored the extent to which Americans had closed ranks behind a firm position toward the Soviet Union, and indicated the degree of intolerance for anyone who challenged the assumptions on which those policies were based. Nevertheless, Wallace pledged to "go on speaking out for peace wherever men will listen until the end of my days."[12]

After leaving Britain, Wallace made brief stops in Norway, Sweden, and Denmark. In Copenhagen, he denied that World War II had resulted from America's failure to arm, asserting that it had stemmed from the country's failure to act as a creditor state and assume its proper economic relationship with the world. He declared that "a harmonious economic approach is the road to peace." He pursued that theme after arriving in Paris on April 23, 1947. Wallace proposed a large American loan to the Soviet Union as a first step toward easing world tensions. Although he opposed "political strings" on loans, he thought a loan to Russia could be tied to settlements on Germany and other areas. He contended that if the United States extended low-interest credit to the Soviets, they would no longer need reparations from Germany, and an agreement could be achieved. Wallace also urged that the United States engage in direct discussions with Stalin. When newsmen reminded him that Secretary Marshall had just been in Moscow, he retorted: "Do you think he could dissipate distrust with the men who surround him?"

When Wallace returned to the United States in late April, he accused the press of distorting his speeches and statements in Europe, and producing "a fearsome-looking character." But he maintained that he had "forced an increased discussion of Truman's proposals," and that it was "plain that an awareness of the crisis is reaching the consciousness of the American people."[13]

Shortly after his return to the United States, Wallace took his case to the American people. In a nationwide speaking tour, he outlined his "constructive alternative" to the Truman Doctrine. Wallace proposed that America underwrite a $150 billion spending program over a period of ten years, administered by the United Nations, that would restore wartorn areas and raise living standards throughout the world. He admitted that his plan involved sacrifice and enormous costs, but argued that it would be "far less than the cost of continuous spiritual warfare backed up by military adventures in every corner of the world." The Truman Doctrine, he asserted, was "the single most destructive policy ever announced in our 170-year history as a nation." Denouncing bipartisanship in foreign policy as "undemocratic, one-party government," Wallace accused the administration of demonstrating a "spirit of meanness and selfishness and shortsightedness and fear" that betrayed "every principle for which we fought in war."[14]

The speaking tour was tremendously successful. Wallace addressed large, enthusiastic crowds wherever he went. In Chicago, 22,000 people came to hear him, and 25,000 filled Gilmore Stadium in Los Angeles. The University of California at Berkeley denied him permission to use campus buildings, but 10,000 students listened to him speak on a street corner. *Time* magazine conceded that Wallace's audiences consisted not only of left-wingers and idealistic students, but also of "thousands of ordinary, bewildered citizens." Even more remarkable than the size of the crowds was that they paid an admission price ranging from 60 cents to $3.60 to attend a Wallace rally. They usually got their money's worth. At a meeting in Chicago on May 14, 1947, the thousands of people who jammed an indoor stadium were aroused to an emotional pitch by a series of speakers, comedian Zero Mostel, and singer Paul Robeson. Then a persuasive auctioneer successfully solicited cash contributions that augmented the substantial amount already received from admission charges. After two hours of preliminaries, the crowd began to chant feverishly,

"We want Wallace." As the former Vice-President walked to the podium, the house lights dimmed and a single spotlight focused on him. The crowd applauded furiously for a full six minutes.[15]

One newsman who covered Wallace's speaking tour confided to Claude Pepper that he "never had an experience like this in my career as a reporter." Amazed that large numbers of people paid to hear "a man without even any fire," he concluded that there was "a lot more concern on the worker level about our foreign policy and domestic trends than anyone in Washington realizes." Gael Sullivan of the Democratic National Committee was deeply alarmed by Wallace's appeal. He believed that Wallace had "captured the imagination of a strong segment of the American public" and concluded that "action should be taken either to appease Wallace or pull the rug on him."[16]

Wallace ended his speaking tour in Washington, D.C., with a discourse on American-Soviet relations. It was his first public appearance in the capital since leaving the cabinet, and he announced that he was pleased to return to the seat of "the greatest Government on earth." He was gratified, he said, by the popular response to his speeches, indicating that "everywhere . . . the people demand peace." Wallace denied the "widespread belief" that he refused to criticize Soviet behavior. But he contended that denouncing Russian actions would not further the cause of peace and stated that he was "primarily concerned with influencing the policies I can help to change." He maintained that the United States was needlessly antagonizing the Soviets and "paving the way to war." Russia, he declared, required peace to rebuild from the devastation of war and earnestly wanted harmonious relations with the United States. Wallace attacked writers who cited Stalin's statements of the 1920s that capitalism and communism could not exist together peacefully. He pointed out that the Soviet leader recently had held interviews with British journalist Alexander Werth, Elliott Roosevelt, and Harold Stassen that "clearly indicated" his desire for peace and cooperation with the West. "I can see no legitimate reason," Wallace argued, "for believing Stalin's statements a quarter of a century ago and doubting his statements in the past six months."[17]

Wallace admitted that Soviet actions had contributed to world tensions, but he maintained that the United States should acknowledge its share of the blame. The only way to assure peace and build a strong United Nations, he believed, was to achieve understanding between America and Russia. He urged Truman and Marshall to meet directly with Stalin and Molotov to work out differences between their two countries. Then, and only then, could agreement be reached on secondary issues such as Germany. Wallace repeated his call for economic aid to the Soviets, which would not only ease frictions, but also provide an important market for American exports. He further suggested that the United States "propose a complete ban on international traffic in weapons of war" to demonstrate its good will and test Russian intentions. Wallace conceded that Congress would never approve economic assistance to the Soviet Union or an agreement to stop sending arms abroad. But he argued that if more liberals were elected to Congress in 1948, such a program could be accomplished. If the Democratic party submitted to "Wall Street domination," then a new party would be needed to help elect a "useful number of Congressmen in 1948" and show that "the United States has not gone completely imperialistic and psychopathic." He had not given up on the Democratic party, however, and still hoped that the Truman administration would reverse its policies and return to the liberalism of Franklin Roosevelt.[18]

On June 5, 1947, speaking to the graduating class of Harvard University, Secretary Marshall announced his famous plan for American economic assistance for European recovery. "Our policy is not directed against any country or doctrine but against hunger, poverty, desperation, and chaos," he declared. Marshall did not talk of an ideologically divided world as Truman had done three months earlier, and his proposal envisioned economic aid to conquer misery and eradicate the conditions that nurtured communism. It was much more limited in scope than Wallace's scheme for massive expenditures to repair war damage and raise living standards throughout the world. But by calling for economic rehabilitation of war-devastated areas and allowing for Soviet participation, the Marshall Plan embodied some important principles he had espoused. Wallace did not publicly comment on the new American initiative for more than two weeks after Marshall's speech. On June 22, he told newsmen that it was a "great advance" over the Truman Doctrine. "The Marshall Doctrine," he added, "looks toward an overall program which is what I have been advocating all along."[19]

Wallace initially expressed general approval of the Marshall Plan in the *New Republic.* He applauded the Secretary of State for recognizing that the "fundamental problem" was economic in character and that Europe must be aided as an integral unit. He was pleased that the United States had not excluded the Soviet Union from participation in the effort to rebuild Europe. Marshall's speech, Wallace wrote, made him think that perhaps the administration had realized the fallacies of the Truman Doctrine and "was prepared to forget it." But he also voiced reservations about the Marshall Plan. He worried that Congress would not appropriate the necessary funds unless it had "assurances that the money would be spent only for fiercely anti-Communist and anti-Socialist objectives." Wallace believed that the program should be administered by the United Nations. Despite the urgent need for immediate relief for Europe, he complained, the United States was ignoring existing UN machinery that could supervise the operation. Moreover, he was concerned that the Marshall Plan would appear to be an extension of the Truman Doctrine to the Soviets. "Russia has been and is being enormously difficult to deal with," he acknowledged, but he maintained that the United States must allay Soviet fears and suspicions.[20]

When the Soviet Union declined to join the Marshall Plan, Wallace was disturbed and disappointed. "I believe that the Soviet government should have accepted the opportunity," he commented. He feared that without Soviet cooperation in the program, the world would become more divided. He remained hopeful, however, that the Marshall Plan represented a "fundamental change" in American foreign policy. If the United States repudiated the principles of the Truman Doctrine, showed its willingness to extend aid to all countries regardless of their political composition, and permitted UN agencies to help administer the program, Wallace believed that Marshall's proposal could contribute to peace. "On this basis, we who work for One World can support the Marshall program as one possible road back to world cooperation for peace," he wrote.[21]

Wallace remained deeply troubled, however, that the United States had "by-passed and ignored" the United Nations. Moreover, he believed that the Truman Doctrine was still "the official policy of our Congress." Gradually, he became disillusioned with the Marshall Plan. In late July 1947, he told a Yugoslav newsman that he opposed the program if it aimed "to revive Germany for the purpose of waging a struggle against Russia." By October, he had become convinced that the administration intended to link economic assistance with political objectives, hoping to prevent the governments of Western Europe from moving toward the left. Wallace thought that the "excellent principle" of the Marshall Plan had been abandoned, and contended that it had become "an enlarged and glorified non-military application of the Truman Doctrine." Instead of reversing its foreign policy, he argued, the Truman administration continued to supply military aid to "reactionary regimes" in China, Greece, Turkey, and Latin America to combat communism and suppress social reform. By December, he had begun to denounce the Marshall Plan as the "martial plan."[22]

Since the end of World War II, Henry Wallace had spoken for a diminishing number of Americans; a great majority had rejected his views before he left the cabinet in September 1946. He had remained an influential figure among liberals, and many of them had echoed his criticisms of the Truman Doctrine. But most liberals, unlike Wallace, backed the Marshall Plan and rallied behind the Truman administration. By the autumn of 1947, Wallace was an isolated dissenter who spoke only for a small band of supporters, including many who followed the Communist party line. A poll taken in October 1947, indicated that 62 percent of the American people thought the United States was being "too soft" on Russia, while 24 percent thought its posture was "about right." Only six percent believed that American policies were "too tough."[23]

A combination of factors induced Wallace to reject the policies that a broad consensus of Americans endorsed. He remained confident that accommodation and cooperation between the Soviet Union and the United States was possible. Although cognizant of Soviet transgressions, he insisted that as the most powerful country in the world, the United States had the obligation and the ability to soothe Russia's traditional fears and suspicions. "I believe that Russian tactics are directed to providing the security she needs," Wallace wrote to Norman Thomas. "I think we can do a great deal to end any abuses on her part by contributing to that sense of security through economic assistance and sincere pledges of friendship with the Russian people."[24] He was certain that the Soviets wanted peace, and he attributed cold war tensions largely to American actions that appeared belligerent to Russia and reinforced its distrust of the West.

Wallace had no liking for communism, and many of his statements were reminiscent of the fears he had expressed in the early 1930s about the dangers of Bolshevism. But he thought that American foreign policy was attempting to combat communism in a way that ultimately would prove futile. Unlike a great many Americans, Wallace did not believe that the Soviets were intent on world conquest in the pattern of Nazi Germany. He denied that communism and fascism were indistinguishable or that the major lesson of the 1930s was that the United States must not appease Russia as England and France had appeased Hitler. Wallace believed that the United States should engage in friendly economic competition rather than a deadly arms race with the Soviet Union. Curiously, he maintained that although Russia could be trusted as long as it was weak, unless the United States won its friendship and allayed its suspicions, it would become a ruthless, vicious enemy after it grew stronger.

Wallace also refused to endorse American foreign policy because he believed that the Truman administration had betrayed the legacy of Roosevelt and the ideals for which the war was fought. Instead of working for harmony and friendship with the Soviet Union, it had adopted an aggressive anti-Soviet position. Instead of sending economic aid abroad to build a century of the common man, it sent military aid to support reactionary governments. Instead of striving to achieve one unified world, it had undercut the United Nations and pursued policies that divided the world into hostile camps. For Wallace, one world was an urgent, compelling necessity, and although he had once proposed temporary spheres of influence, he feared that the Truman administration was causing a permanent rift between the United States and the Soviet Union. He believed that the Golden Rule and the Sermon on the Mount were not only fine principles, but practical guides in international relations, and he retained his mystical faith in the universal fatherhood of God and brotherhood of man. As one perceptive writer, Ed Lahey of the *Chicago News,* observed: "Henry's insistence that we get along with the Russians looks like sheer Communist appeasement to his critics, . . . but it is strictly 'brotherhood of man' stuff to Henry." Wallace, he added, "believes that God loves even Russians."[25]

During the war, Wallace had been gravely concerned that "American fascists" would gain control of the government, destroy his plan for the postwar world, and pursue aggressively anti-Soviet policies.

Those fears had been blunted in the immediate postwar period by Wallace's hope that Truman would carry on the tradition of Roosevelt. By the latter part of 1947, however, he had become convinced that his worst apprehensions had been realized. Speaking at Madison Square Garden on September 11, he decried the preponderant influence of big business and the military in American foreign policy. "Under the Republicans Wall Street ran America," Wallace declared. "Under the present Administration Wall Street is all set to run the world." Two months later, he reminded a Louisiana audience of Huey Long's statement that "when fascism comes to this country it will be cloaked in the language of Americanism," and asserted: "Huey Long's prophecy is coming true." Wallace was contemptuous rather than bitter toward Truman, commenting that he doubted "if the President fully understands the perilous course on which he leads us." Many Americans were becoming increasingly alarmed by the threat of communist subversion in the United States, while Wallace was becoming increasingly alarmed by the threat of right-wing subversion. He denied that there was "any danger" of communism triumphing in America, but he was profoundly disturbed that the country seemed to be heading in the direction of fascism.[26]

Yet Wallace did not despair. He retained his staunch faith in the wisdom of the American people. Certain that his cause was just, he believed that once the people recognized the rightness of what he fought for, they would rally around him. Greatly encouraged by the success of his speaking tours, Wallace failed to realize, or refused to admit, that for every cheering crowd there were many more silent voices that utterly rejected his opinions. "I see hope in America," he wrote in the *New Republic*. "The hopeful sign is that so many people in the United States . . . are eager to see real Christianity and real democracy put into action." By December 1947, he had decided to formalize his campaign for peace by running for president on a third-party ticket.[27]

NOTES

1. Henry A. Wallace, "Jobs, Peace, and Freedom," *New Republic,* 115 (December 16, 1946): 787-88; Wallace, "The UN and Disarmament," ibid., 115 (December 23, 1946): 862-63.

2. Wallace, "An Open Letter to Secretary Marshall," ibid., 116 (Janu-

ary 20, 1947): 18-19; Wallace, "The Moscow Conference Can Succeed," ibid., 116 (March 10, 1947): 20-21.

3. Wallace, "The Challenge of 1947," ibid., 116 (January 6, 1947): 22-23; Wallace, "Churchill's Crusade," ibid., 116 (January 13, 1947): 22-23; Wallace, "Unity For Progress," ibid., 116 (January 20, 1947): 3, 46; Wallace, "The Opportunity for the GOP," ibid., 116 (February 10, 1947): 22-23; Wallace, "Science and the Military," ibid., 116 (February 3, 1947): 26-27; "Jobs, Peace, and Freedom," pp. 787-88.

4. *New York Times,* March 13, 1947.

5. Wallace speech, "Aid to Greece and Turkey," March 13, 1947, *Congressional Record,* 80th Cong., 1st Sess., 1947, Vol. 93, Part 10, p. 1329.

6. Ibid.

7. Wallace, "The Fight for Peace Begins," *New Republic,* 116 (March 24, 1947): 12-13; Wallace, "The Truman Doctrine—or a Strong UN," ibid., 116 (March 31, 1947): 12-13; Wallace, "The State Department's Case," ibid., 116 (April 7, 1947): 12-13; Wallace speech, "Back to the United Nations," March 31, 1947, *Congressional Record,* 80th Cong., 1st Sess., 1947, Vol. 93, Part 11, pp. A1572-73.

8. Wallace, "The Fight for Peace Begins," p. 13; Wallace, "A Bad Case of Fever," *New Republic,* 116 (April 14, 1947): 12-13; Wallace speeches, "Aid to Greece and Turkey," "Back to the United Nations;" Wallace to Clark Foreman (?), April 2, 1947, Jo Davidson Papers, Library of Congress; Norman D. Markowitz, *The Rise and Fall of the People's Century: Henry A. Wallace and American Liberalism, 1941-1948* (New York: Free Press, 1973), p. 234; Alonzo L. Hamby, *Beyond the New Deal: Harry S. Truman and American Liberalism* (New York: Columbia University Press, 1973), pp. 175-77.

9. Wallace to Kingsley Martin, January 6, 1947; Wallace speeches at Westminister, April 11, 1947, and Manchester, April 12, 1947, Henry A. Wallace Papers, University of Iowa; "Wallace Trip," *New Republic,* 116 (April 12, 1947):7.

10. *PM,* April 15, 16, 1947; *New York Times,* April 13, 14, 1947; *Des Moines Register,* April 16, 1947; *Congressional Record,* 80th Cong., 1st Sess., 1947, Vol. 93, Part 3, 11, pp. 3327, 3350-51, A1695; Harry S. Truman to Louis E. Starr, April 16, 1947, Official File 1170, Harry S. Truman Papers, Truman Library.

11. *New York Times,* April 14, 16, 20, 1947; *The Times* (London), April 14, 17, 1947; *Washington News,* April 16, 1947; *PM,* April 15, 1947; *Washington Post,* April 15, 1947; "How Wrong Is Mr. Wallace?" *Christian Century,* 64 (April 30, 1947): 550-51; Eleanor Roosevelt to C. B. Baldwin, April 17, 1947, Eleanor Roosevelt Papers, Roosevelt Library.

12. *New York Times,* April 14, 15, 16, 1947.

13. Ibid., April 21, 24, 25, 26, May 3, 1947; Wallace, "Report from Britain," *New Republic,* 116 (April 28, 1947): 46; Curtis MacDougall, *Gideon's Army* (New York: Marzani and Munsell, 1965), Vol. I, pp. 140-42.

14. *New York Times,* May 15, 18, June 10, 1947; *Chicago News,* May 15, 1947; *Baltimore Sun,* June 8, 1947; Wallace, "The Constructive Alternative," *New Republic,* 116 (May 19, 1947):11-12.

15. "Old Lochinvar," *Time,* 49 (June 9, 1947):25-26; Marie Hochmuth, "Henry A. Wallace," *Quarterly Journal of Speech,* 34 (October 1948):323; MacDougall, *Gideon's Army,* Vol. I, p. 155.

16. Edwin Lahey to Claude Pepper, n.d., Claude Pepper Papers, Federal Records Center, Suitland, Maryland; Gael Sullivan memorandum, "Re Wallace Situation," June 2, 1947, Clark Clifford Papers, Truman Library.

17. *New York Times,* June 17, 1947.

18. Ibid.

19. Ibid., June 6, 23, 1947.

20. Wallace, "Bevin Muddies the Waters," *New Republic,* 116 (June 30, 1947):11-12.

21. Wallace, "What We Must Do Now," ibid., 117 (July 14, 1947):13-14.

22. Wallace to K. Zilliacus, July 22, 1947, Wallace Papers; *New York Times,* July 21, December 5, 1947; Wallace, "The UN—Our Hope," *New Republic,* 117 (July 21, 1947): 12-13; Wallace, "Too Little, Too Late," ibid., 117 (October 6, 1947): 11-12; Wallace, "Look East and South," ibid., 117 (November 24, 1947):13; "What We Must Do Now," p. 13.

23. Markowitz, *People's Century,* p. 247; Hamby, *Beyond the New Deal,* p. 187; *Public Opinion Quarterly,* 11 (Winter 1947-48): 653.

24. *New York Times,* July 6, 1947.

25. Quoted in MacDougall, *Gideon's Army,* Vol. I, p. 161.

26. Ibid., p. 221; *New York Times,* September 12, 1947; *Baltimore Sun,* September 12, October 8, 1947.

27. Wallace, "Thoughts at Christmas," *New Republic,* 117 (December 22, 1947):13.

13

Year of Defeat: 1948

In a nationwide radio address on December 29, 1947, Henry Wallace announced his independent candidacy for president of the United States. He had decided to run in early December after consulting with his closest advisors, particularly Lewis Frank of the *New Republic* and Beanie Baldwin of the Progressive Citizens of America, the organization that sponsored many of his rallies. Both Frank and Baldwin were non-Communist liberals who were utterly disillusioned with Truman's policies and had long favored a third party headed by Wallace. At a meeting in New York on December 2, Baldwin urged Wallace to declare his candidacy soon, because the timing of the announcement would be critical. He pointed out that the third party would need sufficient time to secure signatures on nominating petitions and meet various state requirements for getting on the ballot. He also contended that Wallace should proclaim his intention to seek the presidency before Truman's State of the Union address, which he predicted would be a "very demagogic speech" that would place the new party on the defensive.[1]

Although Wallace was influenced by the arguments of his advisors, the final decision was his own. He was impelled by his fears that the Truman administration was leading the United States and the world toward disaster and by his compulsive urge to do everything he could to alter the course of world events. Wallace thought that significant numbers of Americans would rally behind him, and his determination to run for president was entirely consistent with his earlier pronouncements. During previous months, he had frequently stated that if the Democratic party became dominated by Wall Street, a new party would be needed to rally peace sentiment and help elect a liberal bloc to Congress. By the fall of 1947, he had become convinced that the Democrats had succumbed to the influence of big business and the military, and he had long detested the Republican party as the stronghold of reaction. "The bigger the peace vote in 1948 the more definitely the world will know that the United States is not behind the bipartisan reactionary war policy which is . . . making inevitable the day when American soldiers will be lying in their Arctic suits in the Russian snow," he declared in his radio address.[2]

Wallace believed that the time was ripe for a new political configuration and compared his movement to the emergence of Thomas Jefferson's Democratic party and Abraham Lincoln's Republican party in the nineteenth century. Convinced that there was "no real difference between the Democratic and Republican Parties on the important issues confronting the American people," he asserted that "this one-party rule" would ultimately lead to "open dictatorship." The new party would not be "a transient party of protest but a major and lasting party" that would "provide an articulate voice for the large sections of the people who oppose the war and depression policies of the Janus-faced political machine of monopoly."[3]

In announcing his candidacy, Wallace reiterated his opposition to the Truman Doctrine and the Marshall Plan because both divided Europe into "two warring camps." He attacked the President's proposal for universal military training as a "decisive step on the road toward fascism." His party, he insisted, favored neither communism nor the Soviet Union, but intended to fight "Hitlerite methods when we see them in our own land." Wallace affirmed his opposition to imperialism by any country, but he recognized that he and his followers would be vilified as "Russian tools and Communists." In response to the widespread charges that he advocated a policy of appeasement toward the Soviet Union, Wallace commented privately and publicly that he was "more fearful of appeasing native-born fascists than . . . of appeasing Russia."[4]

The American Communist party endorsed Wallace's presidential bid, despite the reservations of many of its members who disapproved of his ideological deficiencies. The Communists performed important tasks such as helping to organize the new party on the local level and obtaining signatures on state nominating petitions. Although Wallace realized that the Communists backed his candidacy, he was oblivious to the significant role they were playing in the party. His attention centered on policies and principles rather than organizational details involved in launching the campaign. He dismissed American Communists as "a very sadly confused lot" and told former aide Louis Bean that it would be inconsistent with democratic ideals to "tell a man he can't join you because he has a certain political belief." Wallace was denouncing the Truman administration for a "witch hunt" against alleged communist subversives, and he had no intention of initiating a purge of his own party. The conspicuous Communist support for Wallace's movement resulted in allegations that it was dominated by the Communists and crippled the new party at its inception.[5]

The reaction to Wallace's third-party candidacy followed predictable patterns. The *Daily Worker* exulted. Republicans, who thought that Wallace's announcement doomed Truman's chances for reelection, were equally elated. Democratic National Chairman Howard McGrath stated that a vote for Wallace represented a vote of approval for Stalin and Molotov. The *New York Times* editorialized that "Mr. Wallace's formula for keeping peace with Russia seems to be essentially the formula which Mr. Chamberlain employed in the hope of keeping peace with Germany." Max Lerner wrote that although he still admired Wallace's ideals and liberal convictions, he regretted that those convictions "shone out from a rickety framework of half-analysis and distorted analysis which does not do justice to Wallace." David Lawrence hoped that Wallace would receive a hearing because he provided an alternative point of view to "the impression created by official speeches and a wave of editorial support . . . that everything the United States has done is correct and everything Russia has done is wrong."[6]

On December 30, 1947, the day after Wallace announced his decision to run for president, he spoke in Milwaukee and outlined his alternative to the Marshall Plan. He lauded the "fine words" of the original proposal, but reiterated his belief that the Marshall Plan had turned out to be an extension of the Truman Doctrine. It was, he said, the brainchild of the "Truman-led, Wall Street-dominated, military-backed group that is blackening the name of American democracy all over the world.'' It ignored the United Nations, divided the world, and opened the way for American intervention in the domestic politics of the countries of Western Europe. Wallace proposed that the United Nations administer a program of economic recovery and reconstruction for the wartorn countries of Europe and Asia, using funds provided by the United States and other nations ''possessed of the means.'' He urged that the money be allotted ''to those nations which suffered most severely from Axis aggression . . . without regard to the character of the politics and social institutions of the recipient nations.'' He insisted that grants and loans be made without conditions and that each country be allowed to develop its own economy as it chose. Wallace added the stipulation that the allocation must be ''used exclusively for peaceful purposes'' and not for any military applications. He was confident that the American people would support such a program.[7]

In an appearance before the House Foreign Affairs Committee on February 24, 1948, Wallace reemphasized his objections to the Marshall Plan, denounced it as ''a blueprint for war,'' and stated his proposal for world recovery. He attacked the Marshall Plan as a device for Wall Street monopolists to expand their foreign trade by selling goods that Western Europe normally would buy from Eastern Europe. The United States had already forced Britain and France to abandon plans for nationalization of key industries, he charged, and subjected Europe's ''weak industries to the inroads of American monopoly.'' Wallace asserted that the Marshall Plan increased the opportunity for big business ''to gain control over key sectors of the Western European economies'' while the American people paid the costs and assumed the risks. Pointing to American embargoes, import quotas, and high tariffs on some products, he denied that the United States sincerely wanted to promote free trade. Despite his adamant opposition to the Marshall Plan, Wallace wrote privately that he favored interim American assistance to Italy and France until a United Nations program could be established.[8]

Wallace's presidential campaign began auspiciously. Even unfriendly observers conceded that his party might draw as many as eight million votes; the general consensus was that he would attract at least four or five million. In February 1948, Senator Glen Taylor, a young, energetic, liberal from Idaho, agreed to serve as Wallace's running mate. In the same month, Leo Isacson, a Wallace-backed candidate in a special congressional election in New York City, achieved a surprisingly easy victory over three opponents. In a district with a large Jewish population, Isacson and Wallace effectively appealed for votes by denouncing Truman's policies toward Palestine. Wallace had long sympathized with the Jewish quest for a homeland, and as Secretary of Commerce had actively promoted that cause. "The most ironic development of World War II is the continued homelessness and persecution of Jews after the defeat of the anti-Semitic enemy," he wrote shortly before he left the cabinet. Wallace had journeyed to Palestine in November 1947, and had been enormously impressed with the spirit, determination, willingness to sacrifice, and the collective effort among Jewish emigrants.[9]

In campaigning for Isacson, Wallace attacked Truman for failing to use American power and influence to back up the United Nations partition of Palestine. Palestinian Arabs had refused to accept the UN decision, and had taken up arms against the Jews. Wallace accused the administration of seeking to appease Arab "feudal lords," catering to "oil trusts," and weakening the UN. The President, he said, "talks like a Jew and acts like an Arab." Isacson trounced his closest competitor, Democrat Karl Propper, winning nearly 56 percent of the total vote. Although observers pointed out that Wallace and Isacson had capitalized on dissatisfaction with Truman's Mideastern policies in a heavily Jewish district, some also interpreted the election as a boost for Wallace's candidacy and an indication of the third party's potential political strength. The Democratic National Committee was alarmed about losing Jewish votes, but Truman was unmoved. In early March 1948, he told Jack Redding, the Committee's Public Relations Director, that he would handle the Palestinian problem without regard to politics. Isacson's victory had no immediate effect on American policy in the Mideast. But it is likely that it helped prompt Truman's decision to extend recognition to the newly created state of Israel two months later.[10]

In February 1948, a Communist coup d'etat occurred in Czechoslovakia after a group of moderate and right-wing cabinet members resigned from the government in protest of Communist attempts to gain control of the country's police force. The Czech Communists, with the aid of pressure applied by the Soviet Union, quickly consolidated power. Americans were outraged, and cold war tensions escalated to new heights. When Czech Foreign Minister Jan Masaryk died under mysterious circumstances shortly after the Communists seized power, most people in the United States assumed he was the victim of foul play.[11]

Henry Wallace declared in a speech in Minneapolis on February 27 that the Czech coup was an inevitable outgrowth of the Truman Doctrine. As long as the United States pursued anti-Soviet policies, he argued, the Soviets would continue "to respond with acts of pro-Russian consolidation." At a press conference a short time later, Wallace told incredulous reporters that the United States shared responsibility for the Czech tragedy because American Ambassador Laurence Steinhardt had helped provoke the crisis. Steinhardt, he contended, had put out a statement designed to assist the "rightest cause" just before those ministers left the government. He also suggested that Masaryk had committed suicide because he had cancer, but did not elaborate. Steinhardt responded angrily to Wallace's accusation, calling it "unfounded information" that must have come from Wallace's "Communist associates." Wallace retorted that Steinhardt had issued a "provocative statement" by publicly expressing his hope that Czechoslovakia would participate in the Marshall Plan. Since America extended aid only to governments that excluded Communists, he charged, Steinhardt's statement indicated that the United States intended to force left-wing elements out of the government, and had helped create the Czech crisis.[12]

The *New York Times* attacked Wallace's analysis of the Czech coup, commenting that "we have a new standard for measuring just how valuable a contribution Mr. Wallace's Presidential candidacy is now making to the ideology of International Communism." Wallace replied privately in a letter to *Times* publisher Arthur Hays Sulzberger. He maintained that Steinhardt's statement about Czechoslovakia joining the Marshall Plan had been loaded "with explosive possibilities" and "had implicit within it the possibility that it would serve as the final straw to throw the communists out of the government." He confided to another correspondent that the United States shared the blame for the situation in Czechoslovakia, and added: "The Czech crisis is clearly another fruit of the utterly stupid and possibly suicidal Truman Doctrine." Although Wallace did not condone Soviet machinations in Czechoslovakia, he strained to put the best possible interpretation on Soviet actions and the worst possible on American ones.[13]

The Czech coup fomented a major war scare in the United States. On March 5, 1948, General Lucius Clay reported from Germany that he perceived "a subtle change in Soviet attitude," and that a war could break out "with dramatic suddenness." Five days later, Secretary Marshall, not prone to overstatement, told newsmen that the international situation was "very, very serious," and denounced the "reign of terror in Czechoslovakia." Newspapers headlined rumors of pending war. On March 3, Truman wrote his daughter that the Soviet Union was a "Frankenstein dictatorship" worse even than Nazi Germany, and that the United States might have to fight to preserve freedom. A few days later, he confided to Eleanor Roosevelt that the country confronted "the most serious situation we have faced since 1939." Enactment of the Marshall Plan and strengthening the American military, he said, were the "only hope . . . for peace in the World." In a speech before a joint session of Congress on March 17, the President condemned the Soviet Union for destroying "the independence and democratic character of a whole series of nations in Eastern and Central Europe." He urged passage of the Marshall Plan and called for universal military training and temporary reinstatement of selective service. In a speech to the Society of Friendly Sons of St. Patrick in New York the same evening, Truman repeated the same themes and at one point departed from his text to declare: "I do not want and I will not accept the political support of Henry Wallace and his Communists."[14]

Wallace denied that any threat of war existed. In a radio address the day after Truman spoke to Congress, he attacked the President's "hysteria-breeding speeches." He maintained that there was no plausible reason to fight the Soviet Union or to "militarize America." The United States was being hypocritical in denouncing the action of others, he cried, when it interfered in the internal affairs of foreign countries, supported dictators, and suppressed civil liberties at home. The Truman administration was attempting to uphold the status quo in a changing world in a vain effort to stop an idea. Confident that the American people were too sensible to countenance such policies, Wallace attributed the world crisis to "willful men with private interests" who were "dictating our foreign policy." The following day, March 19, Wallace went on radio again to answer

Truman's remark about "his Communists." The President, he said, had used demagogic tactics to discredit the third party "because he could not answer us with reason." Wallace insisted that the "word 'communism' is a much greater menace than the Communists," because the cry of "communist inspired" was used to stifle dissent and free speech in the United States. The people whose thinking was "most dominated by the Kremlin," he argued, were "those who oppose everything the Russians do, whether it is good or bad or inconsequential."[15]

Writing in the *New Republic,* Wallace maintained that "big brass and big gold" were utilizing and staging "war hysteria" to augment their power. Military and big business interests, he declared, intended "to set up an American version of the police state in this country as a necessary part of gaining control of the entire world." In telegrams sent to all members of Congress, he urged them to "quell the war hysteria which is being fanned by the military and cartelist members of the administration. . . . There is no evidence that any nation has threatened our national security." Wallace charged that the administration had fabricated a crisis atmosphere to obscure the failure of the Truman Doctrine. Testifying against Truman's proposal for universal military training before the Senate Armed Services Committee, he asserted that as a result of America's "get-tough policy," both the Soviet Union and communism had gained strength. He denounced compulsory military training as a ploy by big business to enhance profits and by the military to increase its influence. The way to avert war and ensure peace, Wallace believed, was to "take the conduct of our domestic and foreign policy away from the militarists and bankers now in control in Washington."[16]

Wallace remained deeply troubled by the specter of American fascism. "The Judeo-Christian heritage with its prophetic ideals of peace and justice," he wrote, "is today challenged as never before by the present drift toward war and fascism in the United States." In April 1948, he undertook a speaking tour of the Midwest and found evidence that reinforced his fears. In Evansville, Indiana, a large crowd picketed the site of a scheduled rally, chanting: "We don't want him; you can have him; he's too red for us." A small Indiana college discharged a faculty member for serving as chairman of a local Wallace rally, and several other colleges and universities across the country dismissed professors who actively supported the third party. Many towns refused to allow Wallace to speak in public auditoriums, and a number of colleges denied him use of campus buildings. He endured insults, heckling, and occasional egg-throwing. Nevertheless, he drew remarkably good crowds. Speaking to three thousand supporters in Columbia, Missouri, Wallace declared: "It is almost incredible that in less than three years the bipartisans should be able to undermine everything—literally everything—for which we fought. . . . We are only a couple of city blocks from fascism now." He decried a bill designed to restrict the activities of Communists in the United States, recently introduced in Congress by Representatives Karl Mundt and Richard Nixon. Describing the Mundt-Nixon bill as "the most subversive legislation ever to be seriously pushed in the U.S. Congress," he stated: "I personally believe there is a thousand times as much likelihood of totalitarianism in the U.S. coming from the right as from the left."[17]

Wallace continued to hope that a personal meeting between Stalin and Truman could ease world tensions, and during the spring of 1948, persistent rumors circulated that the Soviet leader wanted to confer with Truman. In early May, the State Department, with the President's approval, instructed the U.S. ambassador to the Soviet Union, Walter Bedell Smith, to present a statement to Molotov expressing America's willingness to discuss their differences. The department also directed Smith to emphasize that the Soviets should not be misled by election year oratory or surmise that Wallace's campaign would alter America's position in foreign affairs. Smith saw Molotov on May 4, and read a lengthy statement blaming American-Soviet discord on Russian behavior in Eastern Europe but declaring that "the door is always wide open for full discussion of our differences."[18]

Molotov responded five days later. Predictably, he blamed American actions for existing tensions, but he also stated that the Soviet government was "in agreement with the proposal to proceed . . . towards a discussion and settlement of the difference existing between us." Smith promised that he would relay Molotov's message to Washington. The next day, May 10, Smith was shocked and chagrined when Radio Moscow broadcast an edited version of his original statement and the text of Molotov's reply. Not only had the Soviets published a confidential diplomatic exchange, but they had given the impression that they were agreeing to an American proposal for bilateral negotiations. Although Smith was outraged, and the State Department was embarrassed, hopes for peace soared throughout the world. An official of the Greek government thought that discussions between America and the Soviet Union could end the civil war in his country. "No more cold war," headlined one French newspaper. "The ice is broken." The British *Manchester Guardian* lauded the American "act of statesmanship." Many Americans were equally euphoric.[19]

The State Department acted quickly to clarify its position. Besieged by inquiries from European diplomats, Marshall explained that Smith had made no specific proposal for negotiations with the Soviets and gave assurances that the United States would not engage in bilateral talks that circumvented the countries of Western Europe. The primary purpose of Smith's note to Molotov, he said, was to make it clear to the Soviets that election year politics would not affect American diplomacy. Both Truman and Marshall stated publicly that there had been no change in the foreign policy of the United States. "General Smith did not ask for any general discussion or negotiation," Marshall told newsmen on May 12. "We have had a long and bitter experience with such efforts." The disappointment was acute. The *Manchester Guardian* commented that the United States had "sadly bungled," while a Berlin newspaper headlined: "Marshall Does Not Want Discussion." The State Department's policy planning staff agreed that the Soviets had "scored a temporary propaganda victory," and concluded "that they have no desire seriously to enter into discussions on points at issue."[20]

Henry Wallace was greatly encouraged by the Smith-Molotov notes. On May 11, the day before Marshall's news conference, he delivered an address to a capacity crowd at Madison Square Garden that he privately described as "the most significant I have ever given." The Smith-Molotov exchange, he declared, introduced "a new hopeful phase of international relations." Then he disclosed that he had prepared an open letter to Stalin, which he had written several days before and revised after publication of the Smith-Molotov statements. Wallace's letter to Stalin expressed regret that the notes of both Smith and Molotov were "characterized by the same self-righteousness which has led to the international crisis." Nevertheless, he insisted that "the letters assume . . . that the war-time co-operation between the two powers can be rebuilt and strengthened in time of peace." He called for a meeting between Soviet and American representatives to discuss their mutual grievances.[21]

The open letter outlined Wallace's proposals for ending the cold war. Both the United States and the Soviet Union, he argued, must take "definite, decisive steps" toward reducing armaments and abolishing "all methods of mass destruction"; cessation of arms shipments to foreign countries; establishing "unrestricted trade" with one another; insuring the "free movement of citizens, students and newspaper men between and within the two countries"; allowing "free exchange of scientific information" between each other; and setting up a UN agency to administer a world relief program. In addition, Wallace urged that both the United States and the Soviet Union refrain from intervening in the domestic affairs of foreign states, maintaining military outposts "in other UN countries," and using economic pressure or "secret agents" to achieve political changes in other nations. Both countries should cooperate with the United Nations "in furthering the political, economic, and cultural health of the world." In order to soothe misapprehensions widely held in both countries, Wallace suggested that the United States make it clear that it did not intend to invade the Soviet Union, and that the Soviets make it clear that they did not want to "conquer the world." "There is no misunderstanding or difficulty between the USA and the USSR which can be settled by force or fear and there is no difference which cannot be settled by peaceful, hopeful negotiation," he declared. "There is no American principle or public interest, and there is no Russian principle or public interest, which would have to be sacrificed to end the cold war and open up the Century of Peace which the Century of the Common Man demands."[22]

Wallace's formula for peace contained elements unacceptable to both the United States and the Soviet Union, but it was a balanced appeal that blamed both countries for provoking the cold war and charged both with the responsibility for ending it. American newspapers gave the open letter little notice. The Soviet press, on the other hand, seemed interested. *Pravda* commended its "realism" and "consistency," and quoted a recent statement of Stalin, who said that "of course" the United States and the Soviet Union could cooperate. "If the two systems could collaborate during the war, why could they not collaborate in peacetime?" *Izvestia* hailed the Wallace letter as "very positive and comforting." It asserted that "there were no differences between the two nations that could not be settled through peaceful discussion."[23]

On May 17, Radio Moscow broadcast a reply from Stalin to Wallace's letter. Calling it "a good and fruitful basis for . . . an agreement" between America and Russia, the Soviet leader declared that "Mr. Wallace . . . makes an open and honest attempt to give a concrete program for a peaceful settlement." He also observed that certain aspects of the letter needed "to be improved" and noted that Wallace had not included "all questions of differences" between the two countries. But Stalin asserted that "despite the differences in the economic systems and ideologies, the co-existence of these systems and a peaceful settlement of differences between the U.S.S.R. and the United States are not only possible but also doubtlessly necessary in the interests of a general peace." When Wallace heard about Stalin's statement, he trembled with emotion and said he was "overwhelmed." Coming just days after the Smith-Molotov notes, he was certain that the Premier's reply signaled the opportunity for meaningful discussions between the United States and the Soviet Union. "If I have done anything to further the cause of peace in the world," Wallace remarked, "I shall have felt my whole campaign a tremendous success."[24]

The State Department moved quickly to check speculation that it would enter negotiations with the Soviets on the basis of Stalin's reply to Wallace. On May 18, it issued a press release describing the Premier's statement as "encouraging," but pointing out that the questions Stalin was willing to discuss were not "bilateral issues" between the United States and the Soviet Union. The department challenged the Soviets to back up their words with action by softening their unyielding stand on atomic energy control, a German peace treaty, and other outstanding issues. Privately, James Forrestal voiced "a feeling of frustration at the success of Russian propaganda" to Undersecretary of State Robert Lovett, who said that he was distressed by "the ability of the Russians to capitalize on the ignorance of the American public." At a high-level policy meeting on May 21, Marshall complained of the "unscrupulousness of Russian diplomatic methods and the susceptibility of the American public to propaganda." He deplored the Soviets' "breach of confidence" in the Smith-Molotov exchange and their "direct interference in American politics" by answering Wallace's letter. It underscored, he said, "the difficulties in dealing with Russia on a normal and frank basis." A few days later, the Secretary publicly declared that "the method of modern totalitarian propaganda is to twist, pervert, and confuse and to create an impression which may not in any way represent the true situation or the possibilities for successful action." James Reston theorized in the *New York Times* that the State Department officials were unwilling to undertake negotiations with the Soviet Union primarily because they believed that the Russians would violate any agreements that might be reached.[25]

Wallace commented bitterly that the American refusal to pursue the Soviet offers "would be funny if it were not so tragic. . . . When we don't want to act, we hide behind the skirts of all the other nations. . . . We must recognize that the cold war is between the United States and Russia." He asserted that American policy makers did not want to achieve agreements with the Soviets because the cold war benefited big business interests. Most observers, however, supported the American government's position. Representative Walter Judd argued that Stalin's communication was "loaded with jokers," and Representative John Davis Lodge contended that if the United States entered negotiations on the Soviet terms, it would be in the same position as Neville Chamberlain at Munich. The *Baltimore Sun* called Stalin's statement "unabashed propaganda," while the *Atlanta Constitution* suggested that Wallace be given a trophy for "the citizen most proficient at muddying waters." Walter Lippmann wrote that Wallace's formula for peace "would leave the Red army supreme and unopposed on the European continent" because the open letter had made no mention of reducing the size of the Soviet army. *Newsweek* correctly noted that Stalin's reply had specifically listed several points from the open letter that his country would discuss, but had omitted Wallace's proposals for free movement of citizens and newsmen, and abstention from using economic pressure or secret agents to achieve desired political results in foreign states.[26]

American officials may have been justified in dismissing the Soviet replies to Smith and Wallace simply as devious propaganda. If that were the case, the United States blundered in its response, because by summarily rebuffing the Russian initiatives, it awarded the Soviets a propaganda victory by default. Yet by assuming a rigid and self-righteous position, the United States may have passed up an opportunity for meaningful negotiations on outstanding issues. Twice within eight days, Soviet leaders indicated a desire to discuss their differences with the United States, and each time the Truman administration spurned the overtures without investigating the possibility that the Russians might be serious.

The United States had nothing to lose by entering negotiations with the Soviets. Politically it was feasible; a poll taken May 2, 1948, showed that 63 percent of the American people thought that a meeting between Stalin and Truman was a "good idea." The State Department's publicly stated reluctance to engage in bilateral talks with the Soviet Union did not appear as a major concern in its private discussions of Stalin's reply to Wallace. Leading British and French papers, while skeptical of Stalin's motives, maintained that America would be unwise to disdain the Soviets without ascertaining whether or not they were serious. The London *Times* commented that there was "something to be said for keeping the door open for testing Russian intentions and for letting the world see more clearly what the discussions would imply." By agreeing to negotiations, the United States would not have been binding itself in any way, and although Stalin had omitted points raised by Wallace, he had specifically assented to discuss a broad range of subjects, including the pivotal question of Germany. Furthermore, he had not ruled out other disputed issues. The Soviets violated diplomatic protocol and bypassed normal channels in making their overtures, which aroused American suspicions. But in early 1949, when the United States did respond to an unorthodox Soviet initiative, the two countries reached a settlement that ended the Berlin airlift.[27]

In May 1948, Wallace spoke before large crowds as he campaigned on the West Coast. Although U.S.-Soviet relations remained his primary concern, he also called attention to American policies in other areas of the world. Shortly after Truman extended recognition to Israel, Wallace demanded that the United States deliver an "ultimatum" to Arab leaders and force them to end their armed resistance to the new state. He accused American and British oil interests of undermining the United Nations in the Mideast and urged UN control of oil reserves in that area. Wallace denounced American support for Chiang Kai-shek. By providing Chiang with military supplies that he used against his own people, he charged, the United States had "the blood of un-numbered Chinese on [its] hands."

Although he had abandoned his belief that the Chinese Communists were merely "agrarian reformers" and admitted that they were "real Communists," Wallace insisted that they were also nationalists who were not puppets of the Soviet Union. American aid to Chiang, he argued, was winning the hatred of the Chinese people rather than stopping the Communists. "We cannot serve democracy anywhere in the world by backing feudal lords, kings, fascists, and reactionaries," he reiterated. "We cannot whip the idea of Communism with guns." Wallace also attacked U.S. policies in Latin America. The Truman administration, he contended, had destroyed Roosevelt's Good Neighbor policy. He assailed the U.S. government for sending arms to support dictators, and accused Wall Street concerns of exerting economic pressures in Latin America "which pervert the entire economy to their own interests, impoverish the people, . . . and extract fantastic profits." His hopes for inter-American cooperation and improved living standards throughout the hemisphere, he believed, had been corrupted by "reactionary and militarist diplomacy."[28]

In late June 1948, the problem of the future of Germany, which had been simmering for over a year, erupted into a grave crisis. The United States, Britain, and France, convinced that the economic rehabilitation of Germany was requisite to the stability and recovery of Western Europe, instituted a currency reform in their zones in Germany. On June 23, the Soviets responded by clamping a blockade on the Western powers' land access to West Berlin. The United States refused to abandon Berlin, and began to supply the embattled city by airlift. The ominous course of events incited another war scare in America.[29]

Speculation about an immediate war soon subsided, but the situation remained grim as over three thousand Progressive party delegates gathered in Philadelphia in late July for their nominating convention. Unfriendly reporters were quick to note that Communists were attending the meeting, though charges that "the convention swarmed with Communists and Fellow Travelers" were hardly accurate. The delegates displayed an air of exuberance and spontaneity, constantly singing about "Friendly Henry Wallace" and "Building A People's Party." Wallace remained aloof from disputes about the Progressives' platform, and when the delegates defeated a resolution stating that they should not extend a "blanket endorsement to the foreign policy of any nation," newsmen interpreted the action as proof that Communists dominated the proceedings. The convention nominated Wallace for president and Glen Taylor for vice-president by acclamation. Accepting the nomination before 30,000 people at Philadelphia's baseball stadium, Wallace attacked the Democrats and Republicans for following "policies of militarization and imperialism." Referring to the German situation, he declared that if he were president "there would be no crisis in Berlin today." He argued that Germany would remain a point of contention until the United States achieved a general agreement with the Soviets, and denounced the American plan "to revive the power of the industrialists and cartelists who hailed Hitler and financed his fascism."[30]

Wallace continued to assail the American position in Germany as he undertook a nationwide campaign tour. He repeated his call for strengthening the United Nations, but was outraged when the Western powers submitted the Berlin issue to the UN Security Council after direct negotiations with the Soviets proved fruitless. He charged that the Truman administration had contrived the German crisis, and had purposely avoided reaching a settlement with the Soviets. Then it had taken the question to the UN to use it "as a forum for reckless attacks on Russia." Privately, Wallace wrote that he considered "our German policy the most dangerous of all aspects of our foreign policy," finding it "almost incredible" that "our own leaders should be hard at work rebuilding the Nazi world." Wallace wired Truman, charging that "in the name of combatting appeasement," the United States was "preparing a new and more terrible Munich by rebuilding reaction and militarism in Germany and refusing to negotiate with Russia."[31]

Truman was alarmed by Wallace's potential appeal, and in early October 1948, decided to send Chief Justice Fred M. Vinson to Moscow to make a dramatic gesture of good will toward the Soviet Union. The President's staff began arrangements for a radio address announcing Vinson's trip. When the President consulted Marshall, however, the Secretary adamantly opposed the idea because it would offend Britain and France. Reluctantly, Truman agreed to discard the plan. When news of the proposed mission leaked to the press, Truman was embarrassed, Marshall was dismayed, and the British and French were displeased that the President had considered a unilateral initiative. Wallace commented that the Vinson mission had aborted because Truman was "timid and incapable" and "could do nothing but obey the men who hold him prisoner." The "real masters of our foreign policy," he said, were "the big brass and the big gold."[32]

Truman was unduly concerned about Wallace's political impact. During the fall of 1948, the Progressive party candidate's campaign faltered badly. The Democratic party had blunted his appeal by adopting a liberal platform on domestic issues. Wallace continued to be crippled by the crescendo of attacks charging that he was a Communist dupe. But above all, the Berlin crisis rallied support for Truman's foreign policy and strengthened the conviction that Wallace's call for cooperation with the Soviets was hopelessly fanciful. The crowds that turned out for Wallace's rallies dwindled sharply, and the party's morale visibly suffered. Polls that had indicated in April that Wallace would receive 7.5 percent of the total vote showed in October that he could expect only four percent. On election day, November 2, 1948, he collected just over a million votes, slightly over two percent of the total, as Truman achieved his stunning victory over Thomas E. Dewey. Nearly half of the Progressive party's tally came from the state of New York, and its aggregate vote was less than that achieved by Governor Strom Thurmond's "Dixiecrat" party. The Progressives failed to show significant strength in any section of the country or among any socioeconomic group. The campaign that began with great hopes and high spirits ended in utter defeat. Wallace sent a rather ungracious congratulatory letter to Truman, urging him to "cut loose from the advice of the military and the reactionaries from the South and from Wall Street." The "only practical guide for saving the human race," he added, was the Sermon on the Mount.[33]

Wallace's presidential campaign culminated his opposition to the foreign policy of the Truman administration, but it highlighted the weaknesses rather than the strengths of his cold war critique. His rhetoric was shrill and dogmatic, and his analysis of American diplomacy, particularly in the cases of the Czech coup and the Berlin crisis, demonstrated a lack of balance and careful reasoning. He went beyond credible limits in placing Soviet moves in the best possible light while subjecting American actions to the harshest possible interpretation. Contrary to the assertions of a host of critics, that tendency did not derive from the influence of Communists or a cabal of left-wing advisors who allegedly manipulated Wallace. He had not lost his capacity for independent thinking, and his private correspondence, handwritten drafts of speeches, and personal interviews echoed the same opinions as his public pronouncements.

The strident and polemical tone of many of Wallace's criticisms of American foreign policy suggested that he had taken on the temperament of a zealot. Convinced that his cause was right and that Truman had submitted to the influence of the military and big business, Wallace refused any compromise with policies that he believed to be evil devices of his archenemies. The Marshall Plan embodied principles that he had long advocated, and he could have supported it without giving a blanket endorsement to American diplomacy, but by 1948 he was attacking it as a Wall Street ploy. He repeatedly denounced the Truman administration for bypassing the United Nations, but when the United States presented the Berlin question to the Security Council, he protested with equal fervor.

Wallace recognized some of the dangers inherent in what later became known as the military-industrial complex. But his analysis consisted of a simplistic conspiracy theory rather than a thoughtful consideration of the ultimate implications of growing collaboration between the armed services and big business for the American economy and foreign policy. His portrait of Truman was a caricature that ignored the President's commitment to civilian control of military matters, his liberal instincts, and his dislike of big business. James A. Wechsler, who covered the Progressive party for the *New York Post,* commented at the conclusion of Wallace's campaign: "In this time of terrifying international tension, a reasoned voice, affirming the vitality of free institutions in America, might have offered genuine relief. But this was the voice of doom, negative, rasping, and uncharitable."[34]

Wallace's persistent call for a strong United Nations belied the weakness of the world organization and the reluctance of both the United States and the Soviet Union to attach much importance to it for settling fundamental issues. In addition to his belief that it provided the instrument for promoting world unity, the integrity of his program depended upon a viable United Nations. He advocated foreign economic assistance that would serve to improve living standards abroad, but he opposed meddling in the domestic affairs of other countries. If the United States extended unconditional aid to underdeveloped and wartorn nations, it had no way of assuring that foreign governments would expend the funds for constructive purposes. If it dictated the ways in which its aid was to be used, however, it would be interfering in the political and economic policies of other countries. Wallace attempted to resolve that dilemma by urging the creation of an effective United Nations to supervise and administer economic assistance, but that was an unattainable goal, particularly in the highly charged, distrustful setting of the cold war.

Despite his frequent assertions to the contrary, the American people would not have accepted Wallace's program for sending massive aid abroad. After the end of the war, they were anxious to cut taxes and reduce the amount of foreign spending. The Truman administration secured congressional approval of its much more modest foreign assistance programs only by emphasizing their anti-communist aspects in an atmosphere of crisis and pending doom.

Since the early years of World War II, Wallace had contended that the way to achieve peace and understanding with the Soviet Union was to win its confidence and overcome its traditional distrust of the West. He overestimated America's ability to allay Russia's fears; Roosevelt's efforts to soothe Stalin's phobias, even when the two countries were allied in a common struggle against Nazi Germany, had achieved only limited results. George Kennan complained about Wallace's statements concerning Soviet-American relations in 1946, arguing that "nothing short of complete disarmament, delivery of our air and naval forces to Russia and resigning powers of government to American Communists" would mitigate Soviet suspicions. "Even then," he added, "Moscow would smell a trap and would continue to harbor most baleful misgivings."[35]

Despite the flaws in Wallace's position, he offered perceptive criticisms of American cold war policies. He recognized that Soviet actions were not solely responsible for world tensions and argued persuasively that many American policies were reinforcing Russian suspicions and aggravating discord. Soviet-American relations could not have been as smooth and harmonious as Wallace envisioned. But if the United States had been less self-righteous, more mindful of how its actions appeared in Soviet eyes, and more alert to Soviet needs and sensibilities, the cold war could have been less tense and traumatic.

The most troubling and tragic aspect of Wallace's cold war critique was that he did not receive a fair and respectful hearing. It is clear, in retrospect, that he discerned many of the pitfalls of America's anticommunist crusade in both foreign and domestic affairs. But few people were willing to listen to him. Wallace fell victim to an atmosphere of rabid and frequently irrational fear of communism that emerged in the United States soon after the end of World War II. The mood of the country became increasingly unreceptive to his message of hope for a century of the common man and faith in the willingness of the Soviet Union to cooperate with the United States. After early 1946, neither the Truman administration nor most Americans seriously considered the merits of his arguments, and he never succeeded in stirring a "full and open debate" about American foreign policy after he left the cabinet. His appeal to hope and faith, which had inspired many Americans during World War II, seemed much less compelling than the prevailing fear of communism.

Beginning in 1947, Truman's attempts to "scare the hell out of the American people" to win support for his foreign policies, his anticommunist rhetoric, and his internal security programs inflamed existing fears of Soviet imperialism abroad and communist subversion at home. They fostered an atmosphere that was disturbingly intolerant of dissent.[36] The anticommunist activities and rhetoric of the Truman administration and the refusal of most Americans even to consider an alternative viewpoint intensified Wallace's anxieties that his apprehensions rather than his hopes for the postwar world were being realized. He became convinced that the United States was heading toward a form of domestic fascism, and he too began to appeal to fear. But his hyperbolic warnings about incipient fascism further alienated him from Americans who worried about communism, not fascism. During the 1948 campaign, Wallace's extravagant rhetoric, his sometimes impalpable justifications for Soviet behavior, and his unwillingness to emphatically disavow Communist support confirmed suspicions that he was the naive agent of Communist chicanery. Although he was not a dupe of the Communists, he often sounded like one.

Yet even when Wallace had presented moderate and reasonable criticisms of American foreign policy, as he had done in 1946 and early 1947, he suffered widespread denunciation as a spokesman for communist doctrine and an apologist for the Soviet Union. The shrillness of his rhetoric in late 1947 and 1948 was in part a response to the vehemence of the attacks aimed at him. He was banished to the fringes of American politics for daring to challenge the assumption that the United States was the defender of freedom, democracy, and morality against a ruthless aggressor. He endured both petty indignities and malicious attacks, ranging from having his name removed from the Washington Social Register to facing hostile, angry crowds. In an appearance in Burlington, North Carolina, in September 1948, after being pelted with eggs and tomatoes and shouted down by abusive epithets, Wallace turned to a bystander and asked in anguish: "Am I in the United States?"[37] It was exceedingly unfortunate that as America assumed world leadership and faced grave responsibilities and crises abroad, it allowed so little debate and dissent about the policies it should follow in international affairs.

NOTES

1. Curtis MacDougall, *Gideon's Army* (New York: Marzani and Munsell, 1965), Vol. I, pp. 224-27; Norman D. Markowitz, *The Rise and Fall of the People's Century: Henry A. Wallace and American Liberalism, 1941-1948* (New York: Free Press, 1973), pp. 255-56.

2. *New York Times,* December 30, 1947.

3. Henry A. Wallace, "Why a Third Party in 1948?" *Annals of the American Academy of Political and Social Science,* 259 (September 1948): 10-16.

4. Wallace, "The People Talk," *New Republic,* 118 (February 2, 1948): 9-10; Louis Bean interview, Columbia Oral History Collection; *New York Times,* December 30, 1947; Wallace to Donald Murphy, January 13, 1948, Henry A. Wallace Papers, University of Iowa.

5. Bean interview, Columbia Oral History Collection; *Baltimore Sun,* October 6, 1947; MacDougall, *Gideon's Army,* Vol. I, p. 281; Karl M. Schmidt, *Henry A. Wallace: Quixotic Crusade, 1948* (Syracuse: Syracuse University Press, 1960), pp. 101, 277-78; Joseph R. Starobin, *American Communism in Crisis, 1943-1957* (Cambridge, Mass.: Harvard University Press, 1972), pp. 176-77.

6. *New York Times,* December 30, 31, 1947; *PM,* December 30, 1947; David Lawrence, "The Strange Case of Mr. Wallace," *United States News,* 24 (January 9, 1948):25; MacDougall, *Gideon's Army,* Vol. I, p. 285; Schmidt, *Quixotic Crusade,* p. 39.

7. Wallace, "My Alternative to the Marshall Plan," *New Republic,* 118 (January 12, 1948):13-14.

8. U.S. Congress, House, Committee on Foreign Affairs, *Hearings on United States Foreign Policy for a Post-War Recovery Program,* 80th Cong., 2nd Sess., 1948, pp. 1581-1603; Wallace to Anita McCormick Blaine, April 2, 1948, Wallace Papers.

9. *Diary,* October 23, 1943, July 26, 29, 30, 1946, pp. 265, 606-07; Wallace to Joseph Hager, July 30, 1946, Box 1075, File 104251/6, RG 40, NA; Wallace, "First Impressions of Palestine," *New Republic,* 117 (November 3, 1947): 11-12; Wallace, "The Conquerors of the Negev," ibid., 117 (November 10, 1947): 4, 10-12; MacDougall, *Gideon's Army,* Vol. I, p. 291.

10. *New York Times,* February 11, 16, 18, 19, 20, 1948; "Wallace Gives the Democrats A Scare," *Life,* 24 (March 1, 1948):23, 25; "Politics and Zion," *Newsweek,* 31 (March 1, 1948):18-19; Jack Redding, *Inside the Democratic Party* (Indianapolis: Bobbs-Merrill Co., 1958), pp. 104-105, 149; MacDougall, *Gideon's Army,* Vol. II, pp. 323-25; John Snetsinger, *Truman, the Jewish Vote, and the Creation of Israel* (Stanford: Hoover Institution Press, 1974), pp. 79-81, 119-21.

11. Walter LaFeber, *America, Russia, and the Cold War, 1945-1971* (New York: John Wiley and Sons, 1972), pp. 63-64; Herbert Feis, *From Trust to Terror: The Onset of the Cold War, 1945-1950* (New York: W. W. Norton, 1970), pp. 292-94.

12. *New York Times,* February 28, March 16, 18, 1948; MacDougall, *Gideon's Army,* Vol. II, pp. 332-33.

13. *New York Times,* March 19, 1948; Wallace to Arthur Hays Sulzberger, March 24, 1948, Wallace to Julia Welden, April 2, 1948, Wallace Papers. Wallace could have made a plausible case that the United States indirectly shared responsibility for the Czech coup by exerting economic pressure in a futile effort to draw Czechoslovakia closer to the West. But his contention that Steinhardt played a major role in precipitating the coup merely by making a statement was far-fetched. For a discussion of American economic policies in Czechoslovakia, see Thomas G. Paterson, *Soviet-American Confrontation* (Baltimore: Johns Hopkins University Press, 1973), pp. 121-30.

14. Richard M. Freeland, *The Truman Doctrine and the Origins of McCarthyism* (New York: Alfred A. Knopf, 1972), pp. 269-76; Margaret Truman, *Harry S. Truman* (New York: William Morrow and Co., 1973), pp. 358-60; Walter Millis, ed., *The Forrestal Diaries* (New York: Viking Press, 1951), p. 387; Truman to Eleanor Roosevelt, March 16, 1948, Eleanor Roosevelt Papers, Roosevelt Library; *New York Times,* March 11, 18, 1948.

15. Wallace radio speech, March 19, 1948, Wallace Papers; *New York Times,* March 19, 1948.

16. Wallace, "Whipped-up Hysteria," *New Republic,* 118 (March 29, 1948):10; U.S. Congress, Senate, Committee on Armed Services, *Hearings on Universal Military Training,* 80th Cong., 2nd Sess., 1948, pp. 541-554, 566-67; Wallace to Tom Connally, March 16, 1948, Tom Connally Papers, Library of Congress; Wallace to J. G. Couser, May 11, 1948, Wallace Papers.

17. Wallace to the Independent Religious Committee for Wallace, March 19, 1948, Wallace speech, May 3, 1948, Wallace Papers; Wallace hand-written draft of speech on Mundt-Nixon Bill, n.d., Lewis Frank Papers, University of Iowa; Wallace, "Ferment in the Middle West," *New Republic,* 118 (May 17, 1948):11-12; "Reception for Wallace," *Newsweek,* 31 (April 19, 1948):30; MacDougall, *Gideon's Army,* Vol. II, pp. 362-73; Schmidt, *Quixotic Crusade,* pp. 86-88.

18. Wallace to Louis Bean, April 28, 1948, Wallace Papers; Walter Bedell Smith, *My Three Years in Moscow* (Philadelphia: J. P. Lippincott Co., 1950), pp. 157-62; George F. Kennan, *Memoirs (1925-1950)* (Boston: Little, Brown and Co., 1967), pp. 346-47; Robert A. Divine, *Foreign Policy and U.S. Presidential Elections, 1940-1948* (New York: New Viewpoints, 1974), p. 201.

19. *Foreign Relations: 1948,* Vol. IV, pp. 854-57; Smith, *Three Years in Moscow,* pp. 163-66; Divine, *Presidential Elections,* p. 202; "In and Out of the Potatoes," *Time,* 51 (May 24, 1948): 30.

20. *Foreign Relations: 1948,* Vol. IV, pp. 860-64, 866; Kennan, *Memoirs,* pp. 346-47; "In and Out of the Potatoes," *Time,* p. 30; *New York Times,* May 12, 13, 1948.

21. Wallace to Anna T. Davis, May 10, 1948, Wallace speech, May 11, 1948, Wallace Papers; "An Open Letter to Premier Stalin," n.d., Connally Papers.

22. "An Open Letter to Premier Stalin," Connally Papers.

23. *New York Times,* May 17, 1948; *Washington Post,* May 17, 1948; Schmidt, *Quixotic Crusade,* p. 77.

24. *New York Times,* May 18, 1948.

25. Ibid., May 19, 1948; Millis, ed., *Forrestal Diaries,* pp. 442-43; *Department of State Bulletin,* 18 (May 30, June 6, 1948): 705-706, 744.

26. *New York Times,* May 19, 1948; *Washington Post,* May 19, 20, 1948; *Baltimore Sun,* May 19, 1948; *Atlanta Constitution,* May 19, 1948; "The Stage of Put Up or Shut Up," *Newsweek,* 31 (May 31, 1948):19; MacDougall, *Gideon's Army,* Vol. II, p. 357.

27. *Baltimore Sun,* May 19, 1948; *New York Herald Tribune,* May 19, 1948; *Public Opinion Quarterly,* 12 (Fall 1948):559; Feis, *Trust to Terror,* pp. 355-57.

28. *New York Times,* May 17, 1948; *Hearings on Universal Military Training,* pp. 562-63; Wallace, "American Fiasco in China," *New Republic,* 119 (July 5, 1948):11; Wallace interview with International News Ser-

vice, August 11, 1948, Wallace Papers; "Henry Wallace on U.S. Policy in China," n.d., Progressive Party Papers, University of Iowa.

29. Divine, *Presidential Elections,* pp. 214-16, 221-26; LaFeber, *America, Russia, and the Cold War,* pp. 68-69.

30. Schmidt, *Quixotic Crusade,* pp. 178-201; MacDougall, *Gideon's Army,* Vol. II, pp. 484-586; *New York Times,* July 25, 1948.

31. Wallace to E. Jasinski, October 7, 1948, Wallace draft statement on Berlin, September 21, 1948, Wallace speeches, September 20, October 2, 1948, Wallace Papers; Wallace to Truman, October 8, 1948, Official File 386, Harry S. Truman Papers, Truman Library; Divine, *Presidential Elections,* pp. 230-34.

32. *New York Times,* October 15, 1948; "The Misfire of a Mission," *Newsweek,* 32 (October 18, 1948): 31-32; Divine, *Presidential Elections,* pp. 254-59; Robert Ferrell, *George C. Marshall* (New York: Cooper Square Publishers, 1966), pp. 250-58; Harry S. Truman, *Memoirs: Years of Trial and Hope* (Garden City, N.Y.: Doubleday and Co., 1956), Vol. II, pp. 212-19.

33. Wallace to Truman, November 5, 1948, President's Personal File 1917, Truman Papers; *Public Opinion Quarterly,* 12 (Winter 1948-49):767; Divine, *Presidential Elections,* pp. 275-76; Schmidt, *Quixotic Crusade,* pp. 221-41, 333-35; MacDougall, *Gideon's Army,* Vol. III, pp. 762-70.

34. James A. Wechsler, "My Ten Months with Wallace," *The Progressive,* 12 (November 1948):8.

35. *Foreign Relations: 1946,* Vol. VI, p. 723.

36. For accounts of how the Truman administration's anticommunism led to an intolerance of dissent, see Freeland, *Truman Doctrine and McCarthyism,* and Athan Theoharis, *Seeds of Repression: Harry S. Truman and the Origins of McCarthyism* (Chicago: Quadrangle Books, 1971).

37. "The South Gets Rough with Wallace," *Life,* 25 (September 13, 1948):33-35; *New York Times,* October 3, 1948.

14

Gladioli, Strawberries, and Chickens

Despite his repudiation at the polls, Henry Wallace was neither bitter nor dejected. He was satisfied that his presidential campaign had "accomplished far more than we expected, but in an utterly different way than we had anticipated." Convinced that his candidacy had forced Truman to take a more liberal position on domestic issues, he maintained that "the Progressive Party must stay organized or the Democrats will return to their evil ways." The third party effort, he wrote, had been "necessary and good," and he was confident that "events, sooner than any of us think, will demonstrate the rightness of our program."[1]

Wallace retreated to his farm in South Salem, New York, which he had acquired shortly before leaving the government. He devoted his attention primarily to tending his garden and conducting experiments in genetics with strawberries and chickens. But he did not abandon his interest in politics or alter his opinions about international relations. He insisted that understanding could be achieved between the United States and the Soviet Union, and complained that America's foreign policy was "based on the proposition that we will not talk peace until we are in a position to dictate the terms of peace." When President Truman proposed his famous Point Four program for technical assistance to underdeveloped countries in January 1949, Wallace reported that he "couldn't help smiling" and added: "Eventually they will have to come completely around to my way of thinking or they are going to get into some real trouble." He disapproved of Truman's plan because it disregarded the United Nations and because it was part of the "Holy War" against the Soviet Union. Wallace still considered the President a "poor little man" who was the unwitting captive of the "war mongers." In April 1949, he informed Truman that the Progressive party would continue its efforts "to save the nation from the catastrophe which overtook Germany." The greatest threat to American democracy, he maintained, came "from those who are currently cloaking their fascism as an 'anti-communist' crusade."[2]

Wallace bitterly attacked the formation of the North Atlantic Treaty Organization. American participation in a European military alliance, he told the Senate Foreign Relations Committee in May 1949, would violate the UN Charter "in a most flagrant manner." It would preclude any possibility of achieving understanding with the Soviets and "permanently" divide the world into hostile camps. Wallace argued that a defensive alliance against the Soviet Union was unnecessary because Russia posed no military threat to the West. The NATO pact, he asserted, was a logical outgrowth of the Truman Doctrine and would prove equally costly and futile. As always, he urged that America underwrite a UN program for world disarmament, economic reconstruction, and assistance to backward areas.[3]

Although Wallace continued to attribute world tensions primarily to American policies, during the fall of 1949, he began to make pointed criticisms of Soviet actions. Speaking at a Progressive party dinner given in his honor, he condemned the practice of unilateral assistance to foreign countries as a form of power politics. "This applies as much to Russia as to the United States," he remarked. He attacked the United States, Great Britain, and the Soviet Union for "displays of naval strength and mass troop movements." In October, Wallace declared that "the people of the world should denounce both the United States and Russia for needless acts of provocation" that spawned a "war-mad world." He expressed increasing concern about Soviet suppression of civil liberties in Eastern Europe, and although he affirmed that communism and capitalism could exist together in peace, he thought it "high time that both systems . . . abandon their extreme positions." It was unfortunate, he told a church group in November 1949, that "from time to time the Communists have claimed the world for themselves just like Truman did when he said our ideology was the only one backed by a moral code." In a letter to his former speech writer, Lew Frank, Wallace confided: "The more I see of humanity both east and west right now the better I am impressed with gladioli, strawberries and chickens." Although he had never condoned many aspects of Soviet behavior, his statements in late 1949 indicated that he was less inclined to view Soviet actions mainly as a response to American provocation.[4]

Wallace became increasingly estranged from the Progressive party. Many non-Communists had deserted the ranks after the 1948 debacle, and the role of Communists in the party became proportionately greater. By October 1949, Wallace had decided that the stigma of Communism detracted from his cause, and that the third party must divorce itself from the Communists "in every possible way but without red baiting." He made his position clear at a Progressive party convention in Chicago in February 1950. In his speech, Wallace declared that the United States and the Soviet Union "stand out today as the big brutes of the world," because "each in the eyes of other nations is guided by force and force alone." Then he stated that although he wanted no purges, he believed that Progressive party members should not give their primary allegiance to the Soviet Union. "Our principles are vastly different from those of the Communist Party," he said. "The Communists have their party; we have ours." The Progressives eventually agreed on a platform that acknowledged that "the United States and the Soviet Union have both made mistakes in foreign policy," and for the time being, Wallace remained head of the party.[5]

On June 25, 1950, North Korean troops launched a surprise attack on South Korea. Truman immediately dispatched troops to defend South Korea and the United Nations condemned the North Korean aggression. Wallace supported the American action. In a special session of the Executive Committee of the Progressive party on July 6, he stated unequivocally that he would not countenance criticism of the United States when it was at war. Two days later, he discussed the Korean situation with UN Secretary-General Trygve Lie, who had requested that Wallace meet with him. Lie remarked that the former Vice-President's "importance in world political opinion was very great" and asked him to express his views publicly on the North Korean invasion. Wallace disclosed that he had already prepared a statement and when he read it to the Secretary-General, Lie was enthusiastic. He urged Wallace to issue it as soon as possible.[6]

Wallace complied on July 15. In his statement, he recounted his efforts to promote peace and align the United States with the aspirations of the common man throughout the world. "From the time I left the Government in 1946 I have done my best to save my country and the world from this day," he said. But he blamed the Soviets for the war in Korea and voiced certainty they could stop the conflict if they wanted. "I hold no brief for the past actions of either the US or Russia but when my country is at war and the UN sanctions that war I am on the side of my country and the UN," Wallace declared. He expressed hope that the United States and the Soviet Union could arrive at a just solution to the Korean problem, and begin to cooperate through the United Nations to improve living standards in Asia. Again he admonished Americans that "the US will fight a losing battle in Asia as long as she stands behind feudal regimes." He suggested that as soon as the war in Korea ended, the United States sponsor free and democratic elections to unify Korea rather than supporting "the dictatorial and corrupt" government of South Korean President Syngman Rhee.[7]

Although Wallace approved American intervention in Korea, he neither renounced his earlier views nor gave a blanket endorsement to U.S. diplomacy. Even at the height of his presidential campaign, he had publicly stated that he would withdraw his candidacy and support the United States if it became involved in a war. The United Nations' sanction of America's action further convinced Wallace of the need to resist North Korea's armed aggression. He succinctly summarized his stand by writing: "I am for my country and the UN." On August 8, 1950, after the Progressive party failed to take the same position, he curtly resigned. Many Americans applauded Wallace's decision to back the Korean effort. Truman expressed his gratitude, and the *New York News* headlined: "Wallace Is On Our Side." The *New York Times* was relieved to discover that although the former Vice-President was still "confused," he was "a loyal American at heart." With considerable inaccuracy, *Newsweek* commented that "Henry Wallace has eaten an extraordinary amount of crow."[8]

Wallace had long feared that if the United States failed to win the

trust of the Soviet Union when it was weak, it would become a ruthless, aggressive enemy after it grew stronger. The aggression of
North Korea and reports he received that "Moscow-trained communists" were carrying out a campaign of terror in Czechoslovakia
convinced him that his apprehensions had been realized. "I have
begun to think that Russia wants the cold war and may perhaps
want a shooting war as soon as she is ready," he wrote in the fall
of 1950. When the United States had been the stronger power, Wallace
had argued that it should take the initiative to establish friendship
with the Soviet Union. But the Soviet acquisition of atomic power,
the triumph of the Communists in China, and the North Korean
attack, he believed, signaled a shift in power relationships and placed
the primary responsibility for achieving peace on Russia. "The
events that are taking place now could have been avoided," he
declared, "but since they have taken place viewpoints must change."[9]

Despite the triumph of communism in China under Mao Tse-tung,
Wallace hoped for cordial relations between that country and the
United States. In 1949, shortly after the Communists drove Chiang
Kai-shek off the mainland, he declared that "China is not so much
the symbol of communism on the march as it is of the common
man, unlettered and exploited in all the backward nations of the
world." He denied that the Chinese Communists were simply agents
of Moscow, and urged that they be seated in the United Nations in
place of Nationalist China. When the Korean conflict began, Wallace
regretted that it would delay the admittance of Communist China
to the United Nations, but he continued to advocate close ties between the "New China" and the United States. In September 1950,
at the suggestion of the Voice of America, he addressed a personal
letter to Mao "as one farmer to another." He urged the Chinese
leader to abstain from belligerency in the Korean War, and, while
maintaining friendly ties with the Soviet Union, to avoid blind
allegiance to the designs of Moscow. Wallace pointed out that China
could benefit from trading with the United States, and he encouraged
Mao to "consider the fundamentals of a peaceful understanding
with the U.S." Two months later, however, the Chinese Communists attacked UN forces that had driven far into North Korea to the
borders of China. China's active involvement in the Korean War
persuaded Wallace that Mao had become "utterly loyal to Moscow
in thought, word, and deed." But he continued to believe that China's

nationalism and traditional animosity toward Russia would prevent it from remaining under Soviet dominance.[10]

In late 1950 and early 1951, Wallace asserted that Stalin was "driving straight toward a communist dominated world." He now contended that the Soviet Union presented an "infinitely greater" threat than Nazi Germany because communism offered food and land to hungry, poverty-stricken people in underdeveloped areas of the world. The Soviets were exploiting misery and winning the affections of the common man to further their plan for world conquest. Wallace's formula for combatting communism and promoting peace had not changed. The United States, he insisted, must stop aiding reactionary regimes and align itself with the irrepressible march of the common man. In place of excessive military expenditures and "a piddling point 4 program," America and Western Europe, in cooperation with the United Nations, should embark on a massive effort to raise living standards in Asia. "We shall lose all of Asia," Wallace warned, "unless we of the west have a better program for ending misery than the USSR." He reproached the United States for underwriting French colonialism in Indochina. "Some may say that the US should fight in Indo-China as it fought in Korea because the Truman Doctrine demands that we contain communism at every point," he declared. "I say that unless we spend as many billions for helping the people of Indo-China as we do on arms to blow up the towns of Indo-China we shall surely lose in the long run."[11]

Wallace's resignation from the Progressive party in August 1950 officially marked the end of his political career. Although he occasionally wrote articles and spoke before church and scientific groups, he quickly faded into obscurity. He was content to work with the soil and conduct experiments in genetics at his New York farm. But from time to time, Wallace aired his opinions about international relations. The question of ensuring peace continued to be his primary concern, and he was troubled by forces that undermined stability and threatened war. He worried that the march of the common man would become destructive because the United States had "raised the expectations of the backward peoples without getting them effectively and rapidly into the modern scheme of things." Unless the prosperous countries of the world acted wisely and generously, he feared, the century of the common man could become "one of cruelty and the most extreme violence."[12]

The most dangerous menace to world peace, Wallace asserted in 1961, was Communist China. He depicted China as the hostile leader of the "Have-Not Nations" that would begin relentless expansion as soon as it acquired the atomic bomb and other modern technology. Eventually, he predicted, the Soviet Union would have to seek rapprochement with the West "to stem the advancing eastern hordes." The greatest source of world tension, he declared in 1962, was not the conflict between capitalism and communism, but between the modern industrialized areas of the world and the underdeveloped countries that were motivated by hatred, envy, and nationalism.[13]

Wallace was alarmed and appalled by U.S. involvement in Vietnam. "How we can get out of Vietnam without serious loss financially, politically and in terms of human lives is hard to see," he wrote in April 1965. "Every proposed answer carries with it a penalty of large proportions." He did not blame President Lyndon Johnson for the imbroglio, because he believed that Johnson was "caught by historical, geographic and demographic forces." The origins of America's intervention in Vietnam, he contended, went back to the early years of the cold war "when I was getting the hell kicked out of me for suggesting that we were taking on more than we could chew." The Truman administration had initiated policies that "will make the USA bleed from every pore."[14]

Wallace never regretted his attempt to alter the course of American foreign policy in the late 1940s, and never renounced the stand he had taken at that time. At a testimonial dinner for Truman in 1962, he stated that "Truman had done me a favor by firing me when he did," but he did not repudiate his own position. In July 1965, Wallace read a review of Gar Alperovitz's book, *Atomic Diplomacy,* in which Alperovitz charged that Truman and Byrnes had tried to use America's atomic monopoly to intimidate the Soviet Union immediately after World War II. The former Vice-President commented: "The dumbness of Truman and Byrnes may yet destroy this world." Four months later, on November 18, 1965, Wallace died, the victim of a rare muscular disease. The same day, the Department of Defense announced the death of 108 other Americans who had been killed fighting communism in the jungles of Vietnam.[15]

Henry Wallace was a man of warm humanitarianism, generous instincts, and a noble vision. His ideals and his dream of a century of the common man provided a perspective that gave him insight into some of the pitfalls and fallacies of American foreign policy in the early years of the cold war. Wallace was not a cold war Cassandra who had all the solutions to the difficult problems that faced American policy makers after World War II. But he raised valid questions about American cold war credos and offered perceptive criticisms of U.S. diplomacy. Americans would have profited by carefully considering his ideas and giving him an open-minded hearing rather than ostracizing him as an unrealistic, woolly-minded Communist dupe. Wallace set his goals too high—his hope for the millennium could never have been fulfilled and the kind of postwar world he sought could not have been fully realized. But the world might have come closer to achieving a century of the common man if the United States had not concentrated its ideals, energies, and resources so heavily on the anticommunist crusade that Wallace deplored and vainly tried to challenge.

NOTES

1. Henry A. Wallace to Anita McCormick Blaine, November 9, 1948, Wallace to Donald Murphy, November 18, 1948, Henry A. Wallace Papers, University of Iowa; Wallace to Jo Davidson, December 22, 1948, Jo Davidson Papers, Library of Congress.

2. Wallace to Mary Painter, December 20, 1948, Wallace to Beanie Baldwin, January 20, 1949, Wallace to Rollo Brown, February 8, 1949, Wallace to Harry S. Truman, April 8, 1949, Wallace to Mr. Ginzburg, April 11, 1949, Wallace speech, November 27, 1949, Wallace Papers.

3. U.S. Congress, Senate, Committee on Foreign Relations, *Hearings on North Atlantic Treaty,* 81st Cong., 2nd Sess., 1949, pp. 417-32; Wallace to Hornell Hart, August 29, 1949, Wallace Papers.

4. *New York Times,* September 13, October 25, 1949; Wallace to Lew Frank, October 15, 1949, Wallace speech, November 27, 1949, Wallace Papers.

5. Wallace to Lew Frank, October 15, 1949, Wallace Papers; *New York Times,* February 25, 1950; Karl M. Schmidt, *Henry A. Wallace: Quixotic Crusade, 1948* (Syracuse: Syracuse University Press, 1960), pp. 294, 298-301.

6. Wallace notes on "Korea, Trygve Lie, and the Progressive Party," July 6-12, 1950, Wallace Papers.

7. "Personal Statement by Henry A. Wallace on the Korean Situation," July 15, 1950, Wallace Papers.

8. Wallace to Jess Gitt, July 11, 1950, Truman to Wallace, July 20,

1950, Wallace Papers; *Washington Star,* April 25, 1948; *New York Times,* August 10, 1950; "Oh, Henry!," *Time,* 56 (July 24, 1950):13; "Wallace in Wanderland," *Newsweek,* 36 (August 21, 1950):33-34; Schmidt, *Quixotic Crusade,* pp. 304-307.

9. Wallace to Reuel Stanfield, September 9, 1950, Wallace to Wayne Cottingham, September 11, 1950, Wallace Papers; Wallace, "How I'd Stop the March of Stalin," *Coronet,* 29 (November 1950):105.

10. "Personal Statement . . . on the Korean Situation," Wallace to Frank T. Nye, September 11, 1950, Wallace to Mao Tse-tung, September 30, 1950, Wallace to Arthur Krock, October 14, 1950, Wallace speech, "Where I Stand," January 2, 1951, Wallace Papers; Wallace speech, December 4, 1949, Progressive Party Papers, University of Iowa.

11. Wallace speeches, "A Century of Blood or Milk," November 12, 1950, "March of the Common Man: Constructive or Destructive?," January 21, 1951, "Where I Stand," Wallace Papers.

12. Wallace to Glen Taylor, April 18, 1956, Wallace speech, "World Peace and Justice for All," June 10, 1958, Wallace Papers.

13. Wallace speech, "Looking Ahead," March 1, 1961, Wallace Papers; *Des Moines Register,* September 30, 1962.

14. Wallace to Cyril Clemens, April 1, 1965, Wallace to James Pappathanasi, May 9, July 4, 1965, Wallace Papers.

15. Wallace to Donald Murphy, July 17, 1965, "Memorandum on 21st Anniversary Dinner of Appointment of Truman Committee," February 13, 1962, Wallace Papers; *Life,* 59 (July 16, 1965):14; *New York Times,* November 19, 1965.

NOTE ON SOURCES

There is a rich abundance of material relating to Henry A. Wallace's views on American foreign policy. The main body of Wallace Papers, located at the University of Iowa in Iowa City, contains much valuable personal correspondence as well as a large and useful file of speeches. The Iowa collection also includes the original copy of Wallace's personal diary, which consists of 42 loose-leaf notebooks dealing mainly with the period between 1942 and 1946. The diary is a splendid document not only for students of Wallace's career, but for all scholars interested in the later Roosevelt and early Truman administrations. Much of the important material in the diary is readily available in John Morton Blum's superb edition of *The Price of Vision: The Diary of Henry A. Wallace, 1942-1946* (Boston: Houghton Mifflin Co., 1973). I have examined the entire original diary at Iowa, but since it was opened to the public just before this book went to press, diary citations in the footnotes, unless otherwise indicated, refer to the published edition.

Despite their massive volume, the Wallace manuscripts at Iowa are thin for certain periods and must be supplemented with papers housed at other repositories. Particularly significant is the correspondence in Record Group 16 (Records of the Office of the Secretary of Agriculture) and Record Group 40 (General Records of the Commerce Department) at the National Archives in Washington, D. C. Large collections of Henry A. Wallace Papers covering the vice-presidential years (1941-1945) at both the Library of Congress, Washington, D. C., and the Franklin D. Roosevelt Library, Hyde Park, New York, are laden with routine material, but contain some useful documents. Wallace's contribution to the Columbia Oral History Collection, Columbia University, New York, runs more than 5000 pages and consists largely of a verbatim transcription of his diary. It also includes, however, Wallace's reflections on his career from the perspective of 1951, when the interview was conducted. A carbon copy of the oral history is available at the University of Iowa.

Many other manuscript collections yielded significant material for this study. At Roosevelt Library, the papers of Franklin D. Roosevelt and Eleanor Roosevelt and the Henry Morgenthau Diaries contain a number of important items, and the Samuel Rosenman Papers include copies of the "Guru letters." The Harry S. Truman Library in Independence, Missouri, has relatively little information on Wallace, but there are some helpful documents in the papers of Harry S. Truman, Alfred Schindler, Bernard L. Gladieux, Clark Clifford, and George M. Elsey. In addition to the holdings at National Archives cited above, Record Group 51 (Records of the Bureau of the Budget), Record Group 54 (Records of the Bureau of Plant Industry, Soils, and Agricultural Engineering), and Record Group 59 (Records of the State Department) house correspondence that sheds light on Wallace's views on foreign affairs. At the Library of Congress, the papers of Raymond Clapper, Jo Davidson, Cordell Hull, Tom Connally, William Allen White, Harold L. Ickes, and Jesse H. Jones provide useful material on Wallace's career. A few items of interest can also be found in the papers of Uncle Henry Wallace, Lewis C. Frank, and the Progressive party at the University of Iowa; the papers of James V. Forrestal, John Foster Dulles, and Bernard Baruch at Princeton University Library, Princeton, New Jersey; the papers of George N. Peek, Chester C. Davis, and William Hirth at the Western Historical Manuscripts Collection at the University of Missouri, Columbia; the Henry C. Taylor Papers at the Wisconsin State Historical Society, Madison; the M. L. Wilson Papers at Montana State University, Bozeman; the J. Pierrepont Moffat Diary at Harvard University, Cambridge, Massachusetts; and the Claude Pepper Papers at the Federal Records Center, Suitland, Maryland.

Other important sources supplemented the information available in manuscript collections. Wallace was a prolific writer, and his many books and articles give valuable insight into his thinking about foreign affairs. His editorials in *Wallaces' Farmer* from 1921 to 1933 and the *New Republic* in 1947 and 1948 fill in gaps for periods in which manuscript material is sparse. The *Report of the Secretary of Agriculture* (Washington: Government Printing Office, 1933-1940) is helpful for understanding Wallace's ideas during the 1930s, and his testimonies before various House and Senate committees illuminate his positions on reciprocal trade, the postwar loan to Great Britain, atomic energy, universal military training, the Marshall Plan, and other vital issues. The *New York Times* is the most comprehensive of the newspaper sources, but the *Des Moines Register* is also useful. The *Baltimore Sun* and *Chicago News* give the best day-to-day coverage of Wallace's speaking tours in 1947 and his presidential campaign of 1948. Many articles from a variety of newspapers are available in the clippings files and scrapbooks among the Wallace Papers at the Library of Congress. In addition to his own reminiscences, the memoirs in the Columbia Oral History Collection include a great deal of material on Henry Wallace. Although relatively little pertains to his opinions on foreign policy, a number of the interviews contributed significant information to this study.

Finally, I am grateful to the following friends and associates of Wallace who shared their recollections with me through personal interviews and correspondence: Gladys L. Baker, Louis H. Bean, Earl N. Bressman, Mordecai Ezekiel, Michael Gleiberman, Miriam and Avri Glickman, Mrs. Louis Horch, Wayne D. Rasmussen, and Knowles A. Ryerson.

INDEX

37-38; and isolationism, 11-21, 24-25, 29-30, 36, 40-42, 64, 68-69, 78, 86, 87, 91, 100, 145, 153; Jones feud, 95-97; July 23, 1946 letter to Truman, 143-45, 149, 155, 156-57, 160, 161; Latin America, views on, 65-66, 67-69, 72, 86, 95, 196; liberal opinion, spokesman for, 90, 149, 159, 177; Madison Square Garden speech (1946), 150-54, 156, 166; and Marshall Plan, 175-77, 183, 184-85, 199; and McNary-Haugen bill, 15-19, 25; Open Letter to Stalin, 191-95; personal characteristics, 4, 35-36, 101-102, 199; postwar proposals, 83-87, 90-93, 94, 100, 105-06, 113; religious views, 50-53, 60, 66, 86, 178; and Roerich expedition, 57-60; and Roerich Pact, 53-57, 60; Roosevelt, relationship with, 31, 73, 93, 111, 112-13; Soviet Asian trip, 105, 106-07, 122, 145; Soviet Union, views on, 28-29, 39-40, 65, 88-90, 106-07, 119-22, 126, 129, 130, 135-38, 142-46, 151-53, 156, 160-62, 166-67, 170, 172, 174-75, 176, 177-78, 187-88, 192-94, 197, 200-201, 207-08, 210, 211, 212; tariff views, 6, 11-13, 18, 19-21, 24-25, 26, 29, 37, 41-

46, 69-70, 85, 90, 117-18, 167, 185; Truman, opinion of, 112-13, 121, 162, 179, 198, 207; Truman, relationship with, 121-22, 129-30, 139-40, 150, 155-56, 157-58; Truman Doctrine, attacks on, 168-73, 175, 176, 177, 183, 187, 189, 207; United Nations, views on, 87-88, 119-20, 124, 126, 136, 152, 168-69, 176, 178, 185, 192, 197, 199-200, 207, 208-09, 210, 211; and war debts, 13, 18, 25-26, 27, 70

Wallace, Henry Cantwell, 4, 6, 7, 11, 12
Wallaces' Farmer, 4, 6, 7, 8, 11, 12, 15
Washington Naval Conference, 156
Washington Post, 161
Wechsler, James A., 199
Welles, Sumner, 45, 87, 92
Werth, Alexander, 174
Willkie, Wendell L., 74, 75, 76, 90-91
Wilson, M. L., 35
Wilson, Richard, 142
Wilson, Woodrow, 7, 8, 69, 153
Witherow, W. P., 91
World Court, 30
World Economic Conference (1933), 38

Yalta Agreement, 120, 168

ABOUT THE AUTHOR

J. Samuel Walker is an archivist at the Office of Presidential Libraries, National Archives. He has also been an instructor of history at the University of Maryland, and has had articles published in scholarly journals. His special interest is American diplomatic history.